Legal Dissonance

LEGAL DISSONANCE

The Interaction of Criminal Law and Customary Law in Papua New Guinea

Shaun Larcom

berghahn
NEW YORK • OXFORD
www.berghahnbooks.com

Published in 2015 by
Berghahn Books
www.berghahnbooks.com

Library of Congress Cataloging-in-Publication Data

Larcom, Shaun author.
Legal dissonance: the interaction of criminal law and customary law in Papua New Guinea / Shaun Larcom.
pages cm
Includes bibliographical references and index.
ISBN 978-1-78238-648-3 (hardback: alk. paper) -- ISBN 978-1-78238-649-0 (ebook)
1. Sociological jurisprudence--Papua New Guinea. 2. Customary law--Papua New Guinea. 3. Criminal law--Papua New Guinea. I. Title.
KWH46.7.L37 2015
345.953--dc23

2015006530

British Library Cataloguing in Publication Data

A catalogue record for this book is available from the British Library

ISBN 978-1-78238-648-3 (hardback)
ISBN 978-1-78238-649-0 (ebook)

A.M.D.G

Contents

Illustrations

Figures

Tables

Acknowledgements

This book would not have been possible without the help of many people. In particular, I would to thank Professor William Twining and Professor Timothy Swanson for all their assistance, guidance, insights, encouragement and patience; I am deeply indebted to both of them. In relation to the empirical work I am indebted to a great many people, especially Fr. John Cabrido SDB, Fr. John Dixon SBD and their Salesian communities at Kokopo, Boroko and Battersea. The work of the Salesians in Papua New Guinea is inspirational and they are a true witness to the Gospel. Papua New Guinea can be a difficult place to conduct empirical research, and without Fr. John Cabrido's practical and logistical support it would not have been possible to undertake it. I also owe a great deal to all my other hosts, guides, translators and interviewers in Papua New Guinea, especially: the Billy, Banako and Ka'akau families, and Christopher Torona in the Autonomous Region of Bougainville; the Ikalum family, Br. Otto Kaulan, Sam Raralo and Michael Rabia in East New Britain; and the Ignatius family, Dominic Lorpo and Ralph Utunga in West New Britain – and many others. I am also deeply indebted to all the survey and interview participants for their time and generosity. In relation to developing the questionnaire and survey methodology I am especially grateful to Irma Kurniawan, Dan Rogger and Abhishek Chakravarty. I also owe a great debt to Professor Megan Richardson at the Melbourne Law School for her generosity and for hosting me as a visiting scholar in 2011. I thank Tamara Toolsie for her assistance in relation to the use of tort and criminal law to sanction wrongs in the United Kingdom. I also owe a great debt to Kate Johnston, Greg Hemingway, Clare Hemingway and Francesca Di Nuzzo, as well as to my mother, for their editing and proofreading, and for their enlightening and inspirational discussions. I thank Tim Willems for his extremely helpful insights, discussions and technical assistance throughout this seven year project. I also wish to thank Miranda Forsyth for updating me on the recent legislative changes, and Molly Mosher and Marion Berghahn for agreeing to publish the manuscript. I would like to thank my wife, my parents, and all my family and friends for their help and support.

Finally, I would like to thank the people of Papua New Guinea. Nowhere else in the world would you find more thoughtful, more kind or more hospitable people. The sheer natural beauty of Papua New Guinea would easily have to make it one of the most beautiful countries on earth. It is the Papua New Guinean people themselves who must decide what society they wish to live in, and shape their institutions accordingly. It is hoped that this book will provide food for thought in this exercise. This book focuses on ways to improve the current situation and therefore necessarily focuses on the current problems. This focus, however, should not detract from the many state and non-state officials who work tirelessly (and often with little or no reward) to provide justice and mercy to the people of Papua New Guinea.

Introduction

Papua New Guinea, Legal Pluralism, and Law and Economics

A few years ago, in the arrivals hall at Jackson's International Airport in Port Moresby, I saw a sign that read: 'Welcome to Papua New Guinea. Please Respect our Laws'. While this seems a reasonable request of any visitor, a student of legal pluralism would ask: 'Which laws?' In Papua New Guinea this is not merely an academic question, but one with very real consequences. This is so, as its two most powerful legal orders – customary law and the state law – can differ markedly in what they deem to be wrong and in the sanctions (punishments) they attach to such behaviour.[1] This can create situations where, no matter what one does, a wrong is committed, either under customary law or the state criminal law. Consequently, Papua New Guinea's citizens (and visitors) face circumstances in which they must choose which laws to respect.

On my first day of work in Port Moresby, more than a decade ago, I was instructed on which legal order I should respect. Among other things I was instructed that, if I was involved in a car accident or if I hit a pedestrian, I was not to stop but keep on driving. I was further told not to go to the police, and not to go to home or work, but to drive directly to the airport and get on an outbound flight. The reason for these instructions is that the customary law sanction of 'payback' is practised to varying degrees across Papua New Guinea, including in Port Moresby. Under 'traditional' customary law, it can be permissible to engage in a retributive homicide, regardless of the state law conceptions of fault.

Given this practice it is common for people to flee accident scenes, either by driving on or, if the car is damaged, on foot. While the advice given to me was practical given the circumstances, it is a requirement under Papua New Guinea's Motor Traffic Act 1950, Section 24, for a motorist to stop in case of an accident where there is injury or damage, and to report it to the police as soon as is practicable. Needless to say, a payback killing is an offence under Section 299 of Papua New Guinea's Criminal Code Act 1974 labelled Wilful Murder. If such an accident did occur, the agents for my employers assured me that they would resolve the situation with any aggrieved parties, most likely through a compensation payment – a common customary law remedy for wrongdoing once tempers have cooled.

Following European colonization, conquest and settlement, many societies in the Pacific, Africa, Asia, the Middle East and the Americas were subject to legal transplants that were often very different to their pre-existing legal order, and it is noteworthy that many do not fare well on measures of personal security. The Comaroffs (2006: 6) describe much of the post-colonial world as a 'Hobbesian nightmare of dissipated government, suspended law, and routine resort to violence as a means of production'.[2] Like many parts of the post-colonial world, large parts of Papua New Guinea have a serious crime problem. Foreign Policy (2009) listed Port Moresby as one of its five 'murder capitals of the world', and while comparable crime data are rare, the one cross-country victimization survey that included Papua New Guinea suggested that rates of serious crime such as murder, rape and robbery in Port Moresby were incredibly high, and higher than in Johannesburg, Rio de Janeiro or Manila.[3] More recent crime victimization surveys of Port Moresby (Guthrie, Hukula and Laki 2006a) and Lae (Guthrie, Hukula and Laki 2007) suggest that violent crime rates remain extremely high, albeit seemingly lower than earlier estimates. Regardless of the statistics, the effects of violent crime in Papua New Guinea are destructive and pervasive, particularly in urban centres: many of my colleagues had been victims of robbery and car-jacking, and took extraordinary steps to limit their movements to protect themselves and their families. I also learned of many personal and family tragedies caused through violence. In addition, it became apparent that Papua New Guinea's personal security problems were not restricted to its capital. In many areas of the country, crime and its prevention was a major cost of business, with obvious effects on employment and economic development.

Among the scholars writing on Papua New Guinea and crime, such as Levantis (2000) and Dinnen (2006), the exceptionally high rates of crime are sometimes blamed on high rates of unemployment, poverty, and a low expectation of being punished by the state. It is then argued that this low expected punishment is due to a lack of crime fighting resources, low per capita police numbers, poor policing practices, and a lack of training and equipment.[4] Within Papua New Guinea, the crime epidemic is referred to as the country's 'law and order problem'. In addition to crimes committed by violent *raskol* gangs, and those motivated by greed and malice, customary sanctions such as violent payback and the execution of sorcerers are still common across the country, despite tough penalties imposed by the state if the offender is tried. As Pitts (2001: 131) concludes, some 'traditional' controls 'are crimes against the state', and include tribal fighting and payback which can manifest in burglaries, car thefts, muggings, killings or sorcery.

While the state once sought to distinguish between customary motivations and other more malevolent motivations, it generally no longer does. Indeed, the state seems to have taken aim at customary motivations with the intention of eradicating them. Recent evidence of this is the widely reported repeal of the Sorcery Act 1971 in mid-2013.[5] As will be explained, the Sorcery Act 1971 was an attempt by colonial authorities to deal with the widespread belief in sorcery in Papua New Guinea. It was a practical measure that aimed to deal with the realities of Papua New Guinea, and as such made some acts of sorcery crimes and extended the defence of provocation where the perpetrator of violence was motivated by beliefs in sorcery. While alleged sorcerers *ought* not to be killed, the reality is that there remains a widespread belief in the supernatural causes of events in Papua New Guinea. Most communities have people within them that are identified (or suspected) as sorcerers or witchdoctors, who are considered able to use their powers for healing or death or injury. Many deaths across Papua New Guinea, including in cities and towns, are attributed to the work of sorcerers. Therefore, one effect of repealing the Sorcery Act 1971 could be to create an even bigger chasm between the criminal law of Papua New Guinea and its customary law. Alternatively, the repeal could be seen as an acknowledgement of the fact that state legislation and the (higher) courts have been unable to deal adequately with sorcery cases, and that they are best handled by village courts and various customary processes and tribunals.

This book explores the interactions of Papua New Guinea's two most powerful legal orders, customary law and state criminal law, in relation to crime (or wrongs more generally) using the concept of deep legal pluralism and the economic analysis of the law.[6] It will be argued that the interaction of Papua New Guinea's two most powerful legal orders can see each undermine the other, a phenomenon labelled 'legal dissonance'. Legal dissonance can result in neither legal order being able to do its job. In doing so, this analysis provides an alternative explanation for the extremely low level of personal security in parts of Papua New Guinea. It will be shown that a lack of coordination in the punishing of wrong behaviour can be problematic both for legal orders themselves and for those subject to such a legal phenomenon. This can lead to a situation where an activity can be simultaneously advanced by one legal order and punished by the other, leading to injustice and, perhaps more importantly, to an undermining of each legal order's ability to deter wrongdoing.[7]

Papua New Guinea

People have lived on the landmass and islands that now make up Papua New Guinea for around 60 thousand years.[8] Nonggorr (1993) suggests that the first migrations were from South East Asia by people similar to the Australian Aborigines, followed by later migrations that brought the people who spread out across the South Pacific. At the time of European contact, the population was mainly made up of thousands of small stateless tribal units, often consisting of around two hundred to five hundred people. Narokobi (1996: 28) considers the primary distinguishing factor of Melanesia at the time of European contact was its 'small self-contained communities'. According to the Müller et al. (2000) *Atlas of Pre-colonial Societies* which, as its name suggests, aims to capture institutions, social organizations and production technologies prior to colonization, Papua New Guinean societies mainly consisted of compact permanent settlements, with extensive but relatively rudimentary agricultural activities (that included the domestication of pigs and the cultivation of taro and other root crops) as well as fishing in the coastal areas. Apart from pronounced differences between the sexes in terms of occupation, succession and marriage, Papua New Guinean societies prior to colonization were highly egalitarian, with the vast majority having no hereditary local headmen or class distinctions of any type, and a complete absence of caste and slavery. This is in sharp contrast to neighbouring Polynesia and much of the rest of the world at the time.

Once the people of Papua New Guinea did encounter European colonization, they had four colonial rulers in a period of less than one hundred years. As will be outlined in more detail in Chapter 2, following an agreement to partition the eastern half of the island of New Guinea in 1884, Britain declared the southern part a protectorate and named it British New Guinea, and Germany annexed the northern part and the New Guinea Islands (German New Guinea). Soon after, both governments set up colonial administrations and transplanted their criminal laws. In 1906, the Australian Government assumed control of British New Guinea and renamed the territory Papua, and with the First World War, German New Guinea also came under Australian control in 1914. Both territories remained under Australian control until 1942 when the Japanese Imperial

Army occupied large portions of the territories during much of the Second World War. Following the Allied victory, Australia resumed colonial control until 16 September 1975, when the autochthonous constitution of the Independent State of Papua New Guinea came into force.

Today, Papua New Guinea has an estimated population of just over seven million, which is growing rapidly. Queen Elizabeth II is the head of state, and the country has a vibrant, albeit sometimes turbulent, parliament. Despite some close calls, it has remained democratic since independence from Australia in 1975, with high voter turnout and relatively peaceful changes of government. However, it is a poor country with high levels of income inequality. According to the World Bank (2014) the estimated average per capita income was US$1,790 per year in 2012, with approximately 40 per cent of the population living in poverty. Most people live a traditional lifestyle and Papua New Guinea has the third highest rural population level in the world at 87 per cent. Many others live in settlements surrounding the nation's main towns and cities. Education levels are especially low: the World Bank (2014) estimates the gross secondary school enrolment rate to be 40 per cent for 2012, which is slightly below the sub-Saharan African average.[9] Many families simply cannot afford the fees to send their children to school. The United Nations Development Program (2013) ranks Papua New Guinea 156th of the 187 countries on the Human Development Index.

Like much of post-colonial Melanesia, the Papua New Guinean state is weak. This weakness is characterized by an inability of the state to provide basic services to its citizens. In addition to the poor headline statistics outlined above, other manifestations of this weakness include the first ever reported cholera outbreaks in Papua New Guinea in 2009 and the state's failure to contain them (World Health Organization 2010), an inability to bring most offenders under the Criminal Code to trial, and continued mass jail breakouts that have seen approximately 7 per cent of the prison population escape every year (Papua New Guinea Law and Justice Sector Secretariat 2007).

Forsyth (2009: 1) suggests that the shared Melanesian characteristic is 'diversity' and Papua New Guinea, Melanesia's largest state, is the flag bearer. While there are often clear ethnic distinctions between the people of the Highlands, the Sepik, the Papuans and the Islanders, there are also marked distinctions and deep cleavages within these broad groups. With at least 853 different languages spoken, Reilly (2008) suggests Papua New Guinea is the most ethno-linguistically diverse country in the world. Levine (1997) suggests that Papua New Guinea may have more than one thousand ethnic groups, broadly defined as having their own language, customs and memories that cause them to distinguish themselves from other groups. Within these 'tribal' groupings are 'clans' or extended family groupings. The loyalty displayed to one's own tribe or clan is referred to as the *wantok*[10] system, where primary loyalty belongs to the people of one's own family, clan, language group and region over other groupings, including the central state. Ethnic tensions can be high and sometimes spill into violent raids and fierce fighting, including in Port Moresby and other urban centres. Nonetheless there is a strong sense of national identity and the state does enjoy a degree of legitimacy, but other loyalties come before it.

The ethnic diversity can, at least in part, be explained by geographic factors. Papua New Guinea is a mountainous country, with large plateaus and deep valleys, and with a large population living on islands. The Highlands run through the centre of the mainland and effectively separate the north from the south. There are no roads that connect the two main cities on the mainland, Port Moresby and Lae. Terrain within the regions is also believed to have led to isolation and the creation of individual cultural identities. Today, due to limited, expensive and sporadic transport, many regions and villages remain relatively isolated. Although from empirical work undertaken in the New Guinea Islands for this book, it was striking how many people, even in the most remote parts visited, have lived in or visited Port Moresby (or beyond) during some part of their life.

Introduction to Legal Pluralism and the Economic Analysis of the Law

Over the decades, there have been a number of academic works on Papua New Guinea's legal arrangements. However, this book is unique in that it combines two seemingly unrelated literatures to form the basis of its analysis: 'legal pluralism' and 'law and economics'. Using the insights and analytical tools of these literatures, the interaction between customary law and state criminal law is re-analysed, for the primary purpose of finding workable policy prescriptions to ameliorate Papua New Guinea's debilitating law and order problem – for none yet have been found. However, given that at least one of these literatures will be unfamiliar to the majority of readers, an overview of the key concepts and insights from both legal pluralism and law and economics is provided below.

Legal Pluralism

Perhaps Moore (2005: 246) best highlights the essence of legal pluralism when she says:

> The rules and institutions attached to governments are only one category of a vastly more extensive set of sites producing rules and obligations … In our society, rules made by legislatures and enforced by the state are only one piece of the existing system of obligatory norm. There are many other ways in which enforceable rules are created, some of which intersect with the formal system … Others include rules made by companies, schools, universities. Often non-official rules are socially enforced … Members of the social milieu must conform or get out … An organization can expel … a member, and a business person may not want to do business with someone who does not play the game. Thus the capacity for enforceable rule making is not found in the courts alone, nor in the legislature, nor in administrative agencies, nor in the police, but also in myriad unofficial sites of policy making. Norm setting and enforcing is found in many legitimate social settings outside of government, and is also found in illegal organizations … In anthropology, when a multiplicity of enforceable rule systems operate concurrently this circumstance has been called 'legal pluralism'.

While there are a number of definitions, I consider legal pluralism is best succinctly described as 'a situation where at least two legal orders assert jurisdiction over the same geographical space and persons within that space' (Larcom 2014: 2). Before unpacking this definition, it is worth highlighting the most important insight that the legal pluralism literature has to offer legal scholars: that the state does *not* have a monopoly on the generation or enforcement of law. That is, legal pluralism highlights the social reality that state law is but one of many that coexist in all societies, and that these other legal orders can gain their legitimacy from completely separate sources from that of the state. Furthermore, the literature insists that legal pluralism is the norm rather than the exception, both in terms of human history and geography. Indeed, Griffiths (1986: 39) argues that legal pluralism is the 'omnipresent, normal situation in human society' – whether that society is post-colonial Papua New Guinea or post-imperial England.

The claim that legal pluralism is the normal (or natural) state of any society may unsettle some readers who might find comfort in the thought that only the state can produce, authorize and enforce law; and for good reason, as sometimes legal pluralism can produce chaotic, unjust and detrimental consequences, which is indeed the focus of this book and will be explored in great depth. Others may consider the supposed ubiquity of legal pluralism to be simply a matter of semantics – hinging on how one defines law. While it is true that what defines 'law' (and 'legal') is highly contested, history (at least in Western societies) does seem to be on the side of the legal pluralists claim that it is the norm rather than the exception. A number of scholars highlight that the current conception of a nation state and its monopolistic claim to 'law' is a relatively new phenomenon, scarcely more than two centuries old. Benton (2012: 26) concludes that '[s]tates' claims to legal hegemony developed in an *ad hoc* and incomplete way, gathering force particularly over the long nineteenth century'. Similarly, Tamanaha (2008: 381) tells us that the 'monopolisation of law by states in Western Europe reduced legal pluralism at home just as a new wave of legal pluralism was being produced elsewhere through colonisation'. Tamanaha (ibid.: 380–81) suggests that it was in the seventeenth and eighteenth centuries that '[s]tate law became the pre-eminent form of law', and that over time customary norms and religious law lost 'their former, equal standing and autonomous *legal* status'. Berman (1983: 10), taking a long-term historical perspective, suggests that '[p]erhaps the most distinctive characteristic of the Western legal tradition is the coexistence and competition within the same community of diverse jurisdictions and diverse legal systems'. He also suggests that legal pluralism had many beneficial aspects:

> The pluralism of Western law, which has both reflected and reinforced the pluralism of Western political and economic life, has been, or once was, a source of development, or growth – legal growth as well as political and economic growth. It also has been, or once was, a source of freedom. A serf might run to the town court for protection against his master. A vassal might run to the king's court for protection against his lord. A cleric might run to the ecclesiastical court for protection against the king.

In terms of unpacking the above definition of legal pluralism, the first important word is *jurisdiction*. It is suggested that jurisdiction can be asserted three main ways: over place, over persons and over behaviours (actions and omissions). For legal pluralism to be present, two (or more) legal orders must assert jurisdiction over the same place and persons. The dictionary definition of jurisdiction refers to the 'the official power to make legal decisions and judgements' or 'the territory or sphere of activity over which the legal authority of a court or other institution extends' (Oxford Dictionary Online 2011). This can be extended to include any legal order's ability to make legal decisions, judgements and to sanction wrongs. Indeed Justice Holmes (c.f. Michaels 2007: 1028) asserted that '[t]he foundation of jurisdiction is physical power'.

The second important term in the definition is *legal* – or law more generally. Some scholars have tried to include all enforceable rules as law while others wish to only include state law (see Griffiths 1986; Roberts 2005). There are risks associated with taking a definition of 'law' (and 'legal') that is too broad; most importantly, the word could simply lose its meaning, making analytical rigour and precision difficult or impossible.

In recognition of this very real risk, some such as Twining (2010) have favoured talk of 'normative pluralism' over 'legal pluralism'. However, there are also substantial costs with an overly narrow definition; not least, we know non-state law can and does exist, with the most prominent examples being various religious legal orders, including Canon Law, Halakha and Shari'a Law.[11] But perhaps more importantly, by denying non-state legal orders the status of *law*, it may imply a hierarchical relationship that simply does not exist, whether this relationship is between state law and religious law or between state law and customary law. While this hierarchical relationship is asserted by most states, including the Independent State of Papua New Guinea, it is also strongly contested by those who consider custom as *law* and that it derives its legitimacy from sources other than the state.[12] By not defining indigenous custom as *law* we run the risk of undervaluing (and undermining) it through the use of language. But more importantly, not recognizing non-state law as law makes us more prone to fall into the analytical trap of 'legal centralism' (Griffiths 1995: 201) and model interactions in a vertical manner when reality suggests they should be analysed horizontally. Given the strength of customary law in Papua New Guinea and its countless parallels with the state legal order (as will be outlined in the next chapter) modelling a vertical relationship, as many scholars have in the past, would be to mis-specify the relationship and could lead us to incorrect conclusions. If one is to accept the reality of different sources of law, which the legal pluralism literature rightly insists, it seems that any definition should not imply a hierarchical relationship – unless this relationship actually exists. For a vertical relationship to actually exist, it would seem that three conditions are necessary: first, one legal order must assert it; second, it must be able to enforce it; and third, this vertical relationship must be recognized and accepted by practitioners (or agents) of *both* legal orders.

While it is argued that there is a need to keep the 'legal' in 'legal pluralism' for both analytical and practical reasons, it is still necessary to distinguish legal institutions from other social institutions.[13] Therefore, a legal order is defined as 'a set of rules and practices that are oriented towards ordering relations between persons with its own source of authority' (Larcom 2014: 2).[14] This definition allows us to separate legal institutions from non-legal institutions, primarily based on their purpose – that is, whether they are aimed towards the 'ordering of relations between persons', or not. Clearly law serves many purposes; however, it seems difficult to deny that a basic job of law is to order relations between persons within a society.[15] Under this definition, Papua New Guinean 'custom' would fit neatly, while other phenomena not normally labelled law, including individual social conventions and internalized morals (often labelled norms) would be excluded, due to the requirement of a set of rules. Other forms of social life which have elements of social control, such as education, would also fall out, as they are 'not oriented towards ordering relations'.

If we are to completely unpack the concept of legal pluralism, the distinction between 'state' legal pluralism and 'deep' legal pluralism also needs to be crystallized. State legal pluralism refers to a situation in which the state is considered dominant and may incorporate laws, norms or legal practices from outside into its own (Griffiths 1986: 8). As Sezgin (2004: 1) suggests, this type of legal pluralism can be seen as a 'mere arrangement within state law', where the legitimacy of non-state norms is considered to rely on state authority. Griffiths (1986: 8) rightly concludes that state pluralism is conceptually flawed and only has a 'nominal resemblance to legal pluralism' as it is based on the idea that law must 'ultimately depend from a single validating source'. Conversely, deep legal pluralism, or simply 'legal pluralism', acknowledges the fact that different legal orders can have different sources of authority and that they can coexist or assert their jurisdiction regardless of the recognition by other legal orders, and hence an order having its own source of authority.

Like much of the legal pluralism literature, the discussion on sources of authority (state versus deep legal pluralism) could be seen as a mere exercise in semantics; but to take this view would be to fail to comprehend legal pluralism's key analytical insight. This can be illustrated with respect to the Papua New Guinean state's recognition of customary law. Prior to the passing of the Underlying Law Act 2000, the state referred to customary law as 'custom', in both the Constitution of the Independent State of Papua New Guinea and the Customs Recognition Act 1963. However, with the passing of the Underlying Law Act 2000, customary law was thence referred to as 'customary law' and is now considered as part of the nation's underlying law. That is, the state has begun to recognize customary law as 'law'. Does this legislative change mean that custom was elevated to law with the passing of the Act? A legal centralist might say yes, however a (deep) legal pluralist would say no because customary law does not derive its authority or legitimacy from the state. Of course, this is not to suggest that state recognition of customary law is not important. Indeed much of this book is devoted to highlighting the interdependencies of state law and customary law, despite having their own sources of authority and legitimacy.

To highlight what legal pluralism is, and what it is not, it is worth testing the above definition against two different legal circumstances: the existence of a separate body of Scottish criminal law coexisting with

English criminal law in the United Kingdom; and the practice of customary law in a peri-urban village in Papua New Guinea. The difference between these two examples is that there is no overlap of geographical jurisdiction in the first, but there is in the second. In the first, even though the two legal orders share the same geographical space of the United Kingdom, they do not assert geographical jurisdictions over one another. The Scottish criminal legal order only asserts its jurisdiction over Scotland while the English criminal legal order only asserts its jurisdiction over England and Wales.[16] However, in a post-colonial peri-urban village both customary law and the state criminal law assert jurisdiction.

While two legal orders may overlap in geographical jurisdiction, they may not in terms of person. Take the case of a foreign diplomat stationed in London, who under the terms of the Vienna Convention on Diplomatic Relations (1961) is immune from prosecution under English criminal law.[17] English criminal law does not assert jurisdiction to diplomatic persons under the terms of the Vienna Convention, and the Vienna Convention applies only to diplomats. Clearly, the two bodies of law overlap in terms of geographical jurisdiction, however not in terms of person. Therefore, such a legal circumstance is not legal pluralism as it is missing one of the key elements in most descriptions of the phenomenon, jurisdictional overlap in terms of persons.[18] It should be noted that the jurisdictional overlap in terms of person only needs to be in one direction for legal pluralism to be present. For instance, a Catholic living in England would represent an instance of legal pluralism, as the English state law asserts its jurisdiction over all persons within England (including Catholics, unless having diplomatic immunity), but Canon Law only asserts its jurisdiction over Catholics (including those who are in England).[19]

Problematic Legal Pluralism

Acknowledging the reality of deep legal pluralism (henceforth 'legal pluralism') is one thing, but it is a completely different matter to ascertain whether it produces good or bad outcomes. For instance, Narokobi (1996) and others have described the injustices that can arise for those people living under customary law who find themselves in a Western court, while Woodman (2012) and others have highlighted the fact that customary obligations can lead public officials to engage in corrupt and criminal activities. While Griffiths (1986: 24) is right in telling us that legal centralism is a 'myth, an ideal, a claim, an illusion' when used as an analytical tool to describe reality, it is also wrong to suggest that attempts should not be made to ameliorate its problematic aspects.[20] Legal pluralism may be ubiquitous; however, this does not mean that it should simply be accepted where it is problematic. Indeed, Watson (1998: 13–15) argues that from a historical perspective, imitation and transplantation are the main methods for legal change, and that 'borrowing has been the most fruitful source of legal change in the Western world'. Importantly, however, he also acknowledges that these transplanted legal rules 'are frequently and for long stretches of time dysfunctional, ill adapted to meet the needs and desires of society at large, its ruling elite or any recognisable group'. Berkowitz, Pistor and Richard (2003b: 171) suggest that societies can be subject to a 'transplant effect', which they define as 'the mismatch between pre-existing conditions and institutions and transplanted law, which weakens the effectiveness of the imported legal order'. Their empirical work supports their hypothesis that the 'mismatch' between the pre-existing law and institutions and transplanted law severely weakens the effectiveness of the state law.[21] Both Montesquieu ([1748] 1914) and Bentham ([1802] 2011) arrived at similar conclusions centuries ago. Both cautioned against legal transplants, particularly in societies with different physical circumstances, norms and habits, and suggested that laws, when transplanted, are often likely to be less effective than in the place they originated.[22] Bentham (1789) also directly discussed the influence of norms, customs and religious convictions on peoples' behaviour and how these can clash with the state's legal order.[23]

Therefore, it would seem to be wilful blindness not to acknowledge the (sometimes) chaotic consequences that can be generated through multiple legal orders asserting their jurisdiction over the same place and people. Tamanaha (2008: 410) notes that: 'Sometimes these clashes can be reconciled. Sometimes they can be ignored. Sometimes they operate in a complementary fashion. But very often they will remain in conflict, with serious social and political ramifications'.

More recently, Tamanaha (2012: 44–45) has tried to establish the key differences in relation to legal pluralism found in many Western societies compared to that often found in post-colonial societies, asserting that merely repeatedly noting the ubiquity of legal pluralism across all societies does not significantly advance the debate. Indeed, he likens this to 'observing the sun shines everywhere, from the Arctic Circle to the Arabian Peninsular'. He argues that the 'pivotal difference' in the legal pluralism often found in post-colonial societies is that many legal orders did not evolve over time in connection with society but have been transplanted from outside through colonization and Western hegemony pushing the virtues of global capitalism and liberal democratic rights. He goes on to argue that Western societies 'have never had to grapple with this sharp normative contrast because capitalism, liberalism and their legal systems collectively developed in sync with their own cultures and societies'. In this regard Narokobi (1996: 182) refers to the colonization of Papua New Guinea 'as a huge tidal wave that swept over the land and its people'.

The State's Relationship with Customary Law

Morse and Woodman (1988: 7) categorized three potential approaches the state can take towards customary law: negative measures, incorporation and acknowledgement. Negative measures include the prohibition of certain conduct, including certain customary sanctions; incorporation refers to the adoption of customary wrongs, sanctions and remedies within the state law; and the final category, acknowledgement, refers to an approach where the state acknowledges that it does not have the 'exclusive capacity to perform certain functions to do with law'. Within this final category there are different types of acknowledgement, including whether the state acknowledges the legitimacy of the other legal order or simply sees itself as conferring power on the other legal order; and whether the acknowledgement sees a withdrawal of the state's assertion of jurisdiction or whether it attempts to maintain concurrent jurisdiction. More recently, Woodman (2012: 136–37) has used the term 'recognition', which he divides into 'normative' or 'institutional' when conceptualizing efforts to reduce conflict and increase harmony between state and customary legal orders.[24] Woodman defines normative recognition as an instance when a legal order accepts certain norms of the other as 'valid and to be observed'. He goes on to suggest that the normative recognition may be passive or active, where active recognition sees one legal order apply the norms of the other in its own institutions. The effect of such a measure of recognition is that weak or state legal pluralism is added to the pre-existing deep pluralism. Woodman (ibid.) considers that institutional recognition is given when one legal order accepts 'as legally valid the decisions reached by institutions of the other', for instance the state accepting the decisions of a non-state tribunal as valid. Institutional recognition can be passive when the state leaves the other legal order to enforce its own decisions, or active when it enforces the decisions of the other legal order. He acknowledges that both forms of recognition require 'considerable knowledge and understanding of the recognised law' especially when it is 'active'.[25]

All states, especially those in post-colonial societies, have formal measures (including legislation) that are not implemented or enforced. Often the same legislation is enforced with marked differences from place to place. Indeed, Griffiths (1995: 213) tells us that '[n]o legal rule produces effects just because it is there. A legal rule, as it leaves the legislative body, is nothing more than so many black ink markings on paper'. Allowing for this reality, Tamanaha (2008) suggests that the state has tended to deal with customary legal orders in three main ways. The first is for the state to explicitly condemn contrary customary rules, but take no action to enforce this condemnation. Such action may result from officials realizing they do not have the power to combat it, or because they are sympathetic to customary law, but pressured by some external group to condemn it (e.g. other countries, international organizations, NGOs). The second is to absorb competing systems by explicitly recognizing them, either in part or whole. Such action may take place out of genuine recognition of the legitimacy of customary law, or a transparent recognition of the lack of power of the state in some areas or spheres of social life, or simple expediency in an effort to keep order at least cost. This can reduce the uncertainty caused by legal pluralism, and could take place in relation to an area of the law, a geographical area, to a group of people, or to combinations of these. The third course of action is to make aggressive efforts to suppress conflicting norms, customs and non-state laws by declaring them illegal and actively working to eliminate them. Tamanaha (2008: 404) notes that efforts at suppression 'raise a direct test of the relative power of the competing systems' and mean the 'state legal system is confronted with a formidable task, which it often falls short of achieving'. While Tamanaha's typology, with its focus on action and consequence, is informative and helps to explain the actual relationship between legal orders, clearly it is not exhaustive.[26]

In a recently re-edited publication of Bentham's *Place and Time* that includes previously unpublished passages, it appears that he went further than much of the more recent literature in providing practical advice for the transplantation of laws and dealing with their potential problematic effects. Bentham ([1802] 2011: 156–57) suggests that before the transplant process, a summary of the 'moral, religious, sympathetic, and antipathetic biases of the people' of the recipient country should be collected to enable 'alterations' to the transplanted law. Bentham (ibid.: 173–74) also sets out a list of eight rules for transplantation:

> 1. No law should be changed, no prevailing usage should be abolished, without special reason: without some specific assignable benefit [which] can be shown as likely to be the result of such a change. 2. The changing of a custom repugnant to our own manners and sentiments, for no other reason than such repugnancy, is not to be reputed as a benefit. 3. In all matters of indifference, let the political sanction remain neuter: and let the moral sanction take its course. 4. The easiest innovation to introduce is that which is effected merely by refusing to a coercive custom the sanction

of the law, especially where coercion imposed upon one individual is not attended to any profit to another. 5. The clear utility of the law will be as its abstract utility, deduction made of the dissatisfaction and other inconvenience occasioned by it. 6. The value of that dissatisfaction will be in the compound ratio of: a. The multitude of the persons dissatisfied. b. The intensity of the dissatisfaction in each person. c. The duration of the dissatisfaction on the part of each. 7. As a means of obviating such dissatisfaction, indirect legislation should be preferred to direct: gentle means to violent example, instruction and exhortation should proceed, or follow, or if possible stand in the place of the law. 8. The slowness of its operation is *pro tanto* an objection to a measure: but if this slowness may be a means of obviating a dissatisfaction which expeditious measures would excite, the former may be preferable.

The most striking feature of these rules is the high degree of caution he displays towards the use of legal transplants – *place*, in contrast to his characteristic zeal for legal reform in England, *time*. These rules provide practical guidance both for those considering a legal transplant and those saddled with one. In particular, Bentham considers that: if one wishes to change local customary law, a clear assignable net benefit must be demonstrated and that 'indirect legislation', such as education, instruction and other policies, should be preferred over coercive or legal means; the transplant process should be a gradual process to minimize dissatisfaction and upheaval; and extreme caution should be used in using the transplanted law to punish those actions that are wrongs under the pre-existing law but not in the origin country. He was thus a forerunner in highlighting the potential dangers of state legal pluralism and appropriation of another legal order's wrongs.

Law and Economics

While the concept of legal pluralism provides us with considerable insight, it is not particularly useful for making recommendations on institutional design in relation to Papua New Guinea's legal arrangements. In contrast, as the rules of transplantation above from Jeremy Bentham (the father of law and economics) attest, the law and economics literature is replete with analytical tools that can be readily used to provide guidance on how to improve problematic interactions between legal orders. Therefore, some useful concepts and insights from this literature are briefly outlined below.

One important concept from the law and economics literature relevant to the study of the interaction of customary law and state law, and the potential effects on the prevalence of wrongdoing, is deterrence theory. At its most basic, the deterrence model, which can be traced back to Bentham (1789) and notably refined by Becker (1968, 1976) and Polinsky and Shavell (2001, 2007), presumes that an individual will commit a crime if the expected pain is less than the expected benefit. Under this most basic approach to law (and human behaviour) people are assumed to have no inherent respect for the law. In this respect, the law and economics literature focuses on the 'external' part of Hart's (1997) internal–external view of the law distinction.[27] Cooter (2000) summarizes the deterrence model as taking Judge Holmes's bad man and giving him rationality. In such a case, the rational bad man commits a wrong whenever the expected gain exceeds the expected punishment. While modelling the state criminal law as external to the individual may be an unrealistic assumption in many societies, such as those where the law co-evolved with the development social values and morality, it seems much more realistic in a society subject to a colonial legal transplant. In transplant societies there is no apparent reason why the transplanted law should mirror internalized values or morality. Therefore, deterrence theory seems particularly well suited for the study of the effectiveness of the state criminal law in Papua New Guinea in minimizing those behaviours it deems wrong.

While some criminologists are sceptical of the empirical validity of deterrence theory, Levitt and Miles (2007) who reviewed the vast empirical literature found that differences in the expected punishment, either through policing or degree of sanction, has a significant effect on the prevalence of crime.[28] However there were some caveats; they found that it is difficult to separate deterrence from incapacitation, and that the marginal increase of already heavy sanctions, such as the death penalty versus life imprisonment, may have little effect.[29]

In deciding whether to commit a wrong, a potential wrongdoer weighs up the expected value of committing the wrong versus not doing so. Specifically, a deterrence model suggests that an individual will commit a wrong, such as a robbery, if the expected gain exceeds the expected cost. That is: $g > p.S$

Where g represents the gain from committing the wrong, p represents the probability of being sanctioned (punished) and S represents the magnitude of the sanction.[30] While deterrence theory is normally applied to state law, it can also be applied to non-state sanctions; indeed the father of economics, Adam Smith (1759), devoted an entire book to the incentive effects generated by non-state sanctions and internalized moral beliefs.[31]

It can also be useful to think of a legal order having its own production function that converts inputs (for example, labour and capital) into the provision and enforcement of law. We can expect that the probability of being sanctioned to vary with the level of enforcement activity and the productivity of enforcement activity. The productivity of enforcement effort will depend on: the technology used by the legal order's practitioners and agents, for example the use of fingerprinting or surveillance cameras; the legal principles used, for example the admissibility of evidence, thresholds for guilt, and procedures for determining guilt; and also the degree of legitimacy that the legal order enjoys within society.[32]

In addition to deterrence theory, there is a considerable literature on the interaction of 'norms' and 'law' following Ellickson's (1991) seminal work *Order Without Law*. On this, McAdams and Rasmusen (2007: 1575) suggest that '[e]conomics is eminently suitable for addressing questions of the various incentives mediated neither by the explicit price of some good nor by the threats of government, incentives such as guilt, pride, esteem and disapproval', which they contend underlie norms, and while they do not explicitly say it, would also include non-state legal orders.

Perhaps the most important insight from this literature for the study of legal pluralism in Papua New Guinea is the distinction between non-state sanctions that serve as complements to state sanctions and those that serve as substitutes, in terms of their deterrent effects. This literature suggests that high-magnitude sanctions (for example, violent retribution or compensation payments) can substitute for state sanctions, while low-magnitude sanctions (for example, shunning or insults) act as mere complements. There is also a body of research (see Diamond 1971; Zasu 2007) suggesting that, over many centuries, the development of high-magnitude state sanctions began to take the place of high-magnitude non-state sanctions in many parts of the world.[33] Zasu suggests that the fall in the magnitude of non-state sanctions in Europe (that resulted in them becoming complements rather than substitutes) was driven by the relative costs of state and non-state enforcement. He suggests that the relative cost of enforcing non-state sanctions to state sanctions depends on the intensity of kinship ties in a society, with strong kinship ties making non-state sanctions a more cost-effective option.

While the law and economics literature focuses on the role of external sanctions in minimizing wrongdoing, there is some acknowledgement of internalized morals and values. Indeed some authors such as Dharmapala and McAdams (2003) and Geisinger (2002) highlight the *expressive* function of state law and suggest the state is able to create and perpetuate internalized norms and morals through its ability to signal good and bad behaviour. Posner and Rasmusen (1999: 382) also suggest that 'bad norms' can be changed by the state by 'diminishing the benefits of compliance with such norms by creating effective legal remedies' and by non-legal measures, such as education, which may be more effective in making such behaviour 'dishonourable'. Bisin and Verdier (2008) suggest that internalized norms are transmitted through both 'vertical transmission' (from one generation to another) and 'horizontal transmission' (within generations). This work suggests that internalized norms that run counter to the state law can persist indefinitely if vertical socialization is stronger than horizontal socialization. Knight (1992) suggests that for a new state law to replace conflicting customary laws, expectations among the population must change through expressive information and the use of state sanctions. He suggests that without a proper enforcement mechanism there is unlikely to be a move from the old customary equilibrium to a new state-based equilibrium. However, Posner and Rasmusen (1999: 381) caution against interfering in bilateral sanctions or weakening the power of groups to enforce their norms, suggesting that '[s]ometimes just staying out of the way is the best policy' as interference may hinder more effective forms of social control. Cooter (1998) suggests that if the state is having trouble with the population obeying the state law it should simply align its law with the prevailing morality. Whether he considered that this prescription should apply to post-colonial societies is unclear. Kahan (2000: 607) provides a basic model to analyse state efforts to change what he calls 'sticky norms', and suggests that 'gentle nudges' can be more effective than 'hard shoves' as agents of the state are more likely to enforce minor sanctions and thus create a 'self-reinforcing wave of condemnation' where the state can increase the severity of the sanction over time.

The Ordering of Different States

Making a claim that one state of affairs is better than another is difficult, and some kind of framework is needed to rank the different states. The one most favoured by economists is utility maximization, or the 'the greatest good for the greatest number' principle. One practical problem with using utility is that it is difficult to measure. Aware of this shortcoming, Bentham (1843a; c.f. Twining 2009: 137) conceived of the 'subordinate ends of Government'. He considered subsistence, abundance, equality and security to be intermediate goals to be pursued to maximize aggregate utility. Security for Bentham was broad and included life, person, reputation, property and status. He also recognized that the subordinate ends would be in competition with each other and therefore ranked security and subsistence above equality and abundance. In doing so, Bentham concluded that '[w]ithout security, equality itself could not endure a single day', and considered that the purpose of law was to create and protect security: 'Without law there is no security; consequently no abundance, nor even certain subsistence. And the only equality which can exist in such a condition is the equality of misery' (Bentham 1843a; c.f. Twining 2009: 139).

Therefore, the various states of affairs that will be primarily considered will be evaluated in respect to how they are likely to achieve security of person and sustenance. Such a ranking method is not without its shortcomings, as concepts such as freedom and diversity are not explicitly considered as part of the evaluation. However, given the foundational nature of personal security for any society to function, it is worth at least considering each state of affairs against this criterion.

Conclusion

The Independent State of Papua New Guinea is a (post) colonial creation. Prior to colonization the people of Melanesia lived in small stateless societies with their own customary legal institutions. With colonization also came a transplanted legal order that was overlaid on these pre-existing legal institutions. This has resulted in a profound case of legal pluralism. Extremely high crime rates and a general lack of personal security are well documented in Papua New Guinea's cities and urban centres. It is also in the cities and urban centres where legal pluralism is most pronounced, as the state has only a limited reach in rural and remote parts of Papua New Guinea. Both the legal pluralism and law and economics literature have much to offer the study of the current state of legal affairs in Papua New Guinea. The legal pluralism literature, while rich in description, historical analysis and conceptualization, is lacking in terms of guidance for institutional design and strategies for dealing with problematic pluralism. However, the economics literature, rich in institutional design and analytical method, mostly fails to recognize the reality of legal pluralism. It is suggested that economic analysis is well placed to better grasp the interactions of state criminal law and customary law in Papua New Guinea. However, this must be adapted for the specific circumstances of Papua New Guinea, where the state is weak and its criminal law does not always mirror society's values. This book aims to gain insight into the interactions of state and customary law and the effects on the overall level of personal security in order to provide some policy advice in ameliorating Papua New Guinea's law and order problem. However, before this analysis can be undertaken, a thorough understanding of how the two legal orders operate and interact is necessary, which is the focus of the next chapter.

Notes

1. The term 'sanction' is used to describe both the customary law and state law remedies and punishments. This term is a compromise, as under both legal orders responses to wrongs may sometimes resemble remedies more than punishments. However, legal responses to wrong behaviour generally involve some harm (or pain) to the wrongdoer, whether it be physical, mental or financial sanctions.
2. Berkowitz, Pistor and Richard (2003a, 2003b) also conclude that notable correlates with such societies are high levels of crime and disorder, and low levels of economic growth.
3. A comparison of crime rate data is discussed in Chapter 3. For actual data, see Egan, Zvekic and Alvazzi del Frate (1995). For a comparison and study of Port Moresby and Papua New Guinea crime rates, see Egan, Zvekic and Alvazzi del Frate (1995), Levantis (2000) and Haley and Muggah (2006).
4. Also see Standish (2001), Lipset (2004) and Miller and Armytage (2008) for an elaboration on the dysfunctional state of the formal state legal order and the prevalence of crime.
5. While the Act was widely reported as being repealed on 28 May 2013 (for example, see Papua New Guinea PM plans to implement death penalty 2013; and Ward 2013), however it was still in force in September 2013 when a man was jailed for twelve months for practising forbidden sorcery under the Sorcery Act 1971 (*Post Courier* 2013). The repeal of the Sorcery Act 1971 has now been certified.
6. The term 'wrong' is used to describe such acts (or omissions) to be avoided, following Narokobi (1996: 156), who concludes the 'criminal and civil law' dichotomy has little or no meaning in Papua New Guinean customary law.
7. Therefore, this book is concerned with that part of the law dealing with prohibiting and punishing crimes – what Hart (1997: 27) termed the imperative element of the law: 'something to be avoided or done'.
8. Papua New Guinea consists of the eastern half of the Island of New Guinea and many islands, including the Bismarck Archipelago.
9. The World Bank's education data for Papua New Guinea are relatively sparse and recent point estimates have varied considerably. This could suggest some degree of measurement error and underscores the difficulty in accessing accurate data for Papua New Guinea.
10. The etymology for 'wantok' in Pisin is literally 'one talk' or 'same language' referring to one's own clan or tribe. Pisin is derived from English, German, Malay and Melanesian, primarily Kuanua, the language spoken by the Tolai people of East New Britain (Mihalic 1989). While English is one of the three official languages of Papua New Guinea, it is usually only spoken on formal occasions, such as lessons at school and university, and in government business. Outside these environments, the vast majority of the population speak their local language, or Pisin or Motu, when conversing in mixed groups.
11. Woodman (2001: 3) takes the extreme position that 'state laws have no distinctive characteristics which are not frequently displayed by non-state laws'.
12. In Papua New Guinea customary law is in general conversation is referred to as *kustom* while the state law is referred to as *govman lo*. Although in Bougainville *kustom lo* was much more frequently used in conversation.
13. North (1990: 3) defines institutions as the 'rules of the game in a society', or 'constraints that shape human interaction'. He considered that institutions structure the incentives associated with human exchange, whether it is political, social or

economic. It should also be noted that when North refers to incentives, he is speaking of both reward and sanction.

14. This definition builds heavily on Twining's (2004) definition of a legal order. The main difference relates to ensuring that there is some boundary to a legal order, as opposed to an agglomeration, and is supported by the von Benda-Beckmanns (2006: 18) who suggest that a 'legal system' is a 'body of legal rules and regulations conceived as a totality'. As in Larcom (2014: 2) it is also suggested that 'each legal order has its own production function that converts various inputs into the provision and enforcement of law'.
15. For example, Twining (2009: 98) concludes that even Tamanaha, who attempts to dismiss the social ordering job of law, mostly uses examples 'concerned with contributing to and maintaining orderly relations'. That is, members of a society have reasonably clear expectations of what are wrong, acceptable and virtuous acts; and what are duties.
16. Of course states do sometimes attempt to assert the jurisdiction of their criminal law extra-territorially. For instance, under the UK Bribery Act 2010 a citizen of the United Kingdom can be prosecuted for bribery even if committed abroad. Such instances do raise the possibility of legal pluralism and the potential associated problems.
17. If the legal orders were to overlap by person – that is, if there was some uncertainty as to whether or not a diplomat was immune from state prosecution because sometimes he or she was, and sometimes not – this would constitute legal pluralism.
18. Griffiths (1986) considered that any definition of legal pluralism should not allow the standard case of diplomatic immunity, where a state cedes its criminal jurisdiction, to fit within it.
19. For instance, the Code of Canon Law (Canon 983) states that it is 'a crime' for a priest to break the seal of confession 'for any reason'. Clearly this can place a priest in direct conflict with the criminal law of the state. Under English common law there is no penitent–priest privilege (Halsbury 2002). Interestingly Bentham (1843c) discussed this issue at some length and concluded that the state should acknowledge priestly privilege (effectively ceding jurisdiction) as he considered the costs of not doing so (in the reduced number of confessions) would outweigh the benefits to law enforcement, which he considered minimal.
20. Griffiths (1986: 7–8) argues that in relation to 'formal acquiescence by the state': 'It is a messy compromise which the ideology of legal centralism feels itself obliged to make with recalcitrant social reality: until the heterogeneous and primitive populations of ex-colonial states have, in the process of "nation building", been smelted into homogeneous population of the sort which "modern" states are believed to enjoy, allowances must be made. But unification remains the eventual goal, to be enacted as soon as circumstances permit'.
21. In addition Licht, Goldschmidt and Schwartz (2005, 2007) and Guiso, Sapienza and Zingales (2006) also provide some evidence based on cross-country surveys that 'culture' can affect state law and policy, which suggests that societies may choose (if they have a choice) state laws more suited to prevailing norms. More recently, Larcom (2013a) using data for eighty-six post-colonial states has shown that countries that had higher levels of private enforcement of high magnitude sanctions in pre-colonial times currently have lower levels of state enforcement and higher levels of crime.
22. Bentham ([1802] 2011: 167) suggests that '[a] bad form of government may, while it subsists, render it ineligible to introduce a set of *laws in populum* – laws of the penal

or civil class – which under a good government would be consummately beneficial: the same thing may be said of a bad religion, and a bad system of manners'. Bentham (ibid.: 178) also concludes that '[l]aws appear the worse for being transplanted' as they are 'no longer veiled by partiality, will display themselves in their genuine weakness and impropriety' and that people will 'endure abuses they have been accustomed to, but they will not endure new ones: they will sit easily under the yoke of their own prejudices; but they will not sit easily under the prejudices of another people'.

23. Bentham (1789) considers the interaction between religious conviction and the laws of the sovereign, when discussing motives for action. He notes that religious conviction can motivate people to break state laws. For example he states, '[i]n order to obtain the favour of the Supreme Being, a man assassinates his lawful sovereign'. He also observes that what might be considered pious in one house in England is called superstitious (or even impious) in another, when referring to the Catholic Church's doctrine of Transubstantiation (*An Introduction to the Principles of Morals and Legislation*, Chapter X, XXIV, 1, p.112).
24. While Woodman (2012: 10) considers the process could involve meta-rules or choice of law rules, such as those proposed by Barron, Smith and Woolcock (2004) he rightfully concludes that '[s]uch meta-rules are not likely to be effective if they are made only in one of the laws, even state law', and in effect would likely result in an attempt to establish 'state law hegemony'.
25. Woodman (2012: 10–11) also considers that the state can aim for 'ascertainment', where it attempts to clarify and publicize customary law, such as through codification. However he notes that customary law changes over time, and in relation to efforts to bring customary law into accord with human rights laws he concludes that 'ascertainment of law projects are producing statements which are inaccurate'.
26. For instance, perhaps the most common approach that states take is simply to ignore customary law. As discussed in Chapter 2, states may also try to manipulate or reinvent customary law for their own purposes.
27. Hart (1997: 89) categorizes views of the law as 'internal and external'; he goes on to say 'it is possible to be concerned with the rules, either merely as an observer who does not himself accept them, or as a member of a group which accepts and uses them as guides to conduct'. In relation to those who view a law as external he suggests they are likely to make what is effectively a cost–benefit analysis in deciding whether to breach it or not. In later chapters, both the external and internal views of laws will be analysed.
28. This is not to say it is the only factor. For instance, Soares (2004) provides empirical support that *inequality* can lead to higher levels of crime using cross-country data.
29. Abrams (2011) attempted to isolate the effect of deterrence from incapacitation. He found that deterrence is a significant factor in addition to incapacitation.
30. In the literature, a density function, z, is often attached to g to acknowledge that gains from crimes differ amongst individuals within society. Adding a density function acknowledges that the gains from committing a crime differ among individuals, including internalized motivations. Such an addition also ensures that corner (all or nothing) solutions are avoided, such as the whole population is expected to commit a crime or no one is likely to commit a crime. Similarly a density function can be added to the punishment term, S, representing differing attitudes to punishment, including risk aversion. For a detailed discussion of the basic models, see Polinsky and Shavell (2007). While such additions increase the realism of the model, they also increase the complexity. As these issues are not the focus of the analysis they are not included here, with little or no loss of its explanatory power. This is so, as the main

focus of this analysis is on the interaction of the two legal orders – in particular, to what extent they are substitutes or compliments and to what extent they produce externalities for one another in providing a disincentive for crime.

31. The importance of social norms in regulating conduct was highlighted by Smith (1759) in the following passage: 'Nature, when she formed man for society, endowed him with an original desire to please, and an original aversion to offend his brethren. She taught him to feel pleasure in their favourable, and pain in their unfavourable regard. She rendered their approbation most flattering and most agreeable to him for its own sake; and their disapprobation most mortifying and most offensive' (*The Theory of Moral Sentiments*, Part III, Chapter II).
32. For a more formal treatment of a legal order's production function, see Larcom and Swanson (2015).
33. There is also a considerable literature on the evolution of norms drawing on the seminal works of Maynard Smith (1982), Hirshleifer (1982), and Axelrod (1984), whose work suggests that 'efficient' institutions (norms and laws) can evolve over time.

Chapter 1

Customary Law and the State Criminal Law

Customary Law

It is asserted that the basic job of law is to order social relations, and before colonization customary law did this job in Papua New Guinea.[1] Like many societies in Africa, Asia and the Pacific, Papua New Guineans lived in small stateless tribal communities that had complex structures to coordinate social interaction and provided basic social infrastructure, including personal security and education.

The following description of customary law in Papua New Guinea can be thought of as an 'ideal type'.[2] The description summarizes the processes, principles and sanctions in relation to wrongdoings under customary law, such as murder, rape, robbery, assault and theft. Such actions are labelled 'wrongs' rather than 'crimes' because, as highlighted by Narokobi (1996), customary law did not, and does not, have a crime-tort distinction like the transplanted state law.

Some Conceptual Issues

This description draws on fieldwork in the New Guinea Islands and on past descriptions from legal scholars, anthropologists and indigenous Papua New Guineans such as Lawrence (1969); Kepore (1975); Strathern (1975); Weisbrot (1982); Narokobi (1996); and Pitts (2002).[3] Given that Papua New Guinea is extremely diverse, both ethnically and culturally, and that each distinct social group possesses its own particular enforceable rules and customary principles of justice, it is likely that any generalizations can be contradicted by the practices of at least one group.[4] In addition, given customary law's intangible nature and its variability in terms of both place and time, it is questionable whether it can be adequately defined or described. My own fieldwork has also highlighted differing views and descriptions of customary law, particularly on current practices, within the same communities and villages, raising serious questions over how customary law can be captured or identified, and who has the ability or authority to articulate it.[5] There is a particular greyness in relation to customary law versus 'traditional values and practices' that does not seem to be easily separated by those who live by it and practice it, let alone by outsiders who try to document it. Like law itself, customary law can be a nebulous and slippery concept. Chanock (1998) contests the very concept, suggesting that it is a colonial invention, and arguing that what was often thought of as customary law was invented by local informants for various purposes, including self-gain and the protection of the sacred. It is also well known that customary law is not static and not easily separable from other legal orders (see Woodman 2002; Merry 2012).[6]

Despite these conceptual problems it is also undeniable that customary law exists, guides many people's behaviour, and sanctions wrongs. Its common distinguishing features are the focus of this description. Indeed some, such as Posner (1983), argue that there are strong institutional similarities across most types of customary law in tribal societies across both place and time.[7] Custom (now 'customary law') is defined in Papua New Guinea's Constitution (1975)[8] as: 'the customs and usages of the indigenous inhabitants of the country existing in relation to the matter in question at the time … and the place in relation to which the matter arises, regardless of whether or not the custom of usage existed from time immemorial'.

This definition was borrowed from pre-independence Ghana and Solomon Islands (see Gordon and Meggitt 1985). While some may quibble with this definition, not least because it is used by the state and is tautological, but it does effectively highlight the indigenous nature of customary law, the importance of context, and allows for the fact that, like state law, it can and does change over time.

The Fluid Nature of Law

In Papua New Guinea customary law seems to be a product of many influences including pre-existing customary law, perceptions of pre-existing customary law, interactions with the state law and religious teaching (see Larcom 2015). Of course it must be remembered that customary law was not static prior to colonization either, and Woodman (1986: 135), for instance, argues that the arrival of the sweet potato on the Island of New Guinea, well before European contact, revolutionized agriculture and society, and no doubt the then legal order.[9] In light of these influences, Narokobi (1996: 19) considers customary law in Papua New Guinea as: '[n]either the "pure" classical Melanesian jurisprudence, nor an adoption of an Anglo-Australian jurisprudence. It is a combination of the classical and the contemporary or the new ideas, whatever their sources or origins'.

Despite the fact that customary law does change and that its authenticity is not beyond question, it is noteworthy how closely the findings of my own fieldwork accord with many of the descriptions of customary law that were written many decades before, suggesting that certain conceptions of wrongdoing, sanctions, practices and principles are more persistent than some authors suggest. Indeed many of the key elements described below were also documented during the early colonial period (see Gore 1965; West 1968; Jinks, Biskup and Nelson 1973; and Weisbrot 1982).

Role of Kinship and Reciprocity

Kinship and reciprocity are the foundations of the customary legal order. As briefly noted earlier, kinship obligations and privileges are referred to as the *wantok* system in Papua New Guinea. Under the *wantok* system, primary loyalty is seen as belonging to the family, clan, language group, and even province over other groupings. In a more general context such kinship obligations are often referred to as tribalism. To some, to talk of tribes and tribalism in relation to customary law may be considered archaic. However, the fundamental importance of 'the group', kinship, and social relations to all aspects of customary law makes it a good literal descriptor. The closer the relationship one has, the stronger the obligations and expectations in all aspects of life, including the enforcement of customary law. The concept of kinship also highlights that under customary law some individuals are either within a group or outside it, which has a significant impact on social relations and the consequences of actions.

Kinship obligations also impact enforcement activity, which is usually delivered through compensation claims or retribution. The enforcement of customary law is the primary responsibility of the person wronged and his or her inner *wantok* group, and is commonly referred to as 'self-help'.[10] Kin are obliged to protect the group and to help to enforce customary sanctions under the principle of reciprocity.[11] The timing of enforcement may be immediate, such as in the case of 'payback'. For instance, as outlined in Larcom (2013b), in the Kieta region of Bougainville traditional customary law required a payback killing to take place on the same day as a homicide. Once the sun rises on the next day, other sanctions, such as a demand for compensation, should be sought. In any case, compensation is often sought from an offender's kinship group rather than retribution. However, if the payment is not forthcoming by an agreed date, the wrongdoer or their family or clan are once again liable for retribution. While enforcement is the responsibility of the wronged, and his or her family, customary leaders on both sides will normally be involved to aid negotiation, to ensure the penalty is enforced, and most of all to ensure that peace is restored to the communities. Family members of the wrongdoer may also enforce punishments, such as shaming the person, seizing property, or even handing over an offender to another clan for execution. Other enforcers of customary law include sorcerers, who may aim to harm a wrongdoer through physical or supernatural means. Also, other members of the kinship group may conduct beatings or executions on behalf of the group as a whole.

Methods of detection and determination of guilt or innocence under customary law also harness kinship obligations and community networks, and sometimes the use of supernatural divination. Clan leaders may meet the leaders from the other group to identify the wrongdoer, and sometimes demand that he is handed over for punishment. If the wrongdoer cannot be identified, particularly in relation to suspected sorcery killings, kin will meet community leaders to reach consensus on the identity of the wrongdoer. Supernatural means may also be used in conjunction with a process of deduction – for example, by asking themselves if any of those who they think practise sorcery might have a reason to kill this person?

In much of Papua New Guinea the fact that someone has been killed means that retribution or compensation demands will be forthcoming, regardless of intention or level of care taken, and therefore the standard of responsibility generally approaches 'strict liability'. For example, if a car driver kills someone through no fault of their own, they are generally considered responsible for taking a life and they can expect retribution or compensation demands to come their way. As stated earlier, it is therefore common for a driver to flee following a car accident, whether at fault or not, because of the fear of immediate retribution.

Types of Sanction

Serious wrongs such as murder, rape and robbery can result in payback attacks. This led Narokobi (1996: 176) to declare that, in Papua New Guinea, 'killing is not a crime, but a punishment'. The decision to sanction a wrongdoer through payback or compensation depends on a number of factors that include the timing of the response, the region of the country, and kinship ties. Kinship ties play an important role as the appropriate sanction primarily depends on the social distance between the two parties, measured by closeness or distance from kinship (including marital) ties.[12] As a general rule, the closer the relationship the less severe the sanction. While violence may be directed towards kin, it is unlikely to be fatal and will be followed by mediation and reconciliation. In resolving a dispute between people with close social ties, the main aim is to restore social relationships and order, as the parties involved are likely to belong to the same or closely related in-group who rely on each other for many aspects of daily life. Self-regulation, social pressure, and sorcery are the main controls of behaviour to prevent wrong action involving persons of the same in-group. Therefore, where there are close kinship ties, retribution is often mild or non-existent, even in cases involving homicide.

Where there is no morally binding relationship between the parties, as with strangers or members of rival groups, retribution or violent payback is much more likely, as scores need to be settled. In some parts, if a wrongdoer's family wishes to avoid payback, they must make a part monetary payment immediately after the incident, to 'let heads cool'. Such a payment displays a willingness to settle the matter non-violently. In the case of a killing, if the payment is accepted, and after a period of mourning, the families and clan leaders will negotiate a settlement consisting of money, and sometimes vehicles and land, and a date by which it must be paid. If the settlement is paid as agreed, the two families will eat together to signify that the matter is finished.

While the actual wrongdoer is more likely to be punished, a member of his or her immediate family may sometimes bear the punishment instead, which approaches joint or 'group liability'. From the perspective of the wronged clan, the question of which actual individual from the other clan is at fault may not be of great importance, therefore the wrongdoer's family may face retribution in the form of a payback killing. While the wrongdoer is not directly punished, he or she suffers the loss of a family member and will be blamed for this death within the group. The offender may have to provide for the family of the deceased, give up lands, and be reminded of the trouble he or she has caused. Compensation payments for serious wrongs are also borne collectively among the wrongdoer's extended family. For example, from data collected in late 2010, a compensation demand for murder often exceeds 100,000 Kina (K) ($40,000) in the Kieta region of Bougainville while on the island of New Britain compensation demands for murder were considerably less, in the range of K20,000 ($8,000) to K30,000 ($12,000). I was told that similar, or greater, amounts are demanded in the highlands region, and by highlanders who have moved to the islands region. In a country where the average income was approximately $1,300 per year in 2010, this is a considerable sum, and help from an extended kinship network is necessary for it to be paid.[13] The wrongdoer is indebted to his or her kin for a considerable period. He or she may have to give up land, take on extra tasks, and be reminded of what they have done and the trouble they have caused their clan. Persistent wrongdoers, who through their actions are deemed to be wrecking the community, can be executed by their own clan or handed over to the clan with the grievance, highlighting the social reality that persistent wrongdoers require incapacitation either through imprisonment or execution. Beatings are also commonly used to punish wrongdoers.

Wrongs

For the most part, actual wrongs under customary law are similar to those under the transplanted criminal law, with three notable exceptions: sorcery, adultery and accidental death.[14] Adultery was considered a grave wrong at the time of European colonization and still is across most parts of Papua New Guinea.[15] The supernatural is considered a powerful force, and sorcery is often blamed for death or misfortune. Where a homicide is deemed to be caused by sorcery, retaliation can include a payback killing while alternative forms of sanction can include demands for compensation or counter-sorcery.[16] Accidental killings are also generally seen to require a sanction, as the taking of a life is seen as a wrong per se, requiring a sanction. It must be stressed, however, that notions of right and wrong and their consequences are again moderated by kinship under what Lawrence (1969: 34) called the 'sliding scale justice', where the sliding scale depends on 'social distance'. The rule of thumb is that social relations are more important than the actual action itself; for example, Narokobi (1996: 71) tells us that notions of 'stealing' over 'taking' often depend on 'from whom one takes'.

Rules of Conduct

Gore (1965: 75) concluded in his memoirs as a Supreme Court Judge in Papua and New Guinea for more than thirty years that while there was 'sensible custom of land tenure and the descent of land and their marriage' in criminal matters, '[t]here were no fundamental rules of conduct upon which to build a criminal system'. While customary law sanctions can be brutal and often privately enforced, and although practice does vary from place to place, his conclusion that there are no fundamental rules of conduct seems to be extreme. Under customary law some actions are rewarded, while others are sanctioned. While this depends on social relations, and not merely on the action, individuals are guided into certain types of behaviour through the customary legal order, both in preventing the commission of a wrong and sanctioning it. People living in such a society should be able to have an understanding of the likely consequences of their actions and are able to predict the behaviour of others. Whether they could be used to build a state criminal system is less clear.

Posner (1983) and Parisi and Dari-Mattiacci (2004) have attempted to provide an economic rationale for the main principles of customary law similar to those described above, such as differential treatment for insiders and outsiders, and the use of group and strict liability. While their analysis has its shortcomings (particularly by ignoring the power of internalized values), it does provide insight into how customary law can be effective in regulating wrongs and ordering social relations. They suggest that given the high information costs and low levels of technology in these communities, customary institutions were generally 'economically efficient'. For example, as close kin rely on each another for survival and protection, the probability that one would deliberately kill another is expected to be very low compared to strangers. Also, even where a serious dispute has arisen, given the close living arrangements and lack of privacy, it is unlikely that an individual would deliberately carry out an offence against close kin as the probability of prevention, apprehension and detection would be extremely high. Therefore, kin are generally presumed to act in a benign manner towards each other, so retribution is generally avoided and compensation is light, and the need for deterrence through punishment is much less compared to that for strangers. In addition, group responsibility in exercising justice (that is, kin organizing meetings, demanding compensation, and carrying out retribution) and liability (where kin are liable for compensation or retribution) also seems efficient by way of the incentive structure it generates for the individual. The group, and the individuals within it, need to provide a credible threat against attack from outsiders. Therefore, if they die or become incapacitated their kin are needed to avenge their death or injury in order to maintain a strong disincentive against future attacks. Also, the likelihood of reprisal is much higher if a number of people are involved. Collective responsibility also serves the purpose of providing a strong incentive for kin to monitor and regulate the actions of each other, and to search for and weed out anti-social members. Customary law of the type described above also seems to be able to generate reasonably high levels of personal security, as evidenced by the peacefulness of many remote villages in Papua New Guinea that effectively have no access to, or interference from, the state criminal law.[17]

The preceding description is very much an ideal type and it is acknowledged that the current practice of customary law is much more complicated. However, it describes the essence and key principles and processes. It should also be noted that while many of the more violent and supernatural aspects of customary law may be considered wrong by many people in Papua New Guinea today, few would fail to acknowledge them as legitimate sanctions under customary law, at least in times past.

State Legal Order

What follows is a description of the state legal order's processes, principles and sanctions in relation to wrongs. Like many post-colonial societies, the Papua New Guinean state is weak and has difficulty in enforcing its will in many respects, including the criminal justice system. Acknowledging the reality of surface law and deep legal pluralism, later chapters analyse how the state and its agents actually administer criminal law, but for now the description and analysis is mainly limited to official state law and policy in the sanctioning of wrongs. There will first be a description of the state criminal law of Papua New Guinea and the processes involved, including a discussion on the philosophical principles that underlie the transplanted criminal law and its evolution. This is followed by a discussion of how the state attempts to accommodate customary law through the Constitution, statutes, judicial interpretations, and the village court system.

The Criminal Law

If a person behaves in a manner deemed to be wrong under the state legal order, he or she faces the probability of being sanctioned under the civil branch, the criminal branch, or potentially both branches of the transplanted legal order. As Williams (2006) tells us, the difference between an act (or omission) labelled a 'crime' versus one that is labelled a 'civil wrong' depends on the *legal consequence* of the wrongful act, and not on the act itself. If the wrongful act is capable of being sanctioned under criminal proceedings it is labelled a crime, if it is capable of being sanctioned under civil proceedings it is labelled a civil wrong, and if it is capable of being sanctioned by both it is labelled a crime *and* a civil wrong.

Under Papua New Guinea's state legal order, wrongs such as murder, rape, robbery, theft, property damage, and assault are capable of being sanctioned under the criminal branch of the law and are therefore labelled by the state as crimes. While also being civil wrongs, it is rare for these actions to be sanctioned under the civil branch in addition to being sanctioned under the criminal branch.[18] While compensation payments are often demanded by those who are wronged in Papua New Guinea, this is mostly done outside of the state legal order or sometimes as part of a criminal sentence under the Criminal Law (Compensation) Act 1991. This Act allows a judge to award up to K5,000 ($2,000) compensation to victims, paid by the wrongdoer. Therefore, the focus of this discussion is on the state criminal law, however when discussing the historical evolution and philosophical underpinnings of criminal law later it will be asked why the civil branch of the law is seen more as a substitute than a complement.

Like in Australia and England, if a wrong is committed, and if it is a criminal offence, the Papua New Guinean state takes it upon itself to prosecute the offender. In Papua New Guinea most criminal offences are contained within the Criminal Code made law by the Criminal Code Act 1974. The Criminal Code is a legal transplant, its origin being the Australian state of Queensland. It was applied to British Papua in 1902 and the former German Territories (New Guinea) in 1921.[19] The Criminal Code was a creation of Sir Samuel Griffith in an attempt to simplify the criminal law, make the content more accessible to laypeople, and reduce uncertainty in relation to substantive rules and processes.[20] Griffith (1897: III) attempted to 'include all rules of the Common Law which are relevant to the question of criminal responsibility and administration of justice in courts of criminal jurisdiction'. In drafting the code, Griffith 'derived very great assistance' from the Italian Penal Code of 1888, and also had 'frequent recourse' to the Penal Code of New York.

Despite these influences, and various amendments through the years, the Criminal Code is very much based on the content and procedures of English criminal law, and like virtually all other Western criminal laws it is based on impartiality, consistency, individual responsibility, concepts of intent and fault, and the denial of the supernatural causes of events. The most notable departure from common law in the Criminal Code is the intentional removal of the doctrine of *mens rea*. Griffith preferred to rely on specific mental elements attached to individual offences, for example wilful murder (Section 299), murder (Section 300), and manslaughter (Section 302). Section 24 of the Criminal Code also states that a person is not criminally responsible for an act or omission 'that occurs independently of his will' or 'an event that occurs by accident'. For practical purposes, the absence of this *mens rea* has had little effect both in Queensland and Papua New Guinea.[21] Common law justifications and defences are also explicitly contained in the Criminal Code. Given its origins, it contains those offences commonly considered as criminal in any Western society; however the legislature in Papua New Guinea has so far resisted pressure, mainly external, to remove homosexuality and abortion from the Criminal Code (Sections 210 and 312). As to be expected, punishments are mostly confined to fines and imprisonment. However the death penalty was reintroduced into the Code by Section 2 of the Criminal Code (Amendment) Act 1991 for Wilful Murder (Section 299) in an effort to combat the country's seemingly ever-increasing crime problem. Since this amendment no one has been executed, although some offenders have been sentenced to death which has been later commuted to life imprisonment on appeal. The Criminal Code (Amendment) Act 2013, parliament's latest law and order initiative, has extended the number of offences to which the death penalty applies. The penalty now applies to the specific new crime of Wilful Murder of a Person on Account of Accusation of Sorcery (Section 229A); Aggravated Rape (347A); and Robbery (Section 386). The same Act also extends the possible methods of execution to hanging, lethal injection, deprivation of oxygen, firing squad and electrocution (Section 614).

Depending on the gravity of the offence, cases are heard either by a District Court magistrate or National Court judge. District Court magistrates have jurisdiction over matters under Schedule II of the Criminal Code which includes over eighty offences including serious assault, indecent assault, theft, dangerous driving of a motor vehicle causing death, and property damage. The most serious crimes, such as murder and rape, are heard by the National Court which also hears District Court appeals. The highest state court in Papua New Guinea is the Supreme Court, which as well as interpreting the Constitution, hears appeals from the National Court.[22] While the Constitution does not explicitly rule out the use of juries in criminal cases (Section 186), magistrates and judges decide on the verdict and determine the sentence in criminal trials.

The decision to prosecute an offender is made by the public prosecutor or the police under delegated authority. The Office of the Public Prosecutor was established under Section 176 of the Constitution and under Section 4 of the Public Prosecutor (Office and Functions) Act 1977, and has 'absolute discretion' to 'give consent or refuse consent to proceed with the prosecution of any criminal offence where his consent is by law required'. For offences heard by the National Court following committal in the District Court, Section 525 of the Criminal Code provides for the public prosecutor, after considering the evidence, to decide whether to indict the offender or decline to lay a charge. In relation to prosecution policy, the Office of the Public Prosecutor (2008b: 8) states that:

> The decision whether or not to prosecute is the most important step in the prosecution process. In every case great care must be taken in the interests of the victim, the suspected offender, and the community at large to ensure that the right decision is made.
>
> It is not the rule that suspected criminal offences must automatically be the subject of criminal prosecution. The first consideration is always whether the evidence which is available, and admissible, is such that a court is likely to convict. If there is such evidence, the next question is whether prosecution is in the public interest.

In relation to consideration of the public interest, the Office of the Public Prosecutor (2008b: 9–10) provides a non-exhaustive list of factors that includes the 'seriousness' of the alleged offence,[23] and goes on to conclude:

> As a general rule, the more serious an offence the more likely it is that a prosecution should proceed. While there may be public interest factors which tend away from prosecution, in the great majority of cases where there is a reasonable prospect of conviction the matter should proceed, unless those factors clearly outweigh the public interest in favour of prosecution. Such factors should, however, be put before the sentencing court for consideration.

Of particular interest is the public prosecutor's unwillingness to allow defendants to avoid criminal prosecution on the basis of making customary settlement. The Office of the Public Prosecutor (2008b: 10) explicitly states that 'defendants must not avoid prosecution merely because they pay compensation'. The non-recognition of customary law by the Office of the Public Prosecutor (2008a: 31) is further highlighted:

> When an investigation is done by police, and where evidence exists, the police may arrest and charge a person with an offence. Once that is done, the charges cannot usually be withdrawn. For example, payment of compensation cannot be used as a reason to withdraw charges. **Payment of compensation does NOT mean that the charges are withdrawn.** [emphasis in original document]
>
> Payment of compensation or interference in other ways may be deemed to be perverting the course of justice. That is a very serious criminal offence. The payment of compensation only means that a prosecutor can tell the magistrate or judge about the compensation payment or other restorative justice process; the judge or magistrate will consider those facts when sentencing the prisoner, [if] he or she is found guilty.

> If it is a family or clan member who has been charged and there has been intimidation of the witness, the charges should still proceed. It is not up to the complainant or witness to withdraw the charges; only a police prosecutor, with approval of their senior personnel, may withdraw charges in the District Court. In the National Court, the public prosecutor may authorise the prosecutor handling the case to withdraw a charge.

In short, the official operation of Papua New Guinea's criminal justice system aims to operate as it does from where it originated, in both content and procedure. While the state guards its prosecution powers, as under current English law, there remains the possibility of a private prosecution. Therefore within Papua New Guinea, while it is extremely rare, any person can bring forward a prosecution for an indictable offence that is not punishable by death. However, given the Constitutional powers of absolute discretions, the public prosecutor is able to intervene in the prosecution and take it up or discontinue it if it is deemed not to be in the public interest.[24]

Key Differences in the Two Legal Orders

It is suggested here that the job of both the customary legal order and the transplanted state legal order is to order social relations, including the control and sanctioning of wrong behaviour. However, it should also be apparent from the preceding sections that the two legal orders have very different processes and measures for doing this job. What follows is a brief discussion of the major points of difference between the two legal orders.

Perhaps the greatest divergence between the two legal orders is the importance of social relations and the concept of kinship in customary law and the lack of it in state law. The recognition of kinship, or lack of recognition, plays an important role in both the process and content of the two legal orders. As described earlier, under customary law whether compensation is demanded or revenge taken, and with what speed and magnitude, depends on the social distance between the wronged and wrongdoer. Customary law's sliding scale justice based on kinship and social distance sees those with close ties sanctioned relatively lightly, while those with distant or no ties face a much harsher sanction. For example, the killing of a close kinsman may result in relatively light compensation, whereas the killing of a stranger would justify a payback homicide. Clearly, the exercise of sliding scale justice is in direct contrast to the transplanted Criminal Code. As noted by Lawrence (1969: 34), the state law comes from 'a society in which the individual has become the indistinguishable, transposable citizen-isolate and which stresses judicial authority at the expense of all other factors as the governing factor in litigation'. For the transplanted law, many would claim that equality before the law is one of its highest ideals.

The customary law concept of self-help is also a major point of difference between the two legal orders. Under the criminal law the state and its agents prosecute, determine guilt or innocence, and punish a wrongdoer, whereas under customary law the victim and his or her kin sanction a wrongdoer. However, vigilantism and self-help are generally seen as an affront to the state and are punished severely under criminal law in most societies, with Papua New Guinea being no exception. Furthermore, under customary law the decision to 'prosecute' and the selection of the type of sanction is made by the victim and his or her kin, whereas under the criminal law it is made by the state.

Issues of intent are given less attention in customary law than under the Criminal Code, despite doing away with the doctrine of *mens rea*. Similarly, the use of group liability, where kin are subject to claims for compensation or violent retribution, is also in direct contrast to the Criminal Code. The combination of strict liability and group liability in customary law can result in many situations where customary law clashes with the transplanted state law or would produce vastly different outcomes.

Another key difference between the transplanted state law and customary law is that some behaviours are considered wrong by one legal order, but not by the another. Similarly, some crimes differ in gravity under the different legal regimes. As will be elaborated in more detail later, this is particularly the case for customary sanctions that are considered grave crimes by the state.

In relation to wrong behaviour, customary law is based on kinship, self-help, group liability, strict liability, and an acknowledgement of the supernatural. Conversely, state criminal law is based on a different set of principles, including equal and consistent treatment of wrongdoers, the use of the state to prosecute and punish wrongdoers and an intolerance of vigilante activity, individual responsibility, a focus on intention, and dismissal of supernatural causes of events.

State Recognition of Customary Law

Given that both legal orders assert their jurisdiction over much of the country, and given their differences in procedure and content, the following section discusses how the state attempts to accommodate and suppress customary law in relation to wrongs. On the face of it, state recognition of customary law in Papua New Guinea is remarkable. Not least, the Constitution recognizes customary law as part of the underlying law of the country and speaks of the development of an indigenous jurisprudence. Despite the Constitutional elevation of customary law, the state attempts to enforce the Criminal Code, based on Western notions of morality and justice, much as the state does in Queensland or England. However, there is one important exception, which will be discussed later in this chapter – the village courts.

The Constitution and Statutes

The Constitutional and statutory recognition of customary law in criminal matters is not straightforward, and therefore it is outlined below in some detail, bearing in mind that the legal orderings of the Papua New Guinean state are generally accepted to be: the Constitution; Organic Laws made by the National Parliament which form part of the Constitution; Statutes of the National Parliament (and regulations pursuant to these statutes); and the Underlying Law consisting of both customary law and English common law.

It is clear that the drafters of the Constitution wished to acknowledge customary law to some extent. The degree of this role is open to debate (see Corrin-Care and Zorn 2001). However, it would not seem unreasonable to suggest that the drafters wished to limit customary law where it clashed with or restricted National Goals and Directive Principles and Basic Rights outlined in the Constitution and where it clashed with the Criminal Code.[25] Despite the Constitution's ambivalence towards customary law, Schedule 2 of the Constitution calls for the development of an 'indigenous jurisprudence'. Schedule 2.1 declares that 'custom is adopted, and shall be applied and enforced as part of the underlying law', except where it is 'inconsistent with a Constitutional Law or statute, or repugnant to the general principles of humanity'. Schedule 2.2 adopted the common law and equity of England which applied immediately before independence, unless it was inconsistent with the Constitution, or a statute, or inapplicable and inappropriate to the circumstances of a country from time to time, or inconsistent with custom adopted under Schedule 2.1. Schedule 2 also specifies how the underlying law is to be developed and that the Supreme and National Courts are to ensure 'that with due regard to consistency, the underlying law develops as a coherent system'.

Schedule 2.6(2) of the Constitution also adopted all pre-independence laws as Acts of Parliament, limiting the role of customary law in relation to criminal matters. This included the adoption of the Criminal Code and the Customs Recognition Act 1963. Shortly after independence this Act was amended, and the clause specifying that customary law shall not be recognized when 'repugnant to the general principles of humanity' was removed as it was explicitly contained in the Constitution. It was in any case considered unnecessary as it was deemed that such custom would contravene the Constitution's human rights provisions (see Corrin-Care and Zorn 2001: 66).[26] Section 3 of the Act also 'allows custom to be recognised and enforced by, and may be pleaded in, all courts except' when: (a) 'its recognition or enforcement would result in injustice or would not be in the public interest'; or (b) 'affecting the welfare of a child under the age of 16'. In relation to criminal law, Section 4 of the Act states that custom may be taken into account subject 'to any other law' only for the purpose of: (a) 'ascertaining the existence or otherwise of a state of mind of a person'; (b) 'deciding the reasonableness of an act, default or omission'; (c) 'deciding the reasonableness or otherwise of an excuse'; (d) 'deciding, in accordance with any other law whether to proceed to the conviction of a guilty party'; or (e) 'determining the penalty (if any) to be imposed on a guilty party'. In addition, Section 4 of the Act also allows for custom to be taken into account 'where the court thinks that by not taking the custom into account injustice will or may be done to a person'.

After considerable delay, the Underlying Law Act 2000 was passed by parliament.[27] The bill was drafted by the Law Reform Commission (1977) around the time of independence, who considered its four objectives to be: to change attitudes of lawyers and judges towards custom; to require custom to become the underlying law's major source over that of common law; to establish guidelines to help lawyers and judges to find the appropriate underlying rule; and to assist courts in developing the underlying law. Section 3 of the Act specifies that the underlying law shall be: (a) the customary law;[28] and (b) the common law in force in England immediately before independence. Sections 3 and 4 also state that customary law shall apply unless: (a) it is inconsistent with a written law; (b) its application and enforcement would be contrary to the National Goals and Directive Principles and the Basic Social Obligations established by the Constitution; or (c) its application and enforcement would be contrary to the basic rights guaranteed by Division III of the Constitution. In contrast, Section 4(3) makes clear that the common law shall not be applied unless: (a) it is consistent with a written law; or (b) it is applicable and appropriate to the circumstances of the country; or (c) it is consistent with the customary law as applied above or consistent with the National Goals and Basic Rights of the Constitution.

Section 4(4) of the Act also requires courts that refuse to apply a principle or rule of customary law to give reasons under subsections (a), (b) or (c) above. Section 5 of the Act also specifies that it is the duty of the courts, especially the Supreme Court and the National Court, to develop a 'coherent' underlying law (where written law does not apply). Section 11 of the Act also specifies that parties to a proceeding shall bring evidence or information to assist the court in deciding whether to apply a principle of customary law, apply a principle of common law, or formulate a rule of the underlying law. It is noteworthy that the limits placed on the recognition of custom under the Underlying Law Act 2000 differ from Schedule 2 of the Constitution. Schedule 2.1(2) of the Constitution states that custom does not apply when it is 'inconsistent with a Constitutional Law or a statute, or repugnant to the general principles of humanity', whereas the Underlying Law Act 2000 (Section 3 and 4) states that custom does not apply when it is inconsistent with: written law; the National Goals, Directive Principles, and Basic Social Obligations; or the Basic Rights of the Constitution.[29] As Section 24 of the Underlying Law Act 2000 repeals Schedule 2 of the Constitution,[30] it would seem that the Constitutional limits on custom considered 'repugnant to the general principles of humanity' no longer applies. However, as late as 2007, both the Supreme Court in *Thomas* v. *The State*[31] and the government[32] have referred to the 'repugnancy' clause in limiting customary law. This would seem to indicate that Schedule 2 of the Constitution may still be in force.[33] While the Underlying Law Act 2000 explicitly repeals Schedule 2 of the Constitution, it is silent on the Customs Recognition Act 1963 which remains in force.[34]

A literal interpretation of the Constitution, (the Organic) Underlying Law Act 2000, and Customs Recognition Act 1963 suggests that customary law in criminal matters should be recognized when it is not inconsistent with the Constitution's human rights provisions or the Criminal Code. Despite this, there is considerable scope provided by the Customs Recognition Act 1963 for the courts to recognize customary law in defences and sentencing under the Criminal Code if they so wish. However the higher courts have taken a very restrictive interpretation, as discussed below. From a Constitutional viewpoint it seems that the only impediment in the recognition of customary law applies to its human rights provisions. However, it should also be noted that Narokobi (1996: 52–53) considers that Papua New Guinea's autochthonous Constitution arose out of customary law itself and is lower in hierarchy than the Constituent Assembly of the Constitutional Convention, which strongly advocated the promotion of customary law and which he considers reflected the will of the people.

The Courts and Sentencing Trends

During colonial times, and immediately after, most judges of the National and Supreme Courts of Papua New Guinea were Australian. Now this situation has reversed, with twenty of the twenty-four judges, including the Chief Justice and the Deputy Chief Justice being indigenous Papua New Guineans (Government of Papua New Guinea 2012). Following independence, some hoped that the practice of customary law in criminal matters would be embraced by the courts, especially given legislative changes that seemed to be more tolerant of customary law, along with the very act of independence itself. They were disappointed. The courts initially maintained the practice developed during the colonial period where the judiciary applied a broad interpretation of the partial defence of provocation (Section 266 of the Criminal Code) and of what was considered 'reasonable' in Papua New Guinean circumstances (Otterly and Zorn 1983). While the practice of customary law was not an excuse or defence against criminal conviction, it usually saw the conviction downgraded and/or the sentence significantly mitigated. In considering the 'reasonable man test', judges considered the level of 'sophistication' of the offender which was determined, among other things, by the level of Western education and the degree of geographical remoteness to the colonial administration.[35] The partial defence of provocation often saw defendants found guilty of less serious crimes, for instance manslaughter rather than wilful murder. The courts also used the concept of de facto provocation, again based on customary law motivations and the concept of sophistication, as a significant mitigating factor in sentencing.[36] It was acknowledged that most offenders were 'not criminals in the true sense of the word' and sentenced accordingly (Gore 1965: 88). Those who committed homicide and came to the attention of colonial authorities and were motivated by customary law were usually sentenced from the rising of the court to three or four years imprisonment (ibid.: 77–114). As will be discussed in Chapter 2, throughout much of the colonial period, customary law, while seen as inferior to the transplanted state legal order, was acknowledged as an important social control.

However, since independence, sentences for crimes committed through customary law motivations have steadily increased, and since the passing of the Underlying Law Act 2000, which was aimed at increasing the recognition of customary law, the lack of recognition has increased further. While continuing to some degree, the earlier practice of allowing customary law motivations as a mitigating factor in sentencing has, rather than increasing the scope of recognition, been limited to fewer circumstances.[37] In addition, and perhaps more importantly, the reduction in sentencing due to customary law considerations has been considerably lessened. In short, the higher courts either punish customary motivations or sanctions, or ignore them. This intolerance of the courts towards customary sanctions and self-help has been largely driven by efforts to deter violent crime, given its ubiquity and seemingly constant escalation. Rather than seeing customary law sanctions as a form of control against wrongdoing, the courts now see it as a cause. The Supreme Court is a strong believer in deterrence theory. In 2004, in *Thomas* v. *The State*, the court considered that current sentencing practices in relation to serious crimes were too lenient:[38]

> Indirectly, we may be contributing to the escalating prevalence of the crimes when we let serious violent offenders walk free or impose very inadequate or suspended sentences on serious violent crimes as has been seen in more recent times. … [I]gnoring the community's concerns may lead to distrust in the judicial system and may provide the catalyst for destructive self-help schemes such as payback. That would in turn prove a good recipe for a serious breakdown in law and order, and anarchy. We are now experiencing an unprecedented and a high level of crime. Judges now have the serious responsibility on behalf of the society to ensure this does not get out of control by paying close and serious attention to the kind of penalties imposed for those who are found guilty of committing serious violent offences like rape, murder, wilful murder and armed robbery.

In the following year, 2005, the Supreme Court set much tougher sentencing guidelines for all homicides, in *Kovi* v. *The State*. The court endorsed the trend of increasingly tougher sentences imposed on homicide offenders and developed a sentencing schedule that depended on various aggravating and mitigating circumstances ranging from 8–12 years imprisonment for Category 1 Manslaughter to the death penalty for Category 4 Wilful Murder. While the court acknowledged that de facto provocation can be a mitigating factor in sentencing, there was no specific mention of customary law motivations.[39]

In 2004 in *The State* v. *Gena*, the National Court attempted to rule out the motivation of payback being a mitigating factor in sentencing.[40] However, the Supreme Court has made it clear that custom should be considered along with other relevant factors, but that it has no special status. In *Ume* v. *The State* in 2006, the Supreme Court restated the general principles for the sentencing of wilful murder.[41] It stated that examples for reducing[42] the sentence included 'de facto provocation, duress or coercion, the degree and extent of the offender's participation, the offender's medical condition such as psychopathic personality, offender's lack of sophistication or traditional customs, practices and beliefs which influence the offender to act in the way he did'. The court found that, among other things, the trial judge 'failed to consider relevant customary considerations which influenced the killing'.

In 2010 in *The State* v. *Kepao*, the National Court ruled that customary law can be taken into account as evidence of motive for convicting an offender of wilful murder.[43] In addition, in an unreported case in 2010 that attracted media attention, *The State* v. *Monodoao*,[44] a National Court judge sentenced a man convicted of wilful murder to life imprisonment for a payback killing. In his judgement he told the prisoner he should have been handed the death penalty but for lack of warning, as no one had been executed by the state for some time. He put future payback killers on notice that a death penalty will be forthcoming to serve as a deterrent. In conclusion, Justice Ellis said:

> The incidence of payback killings and deaths from tribal fighting has become a cause for concern. Right-thinking people regard such conduct as offensive. However, as there [are] still some in this country who regard payback killings as an age-old custom, it is necessary to change such attitudes and to change the conduct of those who commit payback killings, regardless of whether they occur in a village, a rural town or the national capital. (Kelola 2010)

While the courts have been getting increasingly tough on the enforcement of payback, the repeal of the Sorcery Act 1971 and the accompanying Criminal Code (Amendment) Act 2013 that applies the death penalty to the new crime of Wilful Murder of a Person on Account of Accusation of Sorcery (Section 229A) has taken the state's combative stance towards customary motivations to a new level, and one never seen before in Papua New Guinea. Prior to the recent legislative activity, under Section 7 of the repealed Sorcery Act 1971 the practice of 'forbidden sorcery' could attract a prison term of five years, while Section 16 explicitly stated that an 'act of sorcery may amount to a wrongful act or insult' for the (partial) defence of provocation. As discussed earlier, the practice of sorcery is considered a grave wrong across much of Papua New Guinea, and is potentially punishable by death in some parts. While sorcerers are often believed to use supernatural means to cause death or injury, they can also use more practical means – for example, poisoning (Goddard 2009). These amendments seemed to be partly in response to some highly publicized horrific killings of alleged sorcerers, a Law Reform Commission report, and sustained pressure from human rights groups (Amnesty International 2009, 2013). The Papua New Guinean Government's motivations for the recent legislative changes are best expressed by the Second Reading Speech for The Sorcery (Repeal) Act 2013:

> I move that the Bill be read a second time.
>
> Mr Speaker, this Act repeals the Sorcery Act in its entirety. The Sorcery Act belongs to another era. The Sorcery Act distinguished between innocent and forbidden sorcery.
>
> Mr Speaker, sorcery is no longer any excuse for committing a crime. Anyone who commits a crime in the name of sorcery will be dealt with by the full force of the law.
>
> Mr Speaker, any criminal act committed in the name of sorcery is unacceptable and will now be dea[lt] with under the Criminal Code. The killing of innocent women and sometimes men under the veil of sorcery will no longer be tolerated.
>
> Mr Speaker, the repeal of the Sorcery Act sends a strong message that the Government is tough on crime, and sorcery is no longer an excuse for committing a crime.
>
> I commend this Bill to Parliament.

While it is difficult to believe today, in the years immediately after independence there were calls for legislative change to treat those who killed alleged sorcerers more leniently (than in colonial times), however this was resisted by parliament (see Chapter 2). Unperturbed, Acting National Court Judge Bernard Narokobi attempted to engage in some judicial activism, however his efforts were overruled by the Supreme Court. Since then the courts have become evermore punitive in relation to the killing of alleged sorcerers. In this sense, and as briefly outlined below, the recent legislative changes can be seen as the culmination of an increasingly tough stance on crimes motivated by a belief in sorcery.

Not long after independence in 1980, in *The Acting Public Prosecutor v. Aumane, Boku, Wapulae, and Kone*, four men from a remote village in Enga Province were convicted of killing a woman they believed to be a witch and responsible for twenty deaths. Acting National Court Judge Narokobi sentenced the men to three months jail in addition to the four months they had already served in custody. He ruled that the sentence was mitigated primarily due to the use of the defence of provocation under Section 16 of the Sorcery Act 1971. However, the Supreme Court replaced the sentence with six years' imprisonment, considering the previous punishment grossly inadequate for a crime of wilful murder. In the judgement, the court confirmed that custom should be taken into account as a significant mitigating factor, but that it 'should not override the clear dictates of Parliament', presumably in relation to the Criminal Code.[45] They also considered that the trial judge 'over-emphasized the belief in sorcery. In fact, he went so far as to state that the deceased had killed about twenty people by sorcery'. Indeed, Acting National Court Judge Narokobi referred to the act of killing the deceased, a reputed sorceress, as 'honourable'.

In *Baipu v. The State* in 2005, the Supreme Court revisited the circumstances under which belief in sorcery can be treated as a significant mitigating factor in sentencing.[46] The court ruled that 'we are of the view that all the aspects of social change in Papua New Guinea have permeated to even remote parts of the country'. It went on to say that while actions taken on 'the spur of the moment motivated by fear and self-preservation can be significant mitigating factors', factors once referred to as relating to 'sophistication' such as educational levels and remoteness should be given less weight than in the past.[47] The court ruled that this is: '[n]ot because the belief in the effectiveness of sorcery may be diminished, but because the belief that taking the law into the defendant's own hands as the only effective means of dealing with the problem should and ought to be diminished'.

The court then went onto suggest that the appropriate sentence for a killing motivated by sorcery was now around twenty years' imprisonment, up from ten to twelve years a decade earlier, due to the spread of 'education and development', and that 'sentences for serious offences involving a belief in sorcery will tend over time to come closer to sentences for the same offence where no belief in sorcery is a factor'.[48] In 2007 in *Thomas v. The State*, the Supreme Court confirmed that it was inappropriate to readily treat a claim of belief in sorcery as a mitigating factor. The court ruled that there needed to be deterrence against claims of sorcery and resultant killings. The court considered the sentence imposed by the National Court of 18 years to be too low, and increased the sentence to twenty-two years' imprisonment with hard labour. In making its judgement the court condemned the appellant on the grounds that he acted outside the state law as 'accuser, prosecutor, jury, judge and executioner'.[49]

Other grave wrongs under customary law include adultery, and death by accident (such as a car accident). Such offences can also attract a customary sanction of death or a hefty compensation payment. Under the state legal order adultery is treated as a civil wrong under the Adultery and Enticement Act 1998, with damages of up to K1,000 ($400) being awarded. While most adultery cases are sanctioned by local tribunals or village courts, usually through compensation, those who are convicted of killing an adulterer are treated more leniently by the courts than many other customary law motivations and generally face a prison sentence of between ten and twenty years.[50] In relation to car accidents the courts often face considerable pressure to find the defendants guilty of dangerous driving where a death has occurred, regardless of fault. However, and as would be expected under the principles of the Criminal Code, the National Court in *The State* v. *Bonot* maintained that the onus is on the state to prove that the driver of a motor vehicle drove at an excessive speed or in a manner dangerous to the public.[51]

In practical terms, the courts place little weight on customary settlements that involve compensation payments for grave crimes. Section 2(1) of the Criminal Law (Compensation) Act 1991 does permit a court to order an offender to pay compensation in addition to any other punishments imposed. However, in doing so it also explicitly states that the 'payment of compensation is not specified as a punishment for an offence'.[52] In *Kovi* v. *The State* in 2005, the Supreme Court also ruled on the effect that compensation payments should play in sentencing decisions.[53] The Supreme Court noted that while the amount of compensation often varies and that despite the maximum amount of compensation that the courts can order under the Criminal Law (Compensation) Act 1991 being K5,000 ($2,000), in actual fact compensation payments negotiated between the parties prior to going to court often exceed K10,000 ($4,000) for homicides. It concluded that substantial compensation payments, those in the range of K5,000 ($2,000) to K10,000($4,000) or more, do place them in the special mitigating factor category for sentencing. However, the court also went on to rule that the weight given to ordinary and special mitigating factors will vary, and that for grave crimes such as homicide, rape and robbery, while depending on the particular case, their gravity can far outweigh the ordinary or even special mitigating factors, and thus render substantial compensation payments as insignificant. From reviewing recent sentences for grave crimes, payment of compensation sees the headline sentence reduced by between two and five years for a long (twenty-five to thirty year) sentence.[54] Compensation demands can also be considered a criminal offence. Under Section 309A of the Criminal Code, demanding compensation is an offence carrying a penalty of up to seven years' imprisonment, and the state does sometimes prosecute offences. For instance, in *The State* v. *Parakua* in early 2011, two men from Kimbe were convicted and imprisoned for demanding compensation for the killing of a pig.[55]

Ironically, despite the passing of the Underlying Law Act 2000, the purpose of which was to promote the use of customary law, the courts of Papua New Guinea have continued to limit the applicability of customary law in criminal cases and have been seeing it as a source of wrongdoing rather than as a source of control. While from a Western viewpoint many may consider this necessary, the overall effect is that the courts punish those who enforce customary sanctions involving violence and do not acknowledge customary compensation settlements as a substitute for criminal punishment. However, it must be remembered that few offences under the Criminal Code are in fact likely to come to the attention of the courts due to the weakness of the Papua New Guinean state, which has been caused by *wantokism*, poor resourcing and weak government institutions, and the desire of many communities to deal with even the most serious wrongs themselves. Even those who are imprisoned have a real probability of escaping, given the frequency of mass jail break outs.

Village Courts

In terms of volume of cases, the village courts are the main state institution for sanctioning and remedying wrong behaviour in Papua New Guinea. Under Section 57 of the Village Courts Act 1989 they are directed to apply 'any relevant custom' when making judgements 'whether or not it is inconsistent with any Act'.[56] They are also exempted from Section 37 of the Constitution which outlines the various procedural protections granted to an offender under the 'right of protection under the law'. Their only requirement is to act 'in accordance with the principles of natural justice'.[57] The Papua New Guinea Department of Justice and Attorney General (2009: 53–54) estimated that there were 1,419 village courts in operation, with 681,120 complaints lodged in a year. Of these there were 340,560 cases before full court, 170,280 adjourned or dismissed, 119,196 compensation orders, 34,056 fines, 17,028 community work orders, and 8,515 imprisonment orders (for failing to comply with village court orders).[58] Given that Papua New Guinea's population was less than 7 million at the time, and that there are often many more than two disputants involved in each case, these figures demonstrate that an extremely high proportion of Papua New Guineans come into contact with the village court system in both rural and urban environments.[59]

The formal criminal jurisdiction of the courts is limited to offences listed under Section 3 of the Village Court Regulations, and covers injury to person, damage to property, stealing property under the value of K100, disturbance of the peace, slander and insulting language, breaking of a customary rule, sorcery, carrying an offensive weapon, and a breach of local council rules. A village court can award compensation up to K1,000 ($400) or a work order for the victim of up to twelve weeks. In cases of bride price or compensation for death, there is no upper limit on the amount of compensation it may order. Village courts do not have the power to impose prison sentences unless a person disobeys the court's ruling, and this is only valid if approved by a District Court magistrate. Village courts also have power to impose fines of up to K200 ($80) and order community work for up to six months. Under Section 92 of the Village Courts Act 1989, a District Court Magistrate can hear an appeal against a village court decision and either confirm or quash the decision. In hearing the appeal, Section 92(2) of the Act states that the decision should be confirmed unless the magistrate is satisfied that the village court 'acted in contravention of any Constitutional Law, Act or subordinate enactment applying to it' or 'exceeded its jurisdiction or its powers', or there was some procedural irregularity.

Village courts can be described as 'hybrid' institutions as they are a state court but they mostly apply customary rules and sanctions. Furthermore, given the actual lack of supervision by other organs of the state, particularly in the more remote areas of Papua New Guinea, the magistrates, in line with community standards, can apply customary law much as they like. The magistrates, who are villagers themselves, are appointed after consultation with the local communities they serve, and must have a good knowledge of local custom. They are, in theory, supervised by the District Supervising Magistrate. The village court magistrates are often, but not always, local elites, which given the usual lack of support from the police and higher courts can be extremely useful in ensuring that the courts are respected and able to enforce their judgements. The procedure of the courts is intended to be informal and there is no procedural distinction made between criminal and civil matters. Under Section 53 of the Act, village court magistrates are first required to attempt to mediate disputes, and only if this fails can the magistrates adjudicate the dispute.

While the official jurisdiction of the village courts is restricted to what the state considers relatively minor crimes, in practice they hear most civil cases and all but the most serious criminal matters. Evans, Goddard and Paterson (2011: 21) conclude that the village courts sometimes hear cases well outside their official jurisdiction, often a result of community pressure on decision makers in the absence of access to higher courts or a resistance to intrusion in community problems from 'outsiders'. In more remote places they have been known to hear murder and rape cases where there is community acceptance of the legitimacy of the village court doing so (see Goddard 2009; Wiessner 2010). While this is a breach of their legislative power, it may not be particularly problematic as they can provide a more acceptable bridge between the two legal orders from all perspectives. Furthermore, village courts that do hear such cases would likely need to be seen as legitimate venues to adjudicate on such matters in their communities. Some, such as Lipset (2004: 66), consider that village courts have 'not displaced indigenous remedies', but occupy a 'regulatory position somewhere in between local society and the state'. The Papua New Guinea Justice Advisory Group (2004) has also suggested that the village courts have become an alternative to both the practice of customary law and the formal state legal order, applying neither customary law nor the transplanted law, but rather some kind of synthesis. However, from my own fieldwork, the demarcation between village courts and other more traditional non-state forums is often blurred on the ground (discussed in Chapter 3).

In applying local custom, Section 52 of the Village Courts Act 1989 requires village courts do so with the aim of ensuring 'peace and harmony' in their communities. Village courts are the most significant form of recognition of customary law by the state in both statutory and practical terms. The degree to which the courts are expected to apply custom can be gleaned from the following case study in the current Village Courts Manual (Department of Justice and Attorney General 2003: 61–62):

> An older woman in a small village in Milne Bay cut open the head of a younger woman with an axe. After the young woman recovered from her wound she took the older woman to the Village Court. After hearing both sides of the case the Court decided to order the husband of the younger woman to give the older woman a pig.
>
> The reason was that the husband of the younger woman had been married to the older woman and had two children with her. He left her one day to live with the younger woman. The older woman tried to make it on her own but when the younger woman teased her and called her names, she got mad and hit her.
>
> The cause of the problem was really the irresponsible behaviour of the man. He left his wife with nothing and went to live with another woman, and he did not stop the new wife from teasing the older woman.
>
> So the Court ordered the man to pay compensation to the older woman because he behaved irresponsibly. It is customary in this village that men must provide for the mothers of their children.

The stated purpose of this case study is to contrast customary law principles with the transplanted criminal law. When introducing the case study, the Village Courts Manual (p. 61) considers somewhat romantically that '[u]nlike Western law, customary law does not seek to punish individuals as much as it tries to repair the damage caused by a crime', and how under custom everyone should 'share in the crime together'. The case study also highlights the effectiveness and legitimacy of self-help, which is in complete contrast to the rulings of the higher courts.

Many commentators celebrate the village court system. However on the whole they consider their jurisdiction should be limited to 'minor' offences and are apologetic when they overreach the authority granted to them by the state in terms of jurisdiction or sanction (Goddard 2009). The Papua New Guinea Justice Advisory Group (2004: 7) lauded the village courts for their 'innovative approaches' in applying customary law principles, and asserted 'that if they did not exist Papua New Guinea's much publicized "law and order" situation would be significantly worse'. The most common complaint put forward in relation to the village courts is that they lack support from the central and provincial governments. For example, it is commonly reported that some magistrates have not been paid for up to a year and inspectors do not have enough funds to purchase fuel to visit the village courts under their watch. There is also a long-standing complaint that police and the higher courts do not support the village courts in enforcing their judgements, thereby reducing their ability to sanction wrongdoers consistent with the statutes.

However, as Goddard (2009) notes, not all evaluations of the village court system have been favourable. There have been concerns over procedure, overreach of jurisdiction, abuses of power, human rights concerns, and concerns over the treatment of women.[60] Attempting to apply customary law principles has also led to controversy when it has been seen to clash with the standards of human rights groups, donor countries, the urban elite and the media.[61] In relation to concerns over the treatment of women, Evans, Goddard and Paterson (2011: 20) conclude that 'rigorous research in several parts of the country has indicated that overall, women disputants fare as well as, and frequently better than, male disputants'. However given the decentralized nature of the village court system and their general lack of state supervision (despite official reporting requirements) any generalizations are difficult. As Goddard (2009: 114) notes, each of the village courts he has observed had a different 'style' and dealt with offenders in a different manner – some focusing on reconciliation, while others focus on punishment.

The village courts also face a number of practical difficulties relating to their mandate of applying customary law. The first difficulty relates to which customs to apply in ethnically diverse urban communities. While there are many common principles to customary law across Papua New Guinea there are also many differences, especially as some ethnic groups have a reputation for expecting higher compensation payments or for more readily using violence than others. The second practical difficulty relates to what is actually meant by 'custom' or customary law.

Customary law is a contested concept, not only for academics but also for those trying to apply it on the ground, particularly as it is often 'reinvented' and 'recreated' in Melanesia (Forsyth 2009: 78). Customary law is influenced by interactions with the state legal order and other important influences, particularly religion. Many Papua New Guineans have taken to Christianity and it would seem that it is now a far more religious society than from where the first missionaries came. In many parts, Christian principles have become firmly embedded in, and intertwined with, what is considered local customary law.[62] Often village courts apply local social norms and standards, rather than 'traditional' customary law which is seen by some in the community, especially the Western-educated local elites, as being at times outdated and uncivilized. The third issue that village courts face is one of legitimacy. In most of the communities I visited it was the local councillors, church leaders, clan heads, and chiefs who played the key role in mediating or sanctioning settlements between disputing groups, rather than the village court system. Often the local village court would be bypassed or be non-operational. Given the weakness of the state and the lack of support, if village court magistrates do not derive their legitimacy from customary sources or if they deliver judgements outside community expectations, the ability to enforce their judgements or settlements is severely limited. Finally, village courts hear many cases outside their official jurisdiction which under the state legal order should be heard by District or National Courts. Therefore, the operation of the village court system in parallel with the application of the Criminal Code can see the simultaneous promotion and suppression of customary sanctions by the state, even for the same type of wrong.

Conclusion

Despite the efforts of the state to bend to customary considerations through the village court system and attempting to crush those elements that it considers repugnant (or in the new language those behaviours that 'contravene human rights') in the higher courts, customary law remains a powerful force in Papua New Guinea. Principles and practices that have long been outlawed by the state – such as strict and group liability, demands for compensation, and payback – are common in both rural and urban areas.

On the face of it the state's efforts do not seem unreasonable. They are based on the notion of recognizing customary law as much as possible while also attempting to hold true to the principles of criminal law and human rights. However, this has created a situation where the two legal orders are often in direct opposition, particularly in relation to grave wrongs. If the job of law is to coordinate the behaviour of individuals within a society, then the coexistence of two very different legal orders can be problematic; it can lead to confusion and conflict for those who live in such a society. Where the two legal orders are sufficiently distant, neither legal order may be able to do its job. This is the focus of this book. However, before analysing this in more detail, it is necessary to understand how the interaction of customary law and the state criminal law reached the point at which it is today. This is the focus of the next chapter.

Notes

1. This is an assertion that may be contested and cannot be proved. Almost universally, European accounts at the time of contact with the indigenous inhabitants of Papua New Guinea speak of chronic tribal fighting, cannibalism and sorcery (see Sack and Clark 1979; Jinks, Biskup and Nelson 1973; and Brown 1969, who all provide original accounts). Despite these practices, customary law's job may still have been to order society and control wrongdoing. Goddard (2009: 5) takes an extreme view and argues that 'peace' and 'harmony' are not as valued in Papua New Guinean culture as they are by 'Westerners'. However, West (1968: 129) tells us that, with greater colonial control, large tracts of land were able to be utilized which had previously been considered by the bordering tribes as 'no man's land', presumably for the purpose of limiting interactions and thereby reducing the incidence of tribal friction, raids and wars – this would suggest that peace and harmony did have a value. Whether or not this is the case is impossible to know. Whether these are transplanted values is open to debate. However, the history of Europe could also be characterized by chronic warfare; but this does not necessarily imply that those in the West have not valued peace and harmony. In any case, regardless of customary law's job before colonization, it currently seems to be able to order social relations and control wrongdoing when unhampered by state interference, or when supported by the state.
2. According to Max Weber's definition (Kim 2008), 'an ideal type is formed by the one-sided *accentuation* of one or more points of view' according to which '*concrete individual* phenomena … are arranged into a unified analytical construct' (*Gedankenbild*); in its purely fictional nature, it is a methodological 'utopia [that] cannot be found empirically anywhere in reality'. Keenly aware of its fictional nature, the ideal type does not seek to claim its validity in terms of a reproduction of, or a correspondence with, social reality. The conclusion also presents Damaska's (1986) ideal types in terms of different approaches to the practice of state criminal law.
3. During the ten years either side of Papua New Guinea's independence in 1975 there was a flurry of activity studying and documenting customary law, spurred on by the brilliant and charismatic Bernard Narokobi, Papua New Guinea's first Chairman of the Law Reform Commission and a former student of Julius Stone. In more recent times, with some exceptions, very little has been written on the practice of customary law.

4. Every author who attempts to describe Papua New Guinean customary law in anything less than a detailed anthropological study offers a similar disclaimer; however it does not stop them, or me, from presenting broad generalizations.
5. It is also acknowledged that this summary is written from a Western viewpoint and therefore is unlikely to fully grasp many customary concepts.
6. Countless authors stress the changing nature of customary law. In relation to its separateness, Woodman (2002) argues that differing legal orders cannot be neatly identified and that mapping legally pluralistic situations is not possible. Perhaps such a view is too defeatist, as while there *is* blurring at the edges, particularly in relation to 'current customary law' and what might be termed 'traditional practices', a distinction between these and state law in Papua New Guinea *is* possible as there are clear distinctions between substantive laws and process.
7. There are many flaws with Posner's (1983) analysis, not least, as he adopts a classic 'evolutionist' approach when considering customary and 'modern state law'. However, he does highlight recognizable patterns found in many customary legal orders, including retribution, group liability, strict liability, the use of compensation payments, and an inclination to think the best of your kin and the worst of strangers.
8. Schedule 1.2.2 of the Constitution. As noted earlier, the Underlying Law Act 2000 now refers to 'custom' as 'customary law'.
9. Similarly, Rouland (1994: 299) highlights the fact that many communities in sub-Saharan Africa still bear the trace of Arab and Islamic influence which occurred well before European colonization.
10. Narokobi (1996: 84) states that '[i]n the absence of a centralized bureaucratic system of control, self-help is an important mode of redress'.
11. Narokobi (1996: 81) concludes in relation to the exercise of customary rights and duties, that if sharing becomes one sided 'eventually reciprocity is extinguished' and a kinsman cannot expect assistance from his own group.
12. *Wantokism*, or group loyalty, can manifest itself in a variety of ways in urban environments, including work colleagues and *raskol* criminal gangs.
13. 100,000 Kina equates to approximately thirty times annual average income. In the United Kingdom, where average annual income is the equivalent of approximately $36,000 it would equate to over $1 million.
14. Except customary sanctions themselves, which are considered wrongs under the transplanted state law. This will be considered in much greater detail later.
15. The Governor of Papua, Sir Hubert Murray, spoke in 1929 of the gravity of adultery under customary law compared to the transplanted legal order (see Jinks, Biskup and Nelson 1973: 129).
16. In Papua New Guinea there is a strong belief in the supernatural generally and in its role in everyday life, not just in relation to wrongdoing. Narokobi (1996: 11) considers that '[t]he place of spirits in Melanesian social order cannot be over-emphasized'. The Law Reform Commission (1978: 1) concluded that '[i]t is interesting however that people with different occupation and influences should be unanimous in acknowledging the existence and effect of sorcery as a reality'. Little has changed.
17. Posner (1983) claimed that some communities operating under customary law in Africa had homicide rates similar to those in the United States. Whether he considers these high or low is unclear. A comparison of crime rates in the survey areas and other places is presented in Chapter 3.
18. Civil sanctions are rarely used in addition to criminal sanctions in common law countries. In the United Kingdom tort in relation to crimes against the person relate to assault, battery, false imprisonment and wrongful death (a statutory tort

almost exclusively confined to accidental death in England; see Law Commission 1999). Sometimes criminal sanctions and civil sanctions are seen as substitutes – for example, if a criminal case fails the victim or his or her family, they may bring civil action and it is normal for courts to stay a civil action while a prosecution is proceeding. However, in England, Jones and Dugdale (2010: 1059–60) note that where a civil action amounts to a 'collateral attack' on the final decision of a criminal court of competent jurisdiction, the civil action will be struck out. This approach is in stark contrast to many civil law countries where a victim can attach a civil claim to a criminal prosecution. The issue of substitutability between sanctions will be discussed throughout this book and in the conclusion.

19. Criminal Code Ordinance 1902 of British New Guinea, and Laws Repeal and Adopting Ordinance 1921 of New Guinea. The Criminal Code of Queensland was also adopted by Western Australia and forms the basis for the criminal codes of Nigeria, Israel, Fiji, the Solomon Islands and the Seychelles (MacKenzie 2002). Given that it was itself influenced by the Italian and New York criminal codes, it highlights the often complex manner in which law is diffused.
20. Sir Samuel Griffith is an important figure in Australia's legal history. At differing periods he served as Premier of Queensland, Chief Justice of the Queensland Supreme Court, and the first Chief Justice of Australia. He was also the principal drafter of the Australian Constitution.
21. In 2008 the Supreme Court in *Kumbamong v. The State* [2008] PGSC 51; SC1017 quoted Chalmers et al. (2001):

    In general, criminal responsibility is today attached to moral blameworthiness, and according to deeply rooted beliefs blameworthiness does not depend simply on what a person did, or on the results caused by those actions. It depends upon the person's knowledge and intentions when he or she acted. The doctrines of *mens rea* in the common law and of dole in the law of Scotland express this element of guilt. There is no reason to think that s24 demands any departure from the basic concept or that it at all attenuates it. The words used reflect the accepted dominant and orthodox view of psychological process and must be read literally.

22. In addition, the Supreme Court also: reviews decisions made by the National Court (concerning matters of which the law does not allow for appeals to be made); gives an opinion or advice on whether a proposed law or a law already passed by Parliament is constitutional (that is, whether it complies with the Constitution or not); develops rules of the underlying law; and enforces human rights as provided under Subdivision C of the Constitution.
23. The non-exhaustive list of factors that the Public Prosecutor (2008b: 9–10) will consider are:

    (a) the seriousness or, conversely, the triviality of the alleged offence; (b) the obsolescence or obscurity of the law; (c) the likely length and expense of a trial; (d) the likely sentence; (e) whether the consequences of any resulting conviction would be unduly harsh or oppressive; (f) the difficulty in detecting such an offence; (g) the prevalence of the offence and the need for deterrence, both personal and general; (h) whether confiscation or reparation is likely to result from the prosecution; (i) the availability and efficacy of alternatives to prosecution (NB defendants must not avoid prosecution merely because they pay compensation); (j) the age of the offence, and whether or not delay has been caused by the defendant or the prosecution; (k) any mitigating or aggravating circumstances; (l) whether the offence involves corruption or other abuse of trust or authority; (m) whether the offence was committed against a person serving the public, e.g. a police officer, prison officer, health worker; (n) the youth, age, intelligence, physical health or mental health of the defendant, victim or witness; (o) the culpability or role of the defendant; (p) the defendant's criminal history; (q) the attitude of the victim; (r) whether the defendant is willing to cooperate in the investigation or prosecution of others, or the extent to which the defendant has already done so; (s) the effect on the public, public order or public confidence of such an offence; and (t) the need to maintain public confidence in State institutions including the Parliament and courts.

24. The Public Prosecutor (2008b:18) concludes that despite Section 524 of the Criminal Code (which only refers to the Public Prosecutor) 'any person may by leave of the National Court present an information (rather than an indictment) against another person for an indictable offence not punishable by death'. The Public Prosecutor also interprets the powers under the Constitution, and the Public Prosecutor (Office and Functions) Act 1997 enables him to 'intervene in private prosecution where it is in the public interest to do so, either to proceed with the prosecution or discontinue it'.
25. In the Preamble to the Constitution (1975) it speaks of 'our worthy customs' which implies that the drafters considered some customs unworthy. The view that the drafters of the Constitution wished to see customary law subservient to liberal ideals and Western criminal law where there was a clash also accords with Narokobi's (1996) interpretation. However it did not stop him from advocating much greater recognition of customary law by the state in all areas, including criminal law (see Chapter 2).
26. In the passage outlining Basic Rights, the Constitution (1975: 5) states:

    all persons in our country are entitled to the fundamental rights and freedoms of the individual, that is to say, the right, whatever their race, tribe, places of origin, political opinion, colour, creed or sex ... [to] life, liberty, security of the person and the protection of the law.

27. Section 20 of the Constitution states that an Act of Parliament shall: (a) declare the underlying law of Papua New Guinea; and (b) provide for the development of the underlying law of Papua New Guinea. Section 21 states that until such time as an Act of Parliament provides otherwise, the underlying law, and the manner of its development, shall be prescribed in Schedule 2 of the Constitution.
28. Note the change from 'custom' in the Constitution to 'customary law' in the Underlying Law Act 2000.
29. The courts rejected payback killings on the grounds of repugnancy to the general principle of humanity in *Public Prosecutor* v. *Apava Keru* [1985], PNGLR 85; the handing over of a child for a death in *The State* v. *Joseph Kure* [1991] PNGLR 404; and giving away single girls as part of a compensation package between two clans in *In Re Miriam Willingal* [1997] NI506 and *The State* v. *Paulus Non Pable* [1999] NI873 (see Chalmers et al. 2009: XIII).
30. This seems reasonable given that the Constitution states that the purpose of Schedule 2 is to 'assist in the development of our indigenous jurisprudence, adapted to the changing circumstances of Papua New Guinea' and that, until such time as the Underlying Law Act 2000 comes into force, the underlying law, and its development, shall be prescribed by Schedule 2.
31. *Thomas* v.*The State* [2007] PGSC 26; SC867.

32. M. Takaku, Minister Counsellor to the United Nations, 'Statement on the Occasion of the 51st Session of the Commission on the Status of Women', 1 March 2007.
33. This reference by the Supreme Court to repugnancy may be an admission of how closely the concept of repugnancy and the human rights provisions in the Constitution are aligned. Alternatively, it may have been an oversight by the court and government officials.
34. Corrin-Care and Zorn (2001) attempt to argue that the Underlying Law Act 2000 may have implicitly repealed the Customs Recognition Act 1963.
35. The concept of 'sophistication' seems to have some empirical grounding. In one study, Papua New Guinea residents were asked to rank crimes according to seriousness. The study found that the ranking by the urban subjects approximated the 'legal' ranks more closely than that by the rural subjects (Wuillenmin, Richardson and Moore 1986). My own research found a strong relationship between education and Western norms, but not urbanization, in fact even an opposite relationship (see Larcom 2015).
36. Like in most things related to Papua New Guinea, one should be careful when generalizing. In relation to defences and mitigating circumstances, Weisbrot (1982: 76) concludes that while this view is generally true, 'a careful review of case law and the writings of administrators reveals that the range of matters in which "custom" is purportedly referred to goes well beyond provocation, while the factor actually taken into account is rarely ascertained and recorded as custom, but rather the relative degree of sophistication of Westernization of defendants'.
37. In 1985 the Supreme Court, in *Public Prosecutor* v. *Aia Moroi* [1985] PNGLR 78, reduced the scope of sophistication when considering a payback killing case, and ruled that the offender's lack of sophistication was only a factor when the offender came from an area so remote as not to know that a Government with courts and police existed and was available to redress wrongs, rather than having to rely on self-help remedies. The court considered there would be very few such people left in the country. The defence of provocation has become more tightly restricted to immediate reactions where (a) force was not disproportionate, and (b) there was no intention to cause death or grievous harm (see *The State* v. *Agua* [2009] PGNC 243; N3932). However, the concept of sophistication can still play a significant role in sentencing. In *The State* v. *Robert* [2010] PGNC 100; N4065, the National Court concluded that an unsophisticated, illiterate and subsistence villager should only be sentenced to a relatively light twelve years imprisonment for manslaughter.
38. *Michael* v. *The State* [2004] PGSC 37; SC737 (not paragraphed).
39. The only reference to customary law considerations was in relation to compensation payments, which is discussed below. In 2008, the Supreme Court further reviewed the sentencing guidelines for *Kumbamong* v. *The State* [2008] PGSC 51; SC1017 and concluded that sentencing discretion remained with the presiding judge and that any other arrangement would usurp the authority of parliament. Despite this, many judgements continue to use the schedule developed in *Kovi* v. *The State* [2005] PGSC 34; SC789 in sentencing.
40. *The State* v. *Gena* [2004] PGNC 142; N2649.
41. *Ume* v. *The State* [2006] PGSC 9; SC836 (Paras 42, 74 and 76 respectively).
42. Interestingly, in this case, the court considers custom and 'sophistication' under the label 'extenuating circumstances' not 'mitigating factors'.
43. In *The State* v. *Kepao* [2010] PGNC 136; N4147, Justice Salika took into account the customary laws of Enga in relation to payback killing and responsibility for a death in convicting a man for a payback killing.

44. *The State* v. *Monodoao* [2010] PGNC; N. Reported by Kelola (2010: no page numbering).
45. *The Acting Public Prosecutor* v. *Aumane, Boku, Wapulae, and Kone* [1980] PGNC: N510 *Kone* [1980] PNGLR 510.
46. *Baipu* v. *The State* [2005] PGSC 19; SC796 (no paragraphing or page numbering).
47. This ruling seemed to be in clear contradiction to the literal wording of the Sorcery Act 1971. Section 16 stated that, in allowing for the defence of provocation, '[i]t is immaterial that the act of sorcery (a) did not occur in the presence of the person allegedly provoked; or (b) was directed at some person other than the person allegedly provoked'.
48. As noted in the Introduction, education levels have actually remained low over this period.
49. *Thomas* v. *The State* [2007] PGSC 26; SC867 (28 August 2007: para. 33). The courts have had some difficulty in determining whether a belief in sorcery should be a mitigating factor in sentencing since this full Supreme Court Decision. The National Court ruled in *The State* v. *Lota* [2007] PGNC 167; N3183 that a belief in sorcery should no longer be used as a bar to impose the death penalty in wilful murder cases, and subsequently sentenced the offender to death. However, in 2009 the National Court in *The State v. Wapsi* [2009] PGNC 84; N3695 ruled that a genuine belief in sorcery can be a mitigating factor in sentencing as long as it can be proved. Satisfied of this, Justice Cannings acknowledged the offender's genuine belief in sorcery was the motivation for homicide and, along with other mitigating factors including his relative unsophistication, the fact that he cooperated fully with the police, and made very early admissions of guilt, sentenced him to twenty-five years' imprisonment.
50. For instance, in *The State* v. *Kove* [2010] PGNC 52; N4063, the judgement refers to another case where a wife who killed a woman she accused of having an affair with her husband was sentenced to fourteen years' imprisonment as the court acknowledged de facto provocation as a significant mitigating factor in sentencing.
51. *The State* v. *Bonot* [2010] PGNC 41; N4042.
52. In *Acting Public Prosecutor* v. *Uname Aumane* [1980] PNGLR 510, the Supreme Court ruled that the state law did not allow courts to impose a customary sanction (in this case compensation) in relation to a criminal offence. Customary compensation could only be taken into account as a mitigating factor in sentencing. According to Chalmers et al. (2009: 668), parliament responded by passing the Criminal Law (Compensation) Act 1991, albeit twelve years later. This legislation was based on recommendations of the Law Reform Commission (1978). However, Forster (2008) notes that various criminal prosecution orders and criminal injuries schemes began appearing in many Western states from the 1960s onwards also.
53. *Kovi* v. *The State* [2005] PGSC 34; SC789. Some years before, in *Kaputin* v. *The State* [1979: 566], the court expected the 'customary society to mould its sanctions to a particular case in the light of what sanction had been imposed in the National Court'. However, for a minor offence in *The State* v. *Paul Pokulou* [1983] N404, the judge released a thief on a good behaviour bond, primary because the matter had been settled under customary law. Banks (1998) highlighted the fact that legislation does not allow customary compensation payments to be considered by the courts and that the maximum amount is too low in relation to commonly held perceptions in parts of the country.
54. For example, see *The State* v. *Korogula* (No.1) [2009] PGNC 124; N3741, *Koe* v. *The State* [2004] PGSC 33; SC739, *Olmi* v. *The State* [2004] PGSC 43; SC872.
55. *The State* v. *Parakua* [2011] PGNC 5; N4199.

56. See Section 57 of the Village Courts Act 1989. The only formal legal limitations on applying custom are those set out in the Constitution (which are now probably superseded by the Underlying Law Act 2000), Sections 2, 3 and 7 of the Customs Recognition Act 1963 which relate to defining custom and procedure in cases where there is conflict between different customs, and Local Government Declarations on what is and what is not custom.
57. In relation to natural justice, Section 59(2) of the Constitution states that a 'minimum requirement of natural justice is the duty to act fairly and, in principle, to be seen to act fairly'.
58. It is unstated how many of the imprisonment orders were actually enforced, but it is likely be a fraction of this total.
59. Assuming a minimum of two people per dispute, 680,000 complaints would suggest that at least 1.4 million people have direct dealings with the village courts each year, which is approximately 20 per cent of the entire population.
60. Jessup (2010) provides evidence of sex discrimination and harsh treatment of women by some village courts in relation to family law matters.
61. In this regard the Papua New Guinea Justice Advisory Group (2004: 18) notes that 'directives that Village Courts follow custom' often puts them in a 'double bind whereby they are sometimes accused of applying unacceptable customs instead of the law, and sometimes accused of applying the law oppressively instead of following custom'.
62. This is highlighted by Demian (2003: 101) who in her search for custom was informed by a local government councillor that 'our custom is Christian'.

Chapter 2

Historical Overview of the State, Criminal Law and Customary Law

It is common to characterize colonial rule as oppressive and brutal, however in Papua New Guinea's case, while the colonial administrations of Germany, Britain and Australia were unashamedly paternalistic, on the whole they showed a considered and sophisticated approach towards customary law in criminal matters, causing Papua New Guinean jurist Narokobi (1996: 114) to remark that '[a]ll too often the new state politicians end up doing even what their colonial masters dared not do'.[1]

While very little has been written over the last decade on Papua New Guinea's legal arrangements, there is considerable literature on the administration and practice of criminal law during colonial times and in the years after independence in 1975.[2] This chapter provides an overview of the three key periods, focusing on the actual recognition shown to customary law in relation to criminal matters in both legal and practical terms, and the reasons behind the different policies taken.

The three periods covered are the colonial period up to 1960, the Derham period (1960–1975), and 'after independence', including the rise and fall of the Melanesian Jurisprudence Movement.[3] While the higher courts now mostly ignore customary law motivations in relation to the commission of serious crimes, this has not always been the case. Despite the strictures contained within various statutes, up until the 1960s the vast majority of Papua New Guineans were able to live by customary law unhampered by the state. While a generalization, there was a system of legal bifurcation whereby the European population lived by the transplanted law, and the rural indigenous population lived by traditional customary law. The principal concern of the various colonial administrations up until the Derham period was to keep order, rather than attempting to recognize or suppress customary law. However, by the late 1960s, guided by Professor Derham, serious efforts were made to unify the criminal justice system and attempt to subject the indigenous population to the Criminal Code. These efforts have continued ever since, despite the rise and fall of the Melanesian Jurisprudence Movement led by Bernard Narokobi. It is important to devote some space to the historical interaction of customary law and state law as it demonstrates that the current problematic interactions have long been recognized. It also demonstrates that the two most obvious reforms to ameliorate these problematic interactions in Papua New Guinea, the attempted suppression of customary law's more dubious practices and the incorporation of substantive customary laws into the state legal order (state legal pluralism), have both been tried and have failed.

Colonial Period to Derham Reforms

Like many other post-colonial states, Papua New Guinea has a complex history and the history of the application of criminal law is even more complicated. At its most simple, the application of criminal law in German New Guinea, which was annexed in 1884, and British New Guinea, which was annexed in 1888, was different but to similar effect. In British New Guinea, one of Governor MacGregor's first tasks was to pass basic legislation, including Ordinance IV which adopted the laws (including criminal law) of the Australian then-colony of Queensland as the Laws of British New Guinea (Jinks, Biskup and Nelson 1973: 66).[4] In 1901, Queensland adopted the Griffith Criminal Code and in the following year it was adopted by British New Guinea under the Criminal Code Ordinance 1902 and applied to the entire population.[5] In 1906, the Australian Government assumed control of British New Guinea, renamed it Papua, and passed legislation that saw the laws previously in force continue to apply. The following year, while the Criminal Code continued to apply to the indigenous population for grave crimes, the Native Regulation Act 1907 was passed (formerly the Native Board Ordinance) to deal with most interactions between the indigenous population and the state. The ordinance also allowed for the establishment of special courts (Courts of Native Matters) with both civil and criminal jurisdiction over the indigenous population, but with colonial magistrates.[6]

In German New Guinea, the Imperial German Government initially granted jurisdiction over the indigenous population to the 'Nue Guinea

Compagnie', including in the 'administration of criminal justice' by Imperial Charter in 1885, but by 1889[7] the German Government assumed political and judicial control over the Territory (Sack and Clark 1979: 127). Initially the administration did not apply the German Criminal Code to the indigenous population. However, by 1888 the German Criminal Code was applied to the indigenous population, but exclusively for the purpose of punishing crimes against whites.[8] By 1900, 'chiefs' (or *luluai*) were appointed by the administration to hear minor matters. In addition, 'whenever substantial public interests' were not 'adversely affected' the indigenous population were encouraged to develop their 'own criminal law and system of justice', primarily based on compensation payments (ibid.: 280). This approach was not without its own problems, and the chiefs' jurisdiction was curtailed due to perceived abuses of power.[9] On the whole, most wrongs were sanctioned under customary law, with or without state authority, due to the administrative policy itself and low levels of effective control.[10] Only those in towns or plantations effectively came under the criminal law, and state court judges sat with assessors in such cases (ibid.: 195).[11]

With the outbreak of the First World War, German New Guinea came under Australian control in 1914. After a period of military administration, the Criminal Code was applied in 1921.[12] As in Papua, where the Courts of Native Matters operated, Courts of Native Affairs were established in the former German territory of New Guinea where a number of summary criminal offences were prosecuted in the Native Courts. These included adultery, sorcery and stealing (Constitution and Law Reform Commission of Papua New Guinea 1975).

Despite officially coming under the criminal codes in 1888 in German New Guinea and 1902 in British New Guinea, most indigenous Papua New Guineans continued to have very limited interactions with the colonial authorities and therefore continued to practise customary law as they saw fit. Generally, for an indigenous person to be tried under the transplanted Criminal Code, the crime would have to be very grave (for example, homicide) and, in addition, be brought to the attention of colonial authorities. The vast majority of Papua New Guineans would settle disputes by custom or be tried in the Native Courts by administrative patrol officers (*kiaps*) who often used considerable discretion in recognizing custom and state law. It was also accepted by the colonial administration that only a small fraction of indigenous disputes or 'crimes' against one another were brought to their attention. Therefore, up until the mid-1960s, as Weisbrot (1982: 66) concludes, the 'received common law was effectively reserved for European residents'.

During the colonial period up to the 1960s, customary law was only really challenged if it posed a direct threat to colonial authority or affected Europeans (who were few).[13] The most likely scenario under which the actions of indigenous Papua New Guineans would have been brought to the attention of colonial authorities and therefore into contact with the formal criminal justice system was through urbanization, or due to large disruptions or massacres brought about by tribal fighting. In relation to urbanization, until the early 1960s the towns and cities were primarily populated by Australians and were little more than colonial administrative centres. This was partly the result of a deliberate policy on the part of the colonizers to discourage urbanization among the indigenous population, and for many decades it was illegal for an indigenous Papua New Guinean to live in cities or towns without a job or a permit (Koczberski, Curry and Connell 2001).[14]

When indigenous Papua New Guineans did find themselves before the courts, the Criminal Code was applied in relation to grave crimes. However, the courts applied a broad interpretation of the partial defence of provocation and of what was considered 'reasonable' in Papua New Guinean circumstances, and used the concepts of sophistication and de facto provocation. This approach allowed offenders motivated by customary law to escape conviction for the more serious offences (such as wilful murder) and therefore avoid the penalties attached. As stated in Chapter 1, homicides that were committed under the motivation of punishing sorcery, adultery or the death of a kinsman (payback) often saw the offender convicted of manslaughter and sentenced from between the rising of the court to three or four years' imprisonment (Gore 1965: 77–114).[15]

However, as Otterly and Zorn (1983) note, those who violated the Criminal Code were rarely totally exempted from state sanctions, and potential defences such as mistake of fact, insanity and self-defence which could have seen total exoneration were rarely admitted by the courts. This was mainly in an effort to use criminal law as an educative tool 'in a manner which would ease the people into it so that it would, with them, too, eventually become conventional' (Gore 1965: 77). The approach taken by the courts was also administration policy, as explained in 1929 by the then Lieutenant Governor of Papua, Sir Hubert Murray:

> [S]o we punish murder and we punish cannibalism, though both may be committed in strict conformity with native custom, but we show our appreciation of the custom by passing sentence which, in the case of natives who are fully under control, may be so light as to be little more than nominal. (Jinks, Biskup and Nelson 1973: 129)

The approach taken by the judiciary and colonial administrators up until the 1960s was partly motivated by a paternalistic civilizing mission and a sense of justice, but perhaps most importantly out of an acknowledgement of the role customary law played in ordering society, and recognition that the state was unable to fulfil this role. In relation to the application of the Criminal Code, Gore, a Supreme Court judge in the territories of Papua and Papua New Guinea from 1928 to 1962, concluded:

> It had to be applied with a respect for their customs and institutions and with proper regard to the tribal creed so that its application would be just. Without some softening, the shock of applying the white man's system would have been too violent – sufficiently violent to overthrow the social structure with grave results. (Gore 1965: 77)

However, over this period the colonial authorities gradually increased their reach to previously uncharted territory and to people who had no prior contact with the state. So although there was no major change in law or policy, there was increasing state involvement in customary matters simply through the expansion of the reach of the state in numerical and geographical terms. Despite this, the vast majority of the population had only slight contact with the state's representatives, and Dinnen (2006) suggests that most villagers would have seen a colonial administrator no more than twice a year, and many others even less frequently.

The Derham Period to Independence

By the 1960s Papua New Guinea was experiencing a transformation. The cities were expanding, economic development was accelerating, and there was growing talk of independence.[16] As part of its response to these developments the Australian Government commissioned a report on the system for administration of the then territories of Papua and New Guinea by the eminent jurist, Professor Sir David Derham.[17] The Derham Report (1960) was to have a fundamental and lasting effect on the practice of customary law. Many commentators consider the Derham reforms as disastrous and the cause of Papua New Guinea's current lack of order and security (see Strathern 1993; Dinnen 2002; Dinnen and Braithwaite 2009).

Derham (1963) considered the development of Papua New Guinea to be both inevitable and necessary, particularly if the indigenous peoples were to govern themselves at some time in the near future. However, he also believed development and the preservation of customary law to be incompatible in a rapidly changing Papua New Guinea. As people from different communities intermingled more and more through improving transport links and the growth of towns, custom would no longer be able to function in resolving disputes, as there would be a clash of different customs. He also argued that custom had no answers for the problems arising from changing methods of agriculture, commerce, and personal relations in urban environments.

Derham (1963: 501) freely admitted that he was engaging in 'social engineering'. He saw the state criminal law as a tool to transform the economic and social structure of Papua New Guinea, and called for an end to the policy of interfering as little as possible in the life of the indigenous communities. In the typology of Damaska (1986: 200), which will be discussed in the Conclusion, Derham wished to implement a hierarchical activist system of justice. He saw the courts, at all levels, as one of the institutions that would develop Papua New Guinea and enable self-government. This meant that the old colonial systems needed to be dismantled and replaced with modern ones. Derham (1960) recommended the end of legal bifurcation between the indigenous and European populations. He concluded that Papua New Guinea needed a Western justice system for all Papua New Guineans, and recommended that indigenous magistrates and judges should serve in the Local and District Courts respectively.

Derham (1963: 499) was fully aware that the attempt to implement a justice system as found in Australia would cause profound disruption for much of the indigenous population; however, he believed that 'development' was necessary, arguing that the plea that the rural communities be left to their own life was 'a plea that belongs to history' and that going back to the pre-colonial period was not an option. Before colonization, Derham argued, highland communities suffered from 'disease and war, combined with head-hunting, cannibalism and wife-capturing raiding parties', and if the colonial administrator were to leave, such abject and barbarous circumstances would likely reoccur. He concluded:

> In any case, the indigenous peoples want the changes that European influence and interference bring. The Highlander wants to be able to walk or ride upon a road rather than to climb the sides of steep hills. He does not want to see his children die in the first years of life. He is not happier with a malarial spleen that will kill him at forty years of age than he would be without it. He does like to supplement his diet with meat, even out of a tin, rather than to live entirely on kaukau [sweet potato] … When the people themselves see such things and such changes as advancements that will make their lives easier, happier and longer, surely it is too late to entertain

> arguments that we should not disturb the 'natural' structures of these communities which are now finding themselves, willy-nilly, caught up into the century. (Derham 1963: 499)

Following Derham's report (1960), a number of key legislative reforms took place in an attempt to implement his vision. Woodman (1986: 151) describes the intent of these reforms as 'a policy of suppression of custom'. In 1963 the Courts of Native Matters (Papua) and the Courts of Native Affairs (New Guinea) were abolished, and the Local Courts Ordinance and the Native Customs (Recognition) Ordinance (later the Customs Recognition Act 1963) were brought into force.

The Local Courts Ordinance 1963 provided for the establishment of Local and District Courts, which were to apply primarily non-customary law throughout the Territory. This saw the demise of the *kiap*,[18] to be replaced by professional magistrates and police. The Native Customs (Recognition) Ordinance 1963 was designed to guide the new higher and lower courts. Among other things, it provided for the requirements of proof of custom and under what circumstances it could be taken into account in criminal cases. In the broad, it restricted the recognition of custom to: the state of mind of a person; reasonableness tests; and sentencing. Some, such as Woodman (1986: 154), suggest that 'the main effect was to exclude custom from some areas and to leave it with an uncertain scope of operation in others'. However, Goddard (2009: 45), amongst others, sees the Ordinance as a move to 'give more recognition to custom in the field of the law', although he considers that in practice it is 'hardly an improvement' on the prior state of affairs.

The aim of the reforms was to bring the indigenous population into the formal court system, but the reforms also highlighted the differences between the state and customary processes. The new formal courts suffered from some serious problems, including being very slow to get established. The new courts' procedures, language and rules were also foreign to the average Papua New Guinean. Dinnen (2002: 5) suggests that this led to a surge in 'self-help' measures and tribal fighting, while Woodman (1986: 154) considers that the introduction of the new system saw 'dispute settlement continue as before, outside the ambit of the state judicial system'.

Serious bouts of tribal fighting did break out in the Highlands in the early 1970s, and colonial authority was violently challenged in other parts of the country.[19] Of particular concern was that tribesmen involved in the fights were beginning to attack the colonial authorities, who in former times would have been able to intervene with relative impunity to restore order (Clifford 1976). It seemed that the new regime was not a viable one for the majority of the population. Derham's vision of the courts as a method for social education and change had not been fulfilled.

Partly in response to these increasingly chaotic circumstances and the rise of the Melanesian Jurisprudence Movement, the village court system was established in 1974. The large number of unofficial courts operating in the early 1970s, despite (or perhaps in spite of) the Derham reforms, was further impetus for the establishment of the village court system.

The actual legislation was in response to a report by two magistrates, Desailly and Iramu (1972), who were asked to enquire into whether the policy of opposition to informal village courts should be changed. They (ibid.: 3–4) acknowledged the failure of the existing legal system to provide adequate means of dispute settlement, but were unenthusiastic about customary courts which would 'perpetuate old ideas in times of change', and acknowledged that some old ideas would 'fail the test of acceptability'. Their recommended compromise was a system of village courts where they would not apply 'strict customary rules', but rather be 'strongly influenced by the customs of the area and by local attitudes and mores' (ibid.: 8). In the end, the establishment of village courts was an attempt to integrate customary law and the state law by creating a forum for the application of mostly substantive customary laws and principles by local magistrates with state authority.

Independence

The independence period can best be described as one of increased intolerance towards customary law in criminal matters, despite significant legislative and Constitutional recognition and the best efforts of the Melanesian Jurisprudence Movement.

Facing mounting pressure from both internal and external sources, including the United Nations, Australia accelerated the process for the independence of its only colonial possession. In 1972 Papua New Guinea was granted self-government, and Michael Somare was elected premier. In that same year the Constitutional Planning Committee, made up of local parliamentarians, was established (Ghai 1997). At the time, anti-colonial sentiments were high and the merits of customary law were celebrated. Europeans had dominated affairs up to this point, in part by deploying the coercive power of the state, and while many within the colonial administration had shown great sensitivity, many had displayed contempt. In addition to the anti-colonial vitriol emanating from parts of Papua New Guinea's indigenous elite,[20] many argued that state law and customary law needed to be reconciled for both practical reasons (especially following the chaos caused by the Derham reforms) and for reasons of justice. A champion of this view was the Chairman of Papua New Guinea's Law Reform Commission, Bernard Narokobi.[21] While customary law advocates spoke boldly for greater recognition of customary law in the Constitutional Planning Committee, Narokobi (1996: 55) considered that the 'grafting' of custom onto the Constitution of Papua New Guinea, via a Schedule, to be more of an 'afterthought' and done 'amidst overwhelming distrust for custom' exhibited by all colonial administrators, lawyers and judicial officers.

Therefore at the time of independence, despite Schedule 2 of the Constitution calling for the development of an 'indigenous jurisprudence', the criminal laws of the independent state were mostly a continuation of those under colonial rule. However, under Narokobi's leadership and charged with this Constitutional responsibility (under Schedule 2.14), the Law Reform Commission set about trying to facilitate greater recognition of customary law by the state, including criminal law. It prepared a number of draft bills including the Underlying Law Act (Draft Bill) which aimed to promote customary law and remove some of the ambiguities over its recognition in the Constitution.

In the mid-1970s the Law Reform Commission acknowledged that, notwithstanding the lack of recognition by the state, widespread and deeply held beliefs in relation to customary law had continued into the independence period, including killings motivated by payback, strongly held beliefs in sorcery, and harsh penalties for adultery in many communities. In relation to sorcery, the Law Reform Commission (1977a: 4) conceded that the person committing the homicide (which it labelled a 'hangman'), often acted with the approval of his society, or even upon its bidding, and that disputes seldom came before the state courts. The Commission also acknowledged the gravity of adultery, which according to the results of surveys of Papua New Guineans at the time was ranked third in terms of seriousness, behind only wilful murder and conversion of real property rights (Weisbrot 1982). In response, the Law Reform Commission (ibid.: 47) made recommendations based on the premise 'that the criminal law of a country should reflect the perceptions and world-views of that country so that the criminal law reflects their view of what is criminal behaviour and what is not'.

The Commission made a number of specific recommendations, including changes to the principles of criminal responsibility to take greater account of customary law. Specifically, it recommended:

> where a person kills, attempts to kill or does a very serious injury to someone when he is acting under customary law or a traditional perception

> or belief, he be found guilty of an offence, but be given a small punishment of up to three years in jail. In addition we recommend that if he does any other act or omission which does not cause the death of, or serious injury to, a person, when he is acting under customary law, traditional perception or belief, that he should be completely acquitted. (Law Reform Commission 1977a: 59)

However the Law Reform Commission did recommend some significant limitations. First, a person wishing to use this new 'defence' would have to 'satisfy the court' (by providing witnesses) that he or she was acting under the influence of customary law. Second, it would not apply to killings or serious injuries motivated by payback. In relation to the proposed 'defence' not being extended to payback, the Commission (1977a: 48) gave no other reason than that 'national policy must be firmly against payback killings and injuries', although it did refer to 'worthy customs' elsewhere, as does the preamble to the Constitution. In addition, the Commission (ibid.: 45) recommended that courts should be able to take customary law compensation payments into account when determining sentencing and be able to order compensation payments to be paid by the wrongdoer of up to K10,000 ($4000).

Not all of the Commission's efforts were in vain. Both the Underlying Law Act 2000 and Criminal Law (Compensation) Act 1991 were passed by parliament, albeit sometime after they were initially proposed, as were amendments to the Customs Recognition Act 1963. However, the amendments to the Criminal Code (Amendment) Bill 1977 have never been passed. The reason for this was the cautious attitude taken by Papua New Guinea's politicians who, fully aware of the pervasiveness and power of customary law, considered certain elements as being incompatible with the new nation state.[22]

While some may consider the Law Reform Commission's recommendations radical, and many legal academics saw their delayed and incomplete adoption as a lost opportunity for the development of Melanesian jurisprudence, their *full effect* would have seen a restricted version of the recognition of customary law that had prevailed under colonial administrations prior to the Derham reforms.[23] These reforms were proposed using a state-centric or weak view of legal pluralism. It was considered that the state could co-opt those elements of customary law considered worthy and eliminate those considered unworthy. This state-centric view of legal pluralism was highlighted much later by Narokobi (1996: 184) when he called for 'a statute to require courts to enforce custom as law', the Underlying Law Act 2000. As demonstrated in the previous chapter, this Act has had little or no effect on the accommodation of customary law by the state. Indeed, in relation to its lack of impact to date, Corrin (2014: 14) has recently written 'amendments to the law can only do so much. For the Act to fully succeed, the judges must embrace the opportunity to engage in judicial activism'.

Following independence, with effectively no change in the statutes regarding the recognition of customary law in criminal matters, many legal scholars and the Law Reform Commission (1977a: 9) hoped that the courts, 'now freed from the shackles of pre-Independence precedents', would adopt a more favourable disposition. They were disappointed. In the immediate period after independence, the courts continued to apply the notion of sophistication attached to the defence of provocation in assessing whether or not customary law motivations should see a lessening of the gravity of the offence, or de facto provocation as a mitigating factor in sentencing. However, over the years they have gradually taken an increasingly tough stance in relation to crimes motivated by customary law, and limited the defence of provocation and the scope of the use of sophistication to the point where it is now almost totally ignored.[24]

The reasons provided by the courts in explaining their failure to recognize customary law include: the Constitution's human rights provisions and the repugnancy of custom to the general principles of humanity; difficulty in determining which custom should apply, given so many different groups and customs; the lack of resources needed for the courts to conduct research into custom;[25] and inconsistency with specific statutes. Others blamed expatriate lawyers and judges within the justice system for their alleged antipathy towards custom and the legal education system for allegedly giving primacy to the transplanted law. Until the passing of the Underlying Law Act 2000, still others blamed parliament (Jessup and Regan 1996). Corrin-Care and Zorn (2001: 66) consider the failure to recognize customary law was the result of the enduring effect of colonialism on the values and beliefs of the post-colonial society, in which the colonized are thought to 'adopt the attitudes of their colonizers'. Few, if any, have attributed it to the fundamental gap between the legal orders, both in substance and procedure – the belief in sorcery, group liability, and vigilantism are considered anathema to the practice of the transplanted criminal law. More recently, and as explained in Chapter 1, both parliament and the courts have made it clear that they see customary law, and specifically customary sanctions, as a cause of disorder and lawlessness rather than a source of control against wrongdoing. Firmly believing in deterrence theory, they have attempted to eliminate such actions through extremely heavy sentencing, including warning, somewhat ironically, that those who kill motivated by customary considerations will be sentenced to death.

The Legacy of Derham

While the act of colonization was a great trauma for the people of Papua New Guinea, so were the Derham reforms and their continued and more stringent implementation following independence. The period following the Derham reforms coincides with the emergence of serious concerns over Papua New Guinea's 'law and order problem' (Clifford 1976). Violent urban crime was increasing rapidly, outbreaks of tribal fighting re-emerged, and there were violent challenges to state authority. However, it must also be remembered that the late 1960s and early 1970s was a time of rapid change for Papua New Guinea on many fronts. Accompanying the state legal reforms were ambitious schemes for economic development based mainly on commercial agriculture and mining. The 1960s also saw the gradual removal of restrictions on urbanization. The easing of these restrictions and large wage differentials led to rapid urban growth. Obviously, these factors were also likely to have an effect on crime and social dislocation. However, many regard the Derham reforms as a serious mistake and the root cause of Papua New Guinea's current crime problems and severe lack of personal security.

There are two different, but interrelated, explanations for the failure of the Derham reforms. The first is advanced by Dinnen (2002). He considers the Australian *kiap* stationed in Papua New Guinea to be closer to a 'philosopher king' than a district magistrate and administrator. Before Derham the colonial administrators allowed considerable discretion in solving disputes. Dinnen argues that this discretion and the many agency functions and powers of the *kiaps* allowed them to draw upon a number of tools to persuade, reward and punish the population in order to keep peace. Their wide-ranging power meant that they could link dispute resolution to the provision of services or address remedies to groups rather than individuals. He further argues that *kiap* justice accorded more closely with customary law as it treated dispute resolution in a more holistic way than was possible under the Derham reforms. Dinnen (2002: 4) contends that this 'holistic and problem solving approach' produced outcomes that were generally acceptable to the local population and was an important contributor to stability preceding the Derham reforms for which he uses the label 'Pax Australiana'. Dinnen (ibid.) goes on to claim that the new courts 'took much longer and entailed a cumbersome and formalistic process, all conducted in a foreign language', and that '[l]ocal litigants viewed this new system as exclusionary, confusing, and often profoundly unjust'. He suggests this led to dissatisfaction and a return to older traditions of self-help in some areas, and a re-emergence of tribal fighting. Dinnen and Braithwaite (2009) have called for the return of the role filled by the colonial *kiap*.[26]

The second, perhaps more compelling explanation, is that increases in state interference weakened the potency of the customary justice system to keep social order. While the previous regime did its best not to overly interfere with customary law, the new regime took aim at and hoped to eliminate it. Strathern (1993: 721) concluded that customary law got its potency and legitimacy on the sanctioning power of violence, and it 'was precisely this ultimate sanction, however, that state control disallowed'. He argues that this fundamental problem has given rise to many others. By all but ignoring the motivations of customary justice, state authorities could only see killings as a matter between the state and the perpetrator, and not part of a broader effort by the indigenous communities to keep order and exercise justice. Penalizing the indigenous population when carrying out customary violence led to the impotency of the customary justice system, and social disintegration followed. This argument suggests that while the state justice system was able to render the customary justice system ineffective, it was unable to replace its ability to keep order. While the reach of the state justice system greatly expanded, it was not able to fill the place of the customary regime in providing order or security.

Conclusion

This chapter has described the different approaches the state has taken towards customary law in criminal matters. It has shown that the early colonial administrations did not seek to destroy customary law but rather to gently nudge it towards their conceptions of what was right and wrong. This approach was taken primarily in the interests of social order but was also motivated by a sense of justice.[27] The Derham reforms that are still in place, and enforced with great zeal by some, took aim at customary law. They were aimed at using the criminal law to make customary law redundant and to suppress its more unpalatable elements. However, it is unclear whether even Derham would have agreed with the current sentencing trends. This chapter also demonstrates the limits of state legal pluralism, advanced by the Melanesian Jurisprudence Movement, in ameliorating problematic legal pluralism. The following chapter provides an account of the actual sanctioning of wrongs currently being used in the New Guinea Islands.

Notes

1. Colonial rule was often brutal and attempted to oppress the practice of customary law; King Leopold's Belgian Congo is a case in point, as captured by Conrad's (1902) invention of the Brussels-based Society of the Suppression of Savage Customs. It must be acknowledged that this account of Papua New Guinea is more sympathetic than some other authors' characterizations of the colonial administrations, such as Fitzpatrick (1980) and Woodman (1986). Perhaps this is because it is focused on criminal law only. Alternatively, it may be that this account is written at a time when the colonial period can be better compared to the post-colonial period, given that the latter, for the most part, attempted complete suppression of many elements of customary law.
2. For example, see O'Regan (1970); Fitzpatrick (1980); Scaglion (1981); Weisbrot (1982); Otterly and Zorn (1983); Chalmers and Paliwala (1984); Westermark (1986); Woodman (1986); Scaglion (1990); Ottley (1992); Nonggorr (1993); Aleck and Rannells (1995); Ntumy (1995); Narokobi (1996); Banks (1998); Jessup (1998); Settle (1998); Corrin-Care and Zorn (2001); and Dinnen (2010).
3. I label the Melanesian Jurisprudence Movement as the group of scholars and legal reformers (both indigenous and non-indigenous) who aimed to see a greater recognition of customary law in Papua New Guinea around the time of independence. Led by Bernard Narokobi, the movement primarily sought this greater recognition through legislative reform that would see the state legal order adopt substantive customary norms, and enforce them. In this sense the movement can be thought of as a state legal pluralism movement. Narokobi (1996) himself did not refer to customary law as 'law', and while he had great respect for customary law his writings suggest that he was a state centralist.
4. British New Guinea's first governor, MacGregor, considered that when the proper time came it should become part of 'federated Australia, with a native population intact', and one of his first acts was to legislate to protect indigenous land rights (Jinks, Biskup and Nelson 1973: 68).
5. Contrary to what some authors have suggested (see Woodman 1986), the Criminal Code of Queensland was transplanted in 1902 under the Criminal Code Ordinance 1902 of British New Guinea. Prior to that, the laws of Queensland were applied, including its criminal law under Ordinance IV 1888 of British New Guinea.
6. The ordinance also contained a number of regulations covering topics that included: absences from tribal areas, the practice of illegal cults, gatherings, use of fire, clothing in towns, burial rituals, various public health matters, the planting of crops, cooperation with colonial officials, and the appointment and duties of village officials.
7. Royal ascent 15 June 1892.
8. The German Statute of 17 April 1886 decreed that the German Civil and Criminal Codes were to apply to German Protectorates with measures for the purposes of adapting these laws to local conditions being reserved for Imperial Ordinance. At the time the indigenous population 'was excluded' (Sack and Clark 1979: 10). However, Imperial Ordinance (7 July 1888) and Penal Ordinance (21 October 1888) placed the indigenous population under the provisions of the German Criminal Code. As explained in the German New Guinea Annual Report for 1887–88, this was 'for the purpose of bringing the punishment of crimes and offences against whites under the rule of law' and to 'protect those who prosecute and punish offenders from the provisions of the German Criminal Code'. The authors of the report continued: 'Although applicable in principle to punishable actions committed by natives against

each other, the Penal Ordinance is not for the present aimed at these' (German New Guinea Annual Report for 1887–88, quoted in Sack and Clark 1979: 28).

9. Both colonial administrations had trouble with local state officials – the *luluais* in German New Guinea, and the village constables in Papua – using their office in ways they had not intended, by slanting decisions or extorting villagers with the threat of state punishment. See West (1968), Lawrence (1969), and Sack and Clark (1979).
10. However, convictions of the indigenous population under the Criminal Code steadily rose and 886 convictions were recorded in German New Guinea for the year 1913, which is a considerable number even by today's standards (Sack and Clark 1979: 359).
11. Sack and Clark's translations of the official German New Guinea reports make it clear that the indigenous population were technically subject to the transplanted criminal law during the period of German control. This is in contrast to Woodman (1986) who suggests they were not. See also Sack and Clark (1979: 128).
12. In 1920, the former German Territories were allotted to Australia under a mandate from the League of Nations, and the Queensland Criminal Code was adopted the following year under the Laws Repeal and Adopting Ordinance 1921. However, as Woodman (1986: 144) highlights, the Ordinance also provided that 'tribal institutions, customs and usages were not to be affected, and were to be permitted to continue in existence'. While this declaration went much further than any in Papua, it had no real effect, especially in relation to criminal law. Prior to this, the German Criminal Code applied, including a period when it was administered by the Australian Defence Force (Brown 1969).
13. Papua's long-serving Governor Murray (1908–1940) described British New Guinea as an 'extensive and expensive ethnological museum' (Murray 1906; as quoted in West 1968: 62). He was later accused of the same approach, as he maintained a policy of limited disruption to the indigenous population by limiting both European immigration and the exploitation of the territory's numerous natural resources. Governor Murray's administration is described by West (1968: 8) as 'benevolent paternalism'. In the former German territories (New Guinea) a more 'pro-development' stance was taken. However, a 'gradual' policy approach was again taken 'to fit the native to participate in the economic and social life of his country' (Prime Minister's Department [Australia] 1937: 279). Both colonial administrations had very limited resources, both in terms of funds and personnel, which would have made any other approach extremely difficult (Lett 1949; West 1968).
14. Koczberski, Curry and Connell report that in Port Moresby during the 1920s, whistles and bells sounded to indicate the times that indigenous Papua New Guineans were allowed in town.
15. Gore also states that if a wrong under customary law was also an offence under the Criminal Code, sentencing was often adapted to local sensitivities in relation to its gravity under customary law.
16. Australia was facing increasing external pressure from the United Nations to prepare Papua New Guinea for political independence.
17. Derham was Professor of Jurisprudence and later Vice-Chancellor at the University of Melbourne, as well as editor of Paton's Textbook of Jurisprudence, 3rd edition (1963).
18. Derham (1960; c.f. Dinnen and Braithwaite 2009: 11) saw the role of the *kiap* 'as an idiosyncratic and essentially transitional institution on the way of establishing a modern state'. However most modern authors, Dinnen (2006) in particular, seem to

romanticize the *kiap* and his ability to respect customs and keep the peace, and see him as being ideally suited to Papua New Guinea.

19. An official inquiry by Paney et al. (1973) considered the long-term causes of outbreaks of fighting in the Highlands were kin loyalty, a culture that encouraged fighting, failure of the introduced system in settling disputes, lack of government presence in rural areas, and social causes. They considered the immediate causes to be disputes over land, sorcery, killings, women and pigs.
20. The then Minister for Justice, John Kaputin, spoke of the state law at the time as, 'an instrument of domination and oppression by the ruling classes … an instrument of colonialism and a means whereby the economic dominance of the white man was established over us' (Kaputin, Press Release, dated 21 November 1973).
21. Bernard Narakobi is considered one of Papua New Guinea's founding fathers and by all accounts was a brilliant man. He was a lawyer (including a period as a National and Supreme Court judge), politician (including a period as Justice Minister), philosopher, poet, and author. He died in 2010 while serving as Papua New Guinea's High Commissioner to New Zealand.
22. Papua New Guinea's first Prime Minister, Michael Somare, also took a cautious stance in relation to the state's acknowledgement of customary law. While Somare (Amet 1995: 45) agreed that a legal system should belong to the whole population, he also considered that the legal system 'must ensure the orderly and progressive development' of the nation.
23. Under the early colonial administration, grave crimes motivated through customary considerations were treated leniently, including those motivated by payback. While the Law Reform Commission's recommendations would have meant those acting with customary motivation (when able to satisfy the court with evidence) would not face a criminal conviction when a non-serious injury occurred, most of these offences were dealt with in the village courts through compensation payments.
24. The courts' treatment of customary law motivations in criminal cases has been well documented up to the passage of the Underlying Law Act 2000. For a detailed analysis, see Otterly and Zorn (1983); Jessup and Regan (1996); Banks (2001); and Corrin-Care and Zorn (2001).
25. For customary law to be invoked it must be pleaded with evidence and therefore depends on the quality of advocates and on having articulate and convincing witnesses.
26. According to West (1968), Governor Murray, while he commended many of his patrol officers, was also often disappointed with their efforts and constantly sought higher quality men for the role.
27. As a prologue to his memoir, Justice Gore (1965) quotes Voltaire: 'A law carried too far becomes an injustice'.

Chapter 3

Empirical Study of the Sanction of Wrongs in the New Guinea Islands

Compared to the rest of Papua New Guinea, the New Guinea (*Niugini*) Islands have a reputation for low crime rates and high levels of personal security, especially East New Britain and its capital Kokopo (and its former capital Rabaul). Given that these provinces seem to be success stories in the provision of personal security, they provide an ideal location for an empirical study of the interactions between customary law and the criminal law in practice, in order to better understand the potential for reform across Papua New Guinea. The opportunity was also taken to gain some insight into the prevalence of wrongdoing, the likely response of individuals when wronged, the prevalence of customary notions of wrong and sanctions, and the substitutability between customary sanctions and state sanctions. The structure of this chapter is as follows: first there is an overview of the method used for the empirical research, and an introduction to the New Guinea Islands; second there is a description of how wrongs are sanctioned in the areas surveyed; and third there is an overview of the descriptive statistics that were generated by a survey.

Empirical Method

The empirical research took place in October, November and December of 2010 in the island provinces of East New Britain, West New Britain, and the Autonomous Region of Bougainville.[1] The major towns where the research took place are marked in Figure 3.1. From left to right, they are Kimbe, Rabaul, Kokopo, Buka and Arawa. In addition to these towns

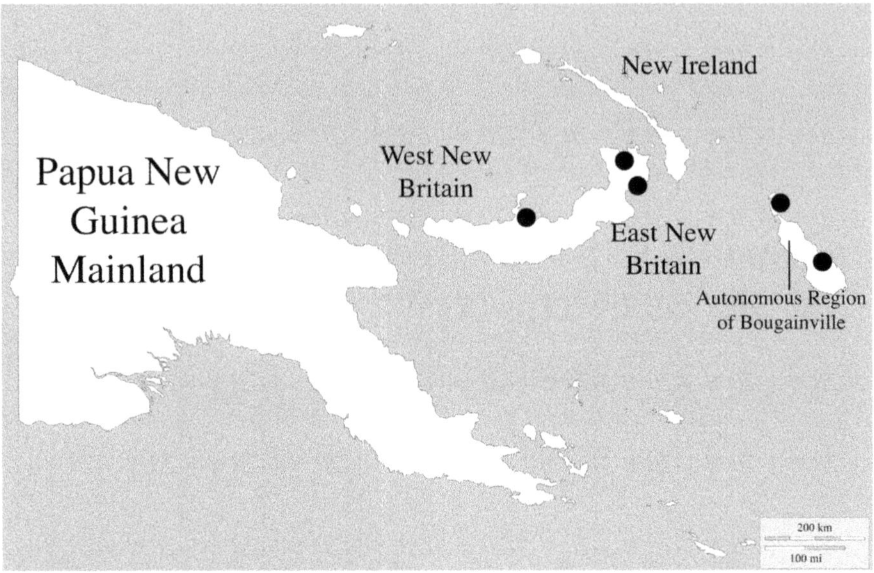

Figure 3.1. Map of Papua New Guinea
Source: The map was downloaded from D-Maps
(http://d-maps.com/carte.php?num_car=17562&lang=en).

and their surrounding villages, the empirical research also took place in rural villages in these provinces.

The empirical component of this book comprised of two elements: a survey questionnaire of two hundred individuals (the survey) from urban and rural areas;[2] and interviews with customary leaders, practitioners, and users of the two legal orders (the interviews). The purpose of the interviews was to gain a deeper and more nuanced account of the sanctioning of wrongs and the interactions of customary law and state law. While the survey enabled precision in research findings, it necessarily also limited their scope. For the most part the interviews were unstructured, using the questionnaire and its content as the basis for discussion. In addition, and in the spirit of Llewellyn (1962), I asked interviewees how wrongs are normally sanctioned in their communities and how this might vary by type of wrong (for instance murder, robbery or adultery) and type of perpetrator (from within the community or outside it) and whether they could draw on specific cases.

Introduction to the New Guinea Islands

In addition to the provinces of New Ireland and Manus Island, the provinces of East New Britain, West New Britain and the Autonomous Region of Bougainville (ARB) are often referred to as the New Guinea (*Niugini*) Islands or Islands Region. As can be seen above, these island provinces lie off the north-east coast of the New Guinea mainland and, despite being extremely ethno-linguistically diverse themselves, they share a common identity within Papua New Guinean society (although the ARB has its own strong unique sense of identity).

Papua New Guinea is a primarily rural country and the provinces visited are no exception. Few people live in the towns themselves, but there are usually many villages and settlements that surround each town, which in many respects resemble suburbs. Residents in villages and settlements in close proximity to a town visit it to purchase supplies, sell their produce, and sometimes to work in formal employment. While residents in the communities surrounding the towns have public transport or are within walking distance of town, many still live a mostly traditional lifestyle, tending subsistence gardens and harvesting small amounts of copra and cocoa on small customary blocks. In the rural villages most residents live a similar lifestyle to those in the villages surrounding town, however they are further away from both the amenities and the drawbacks of the towns.

As explained in more detail below, these islands also share a common colonial and legal history as, along with the north-eastern quarter of the New Guinea mainland, they were: first colonized by the Imperial German government in the late 1800s; then taken over by the Australian military at the beginning of the First World War; under the control of the Japanese military during much of the Second World War; then again under Australian military rule followed by a period of Australian civilian rule; and finally, since 1975, they have all become provinces within the Independent State of Papua New Guinea. A summary of each province visited is presented below.

East New Britain

As its name suggests, East New Britain consists of the eastern half of the island of New Britain, and in 2000 had an estimated population of 220,133 (Turner 2006).[3] Kokopo is the capital of East New Britain and the de facto capital of the New Guinea Islands. The provincial capital was moved to Kokopo following a large volcanic eruption in 1994 that destroyed much of Rabaul and left the rest covered in thick volcanic dust. The last census in 2000 estimated Kokopo's population to be approximately 20,000 and Rabaul's to be 4,000. Despite being partially destroyed and next to an active volcano, Rabaul is being slowly rebuilt, in part due to its near perfect harbour for shipping, which is important to the copra industry. Many villages surround the two towns, which are around 20 kilometres apart. Both towns were former headquarters of New Guinea's various colonial administrations at different times.[4] The Gazelle Peninsular, where both towns are situated, is perhaps the most developed part of Papua New Guinea, with Port Moresby being the only other contender. While it has its problems, East New Britain has a reputation for being a relatively well-run, prosperous and safe province. Given the population's proximity to both the German and Australian administrative headquarters, most villages on the Gazelle Peninsular have had interactions with the colonizers and the introduced state law for more than a hundred years.

Within East New Britain, I conducted the empirical work in the market places of Kokopo and Rabaul, the residential estate of Vunapope, and some villages surrounding these towns, in addition to two remote villages on the Gazelle Peninsula.

West New Britain

The other half of the Island of New Britain is the province of West New Britain which in 2000 had an estimated population of 184,508. Kimbe, its capital, is a boom town with much commercial activity generated through the province's palm oil industry, made possible due to its mainly flat terrain. In 1974 Kimbe was estimated to have a population of 1,000, while in 2000 this had risen to 15,000. Like the East, particularly before the destruction of Rabaul, migrant workers from many parts of Papua New Guinea, especially from the Highlands and the Sepik regions, live in the towns and their surrounds. However, unlike the East, West New Britain has a reputation for crime and *raskolism*, and is referred to by many (in the East) as 'the Wild West'. West New Britain is less developed than the East, and experienced the effects of colonialism much later. In 1914, most of the area that now makes up West New Britain was out of German effective control (Jinks, Biskup and Nelson 1973: 193), and while much of the coastal area became under Australian control, it was less developed than the East (Wilkes 1958: 14–19).

Autonomous Region of Bougainville

Formerly known as North Solomons Province, the Autonomous Region of Bougainville (ARB) was estimated to have a population of 175,160 in 2000. The ARB consists of two main islands, the larger of the two is Bougainville Island and the smaller is Buka Island. Buka Town (on Buka Island) is the current capital of the ARB with an estimated population in 2000 of around 2,000. It is a bustling town that has also become the administrative and commercial hub for the ARB. It is the only town in the ARB with banking facilities, a hospital, an airport, and various government agencies. On Bougainville Island the main town is Arawa, which is the former capital of the province and was estimated to have a population in 1980 of 13,000. However, the current population of Arawa is only a fraction of that, following a bloody civil war (known as the Bougainville Crisis) during which much of Bougainville Island's infrastructure (including bridges, roads, mines, schools, shops and government buildings) was destroyed, and most of it is yet to be rebuilt. The people of the ARB were colonized shortly after the establishment of a settlement on Gazelle Peninsular, with the German administration establishing settlements at Kieta on Bougainville Island (close to Arawa) and Buka and surrounding coconut plantations. Although the islands of Buka and Bougainville are only separated by a narrow strait, albeit deep and fast flowing, they are very different. Buka, with its transport links and much less scarred by civil war, has much in common with the rest of the New Guinea islands, while Bougainville Island still shows the trauma of civil war and is much more isolated. Here the state, including its legal order, has only recently returned after a complete retreat and shows considerable deference to customary law. As part of the peace agreement following the Bougainville Crisis, the province was granted autonomy and has its own constitution and president, while currently remaining part of the Independent State of Papua New Guinea. While each of these provinces share some degree of common identity compared to the rest of Papua New Guinea, the people of the Autonomous Region of Bougainville are closer both ethnically and geographically to the people of the Solomon Islands, and seek complete independence from the Independent State of Papua New Guinea.

History of the Enforcement of Criminal Law

All of the New Guinea Islands have a similar history of state law enforcement, both prior to and after colonization. However there are some recent notable differences, especially with respect to the ARB. In order to understand the current legal circumstances within these provinces it is necessary to provide a brief account of the history of state criminal law enforcement. From reading this historical account it should become apparent that the state has always struggled to enforce its criminal law.

The north-eastern quarter of the main island of New Guinea and the New Guinea Islands to the north, which include New Britain, New

Ireland, Bougainville and Buka, were claimed by the Imperial German Government in 1885, and German Criminal law was soon imposed, at least by statute. By the late 1890s, an administrative system was introduced on the Gazelle Peninsula of New Britain, and was later extended to some other areas, including the islands of Buka and Bougainville.

Under the German administration of the New Guinea Islands, effective control extended only to the Gazelle Peninsula of New Britain (the northern tip where the towns of Rabaul and Kokopo are situated) and some coastal areas, the whole of New Ireland and Buka, the northern part of Bougainville and the area surrounding Kieta. Historians such as Mair (1970: 13) suggest that the Germans focused on making their control fully effective in limited areas of their new territory, and most other areas were left virtually untouched by the colonial administration. Therefore, with the exception of West New Britain, all areas surveyed were exposed to colonial control for at least a hundred years.

The Germans introduced *luluais*, or village chiefs or magistrates, who had certain judicial powers. The *luluais* were elected among the clan leaders and were tasked with keeping order in their villages by enforcing local customs for minor wrongs and carrying out minor duties on behalf of the German colonial administration, such as collecting a head tax. In relation to sanctioning wrongs, for those of a 'serious nature' the *luluai* was required to report them to the colonial authorities, while for those less grave he was instructed to settle the matter himself and report on the outcome to the authorities from time to time. Land disputes and matrimonial cases were also excluded from his jurisdiction, which, along with grave wrongs, were reserved for the colonial court. For his services, he retained 10 per cent of the head tax collected.

However, not long after the *luluais*' introduction, their jurisdiction was redefined and narrowed. Governor Hahl proclaimed in 1903 that they were only to hear issues in their own village concerning quarrels about 'money or *tabu*, about pigs or produce or their other goods' (Jinks, Biskup and Nelson 1973: 190). They were expressly prohibited from hearing cases relating to divorce, land, tribal wars, murder, robbery, arson, property damage, incest, rape, adultery or robbery. For these matters they were required to report to the colonial administration, and deliver the offender (ibid.).

The redefinition and narrowing of jurisdiction stemmed from confusion over their jurisdiction and a view that they failed to act impartially. The German Report on New Guinea 1900–1 states that 'unfortunately, the chiefs appointed by the government are not always equal to the carrying out of the duties of administering justice in the way it is expected of them' (Rowley 1958: 224). This unwillingness, or inability, to act impartially can be explained by Melanesian culture and organization. Traditionally, power was widely dispersed within a village or region among different groupings and families, and while there were village headmen, clan leaders and chiefs, their power was normally limited[5]. Melanesian customary law requires kin to act in a partial manner towards each other, whether it concerns a wrong, or some other matter. Traditionally, the partiality of kin is offset through collective decision making and mediation among families and groupings of roughly even strength. It can therefore be expected that the elected, or appointed, *luluai* would show favour to his kinsmen. In relation to this Lawrence (1969: 35) concludes that: '[I]t was impossible for them, as kinsmen, to operate as impartial officials in a society with a kinship-based structure and morality. They could not be expected, in the name of abstract authority, to sacrifice the interests of individuals on whose daily cooperation they depended for survival in society'.

While the magistrates were formally stripped of much of their power, the German administration only had limited influence over the indigenous population regarding criminal matters, and it is not documented how the *luluais* implemented the new policy. During this period, it is likely that the *luluais* and customary leaders exceeded their jurisdiction, as defined by the state, and that many grave wrongs and sanctions were not brought to the attention of the German colonial authorities (Rowley 1958: 225).

In 1914 the German colonial government capitulated to Australian troops, and the former German colony came under Australian military government. The terms of capitulation required that 'the local laws and customs' were to remain in force, including Prussian criminal law (Rowley 1958: 234–35). Rowley suggests that, given that the new administrators had limited knowledge of German, Pisin or the German criminal law, it was often ignored, by both the Australian military and the indigenous population. According to Mair's (1970: 13) account which was first published in 1948, the practice of criminal law bordered on chaotic, with reports of summary executions and inconsistent enforcement of German criminal law and procedures. However, the reach of the state in criminal matters was even weaker than under the previous administration, where 'regular' patrolling meant 'once a year' (ibid.).

During this period customary law and *luluai* adjudication seems to have been practised mostly without state interference, except in the towns and their immediate surrounds. However, like the German administration, Mackenzie, the chief judge under Australian military rule, considered it the duty of the *luluais* to report any judgements passed on violations of tribal customs and laws, and to notify the district office of any crimes committed in his village or district. Rowley (1958: 225) considers that breaches of the German criminal law in most areas would not have come to the notice of the colonial administration unless it resulted in open tribal warfare, and he cites an Australian district officer who reported at the time that 'no cases whatsoever were brought before the District Office'.

In 1920, the former German Territories were allotted to Australia under a mandate from the League of Nations. With legislative power over the region, Australia enacted the Laws Repeal and Adopting Ordinance 1921, repealing German law and replacing it with English law, comprising of English statutes applying in Queensland and common law and equity at the time, including the Criminal Code. However, the Ordinance provided that 'tribal institutions, customs and usages were not to be affected, and were to be permitted to continue in existence' (Brown 1969: 84). However, New Guinea remained under Australian military government until 1933 when a bill to create Legislative and Executive Councils was passed by the Australian Parliament. The Australian administration retained the system of the *luluais* but wholly stripped them of their judicial function. Despite the change in the state law, they continued to hear and adjudicate on a range of disputes and wrongs across the New Guinea Islands. This was often done with the tacit consent of the local administrative officials (Oliver 1991: 50). Recognizing this fact, an advisor to the colonial administration, Colonel Ainsworth, who had spent time in Africa, recommended in 1924 that the indigenous courts that were being held 'illegally' should be accepted by the state, on the condition that 'serious offences' be brought before the district officer. He recommended that the state should recognize their jurisdiction in all civil matters including succession and adultery, and also in many criminal matters such as theft, assault, sexual offences, and disobedience of lawful orders. He also recommended that the *luluais* should have the state authority to fine the offender and that no limit be set. However, Ainsworth's recommendations were rejected and instead Native Regulations were promulgated in 1924, where Courts of Native Affairs were established and held by the colonial district officer, assistant district officer or the patrol officer in villages or government stations. The regulations covered marriage, divorce, adultery, inheritance, disposal of the dead, real and personal property, and minor wrongs. Serious criminal matters came under the District Courts and the Criminal Code (Jinks, Biskup and Nelson 1973: 256–63).

Despite the changes to statute, the state and its legal order remained weak on the ground. In 1928 there were less than two hundred permanent officers in the whole of New Guinea – including the New Guinea mainland – and efforts to extend effective control were slow (Mair 1970: 36–39).

Officially, New Guinea was divided into four areas of control: areas under 'control', 'influence', 'partial influence', and areas where patrols had entered without establishing friendly relations. Areas under control were those where a full census had been taken and where an unarmed 'native' constable could arrest an offender without danger. In areas under influence, a partial census had been taken and some 'natives' would visit the district officer for advice or the settlement of disputes. Those under partial influence had been penetrated by patrols and succeeded in friendly relations. Mair (1970: 40) reports that by 1936 the whole of the New Britain coast was 'under control', the Gazelle Peninsular almost from coast to coast, and a smaller area across the western tip of the island. The central mountains were almost untouched, but it was later found that they were largely uninhabited. In addition, Buka and the coastal areas of Bougainville were also 'under control'. By the early 1940s the reach of the state was growing, with most of New Britain, Buka and Bougainville under the influence of the colonial authorities; and by 1942 the police force for New Guinea consisted of 794 men (ibid.: 42) Despite this, it still seems that most wrongs were sanctioned within the villages and without the administration's knowledge.

In February 1942 the New Guinea Islands fell to the Imperial Japanese Army and remained under their control for more than three years. Accounts of this period suggest that they demanded complete obedience from the indigenous population and were at times brutal, including the execution of members of the indigenous population for minor offences (Rowley 1958). However, there was heavy fighting on many of the islands, particularly Bougainville, so it is unclear how tight Japanese control was, particularly outside of the towns.

Following the Japanese surrender, the New Guinea Islands reverted to Australian military control. In 1949, not long after civil administration was restored, the Papua and New Guinea Act allowed for the establishment of 'native village courts' and some were set up around Rabaul. However, these were geographically contained pilots, and the colonial administration continued to refuse to recognize the jurisdiction of indigenous courts and tribunals in the New Guinea Islands. The policy of the administration (Annual Report in 1955: 41; c.f. Mair 1970: 77) remained to: 'encourage the people to turn to the greater use of the existing statutory judicial system which provides for them the highest measure of justice, and in due course, and as circumstances permit, the Administration will ensure a fuller participation of indigenous people in the administration of justice within that system'.

While the official policy aimed to replace customary law with state criminal law, albeit in a gentle manner, it was acknowledged at the time that it was both counterproductive and unrealistic. David Fenbury, the

Director of Native Affairs, and an advocate of the native village courts considered: 'that in New Guinea conditions, where everyone knows everyone else's business, elaborate rules of evidence are not necessary to determine guilt and innocence, and if the application of these rules leads to the acquittal of someone known to be guilty it is the prestige of the court that suffers' (Mair 1970: 78).

Fenbury considered the lack of recognition of native tribunals that produced 'two parallel legal systems administering two different kinds of law and justice'; *Kot belong Government* versus unrecognized village tribunals, *Kot bilong mipela* (Fenbury 1965 c.f. Mair 1970: 78). As will be demonstrated from the findings of the empirical research, this situation is still the case.

Regardless of administration policy at the time, the vast majority of Papua New Guineans continued to settle disputes and sanction wrongs using customary law or were tried in the Courts of Native Affairs by administrative patrol officers (*kiaps*) who often used considerable discretion in recognizing customary law over state law. While it does seem to be the case that the majority of indigenous Papua New Guineans sought to sanction wrongs outside the state court system, it would be wrong to suggest that that some did not come into contact with state courts during this period. From my own review of the Supreme Court records from sittings in the New Guinea Islands during the late 1940s and the 1950s (contained in Derham 1960), it is clear that many indigenous Papua New Guineans did come into contact with the formal court system.

However, one striking feature of these records is the leniency in sentencing, with indigenous offenders often receiving headline sentences of four to seven years' imprisonment for the gravest of crimes. It must also be known that the state also accommodated the grave customary wrongs of sorcery and adultery into the state law.[6]

The Current Control of Wrongs in the New Guinea Islands

Customary law plays an important role in the sanctioning of wrongs in the New Guinea Islands; and the state, for the most part, only sanctions wrongdoers when customary law fails to do so. In the provinces of East and West New Britain this is an informal practice, while in the Autonomous Region of Bougainville it has been formalized.

According to the Papua New Guinea Law and Justice Sector Secretariat (2007: 6) the total police numbers for these three provinces is 514, with 271 in East New Britain (the administrative headquarters for the Royal Papua New Guinea Constabulary in the New Guinea Islands), 113 in West New Britain and 130 in the Autonomous Region of Bougainville. In ratio to population, this equates to approximately one police officer for 812 people in East New Britain, 1,633 in West New Britain, and 1,347 in the Autonomous Region of Bougainville. This compares to the national average of one police officer for 1,084 people – but the global average is one per 400.[7] This shows that these provinces have very low policing levels by world standards, as does the rest of Papua New Guinea. The one exception is Port Moresby which contains one-third of Papua New Guinea's uniformed police force, which equates to one police officer for every 156 residents.[8]

Despite this legislative framework that seeks to accommodate customary law, the police in the New Guinea Islands show considerably more deference to the practice of customary law, while village courts often far exceed their legislative authority. While it would be wrong to characterize the current interactions as problem free, for the most part the customary legal order and state legal order have a cooperative and supportive relationship in the New Guinea Islands. Despite the Criminal Code and the official prosecution policy, the primary gatekeepers of the state legal order – which in East New Britain are the police – largely allow customary law to operate unhampered for all but the gravest wrongs, and even then they show discretion. There was a general, but not universal, feeling that the current interaction between customary law and the state law works well.

It must be stressed that within the New Guinea Islands the relationship between the two legal orders varies markedly, both between and within provinces. The main outlier is the Autonomous Region of Bougainville which, having a separate constitution and different prosecution policy, has a formalized cooperative relationship primarily through the public prosecutor's role as a gatekeeper that allows a customary sanction to substitute for a state prosecution and potential sanction. However, even within the Autonomous Region of Bougainville, this relationship varies considerably between Buka Island and Bougainville Island. While a broadly consistent picture emerged, there was some variance, particularly between the town centres (and the communities that surround them) and the rural villages.

The Town Centres and Their Surrounds

The towns in these provinces have few residents as they are primarily commercial and government centres that are surrounded by many villages and settlements that resemble suburbs. Within the towns both residents and visitors enjoy relatively high levels of personal safety and freedom of movement. The police mainly confine themselves to the town centres, and devote considerable effort to policing minor offences, such as traffic offences, shoplifting and littering. From the interviews, a consistent picture emerged: the type of legal order applied – customary or state – strongly depended on *where* the offence occurred. If it occurred within the town centre the victim would seek redress from the state legal order, whereas if it occurred within the village they would use customary law, even if the village was only a short (say, half an hour) walk to town.

While there was a strong expectation that a wrong committed in town should be sanctioned using the state law, if the sanction was seen as inadequate then there was a perception that customary sanctions, including the use of payback, would be permissible. As explained by a retired police officer, in the case of an accidental death a retaliatory killing would not be condoned unless a reasonable compensation payment had not been forthcoming. However, if the killing was deliberate, a payback killing could be condoned if it occurred immediately after the death (that is, on the same day). I was also told that sometimes the police let the prosecution of a killing rest if it complies with customary law principles. Another man interviewed on an urban estate suggested that around K20,000 ($8,000) to K30,000 ($12,000) would be demanded for a killing if the wrongdoer did not face jail. If an offender was jailed for a considerable period, less compensation would be demanded, perhaps K10,000 ($4,000). However, if the demand was not met by a certain date, the family of the offender would be at risk of a payback killing.

While there was widespread acceptance of the state's authority to sanction wrongs within the town itself, and that customary law should only be exercised if the state fails to sanction a wrong adequately, in the surrounding villages this legal ordering is reversed. In these communities customary law is the primary legal order used to sanction wrongs while the state criminal law provides a secondary and mostly supportive role. Within these surrounding villages, I was continually told that if victims go to the police prior to attempting to seek redress in the village they will be sent back to the village councillor or village court.

In these surrounding villages, the community institutions that control and sanction wrongdoing differ in terms of name and proximity to 'traditional' customary law. In some villages elders groups take on this role, while in others they are attached to state or church institutions such as the village council, church peace and justice committees, and sometimes village courts. The village councillors who preside over the sanctioning of wrongs play a similar role to that of the *luluai* set up by the German colonial administration more than a hundred years ago and that officially ceased more than seventy years ago. In places where there seemed to be no clear functioning customary leadership, customary law is primarily exercised through self-help.

In one of these surrounding villages the councillor told me that customary law is used to solve problems in his community and for sanctioning most wrongs. He told me that the community does not rely on the police to deal with crime, rather on a strong community spirit which, he told me, is an extension of custom. He went on to say that if a wrong can be remedied within the community, they do not involve the police. The process of sanctioning a wrong in this community normally begins with taking the matter to the village councillor. If the matter cannot be settled by the councillor or the peace and justice committee, it may be elevated to the village court or be taken to the police. The *wan bel* process, which consists of mediation, reconciliation and compensation, is the main method for sanctioning wrongs, where the magnitude of required compensation depends both on the wealth of the family involved and on the gravity of the crime.

In this village the peace and justice committee meets weekly and normally hears four or five cases. The most common wrongs they encounter are disruptions, violence, and damage associated with drunkenness. For more serious wrongs, the village court magistrate will also help to mediate and adjudicate. However, it is the complainant's decision whether it is the peace and justice committee that hears the case or the village court, and I was told that most choose the peace and justice committee. Even serious wrongs must be dealt with at the community level first, regardless of whether the police take action afterwards. In very serious matters, such as cases of incest, the wrong is initially dealt with in the community – with agreement on compensation, which often includes shell money – and then the community leaders will notify the police. It is then up to the police to decide whether to charge the suspect or not. In this village, the leadership did not see any conflict between the two legal orders, with the councillor telling me that customary law 'is the same [as the] law of the police'.

In this same village, where the village court operates both in parallel and sometimes together with the peace and justice committee, it meets twice a week and most cases relate to bride price disputes and minor thefts.[9] From reviewing a copy of their latest quarterly report at the time (September 2010), all cases related to theft, assault or property damage. The three defendants for theft, one male and two female, were fined a total of K120 ($48) and ordered to pay a total of K340 ($136). The five defendants for assault/fighting were fined a total of K140 ($56) and ordered to pay a total of K350 ($140) in compensation. The court also heard issues relating to failure to comply with summons, a settlement order or fine, bride price, 'marriage problems', and land use. The clerk told me that if fines or compensation payments are not made on time, the court officials will go to the houses to demand payment. If they do not respond, the village court will order jail time and he told me this would be enforced by the police. He, like many others in the village, told me that more serious wrongs, such as rape and murder, are referred straight to the police.

In another surrounding village a similar picture was painted where the law and justice committee consisted of the councillor, the pastor of the church, and other village leaders in conjunction with the village court. Again, I was told that most wrongs are solely sanctioned at the village level, with the exception of rape and homicide. Going through the list from the survey, theft, robbery, property damage, assault, threatening violence and unauthorized compensation (where they disobey the village), adultery, sorcery, spreading false rumours, domestic violence, abandonment, armed robbery, and breaking and entering are all remedied at the village level. In this village I was again told that if a victim approaches the police for any of these matters before making real efforts to settle it within the village then they will be referred back to the village. While the village court is not able to award compensation or fines in excess of K1,000 ($400) for most wrongs, this is sometimes supplemented by requiring the offender to make a payment of shell money in addition to paper money. Shell money is accepted currency in these villages and can be used to purchase goods at the village stores. Despite the order of compensation or fine being levied on the individual, it is expected that the offender's extended family will provide much of it.

In this part of New Britain (the Gazelle Peninsular) I was repeatedly told that payback killings are not part of 'traditional' customary law. However, many talked of sorcery being used as a severe sanction which is widely thought to be able to cause death, as belief in sorcery is almost universal. While sorcerers are believed to have supernatural powers, I was also told they are often said to use more practical means such as contaminating a person's food, drink or clothing with harmful substances. In addition to the use of compensation and sorcery, the community may sanction a beating, for example for an accused sorcerer who denies such activity or refuses to stop his or her alleged nefarious practices. I was told of one accused sorcerer, who in addition to being beaten was also fined a considerable sum of money.[10]

This description of how wrongs are sanctioned and the relationship between the two legal orders in urban centres and their surrounding villages was primarily derived from interviews with community leaders. However, while interviews with the broader population mostly confirmed these findings, there were differing accounts in relation to the scope of police activity and their willingness to recognize the practice of customary law. While there were consistent accounts that the police would be alerted in the case of a killing, others suggested that in cases of rape and abortion they may not be notified as these can be sufficiently sanctioned solely within the village. Others suggested that the police would be informed, but as long as the matter was settled under customary law, the police would let the matter rest. There were also discrepancies concerning the degree to which the police actually turn a blind eye to a killing that has been sanctioned under customary law or is itself a sanction under customary law. On this matter the full spectrum of accounts were expressed; I was even told by one interviewee that a family would go to the police and warn them that the offender's family had not paid compensation and so they were going to execute a payback killing.[11] There were differing views and confusion over what roles customary law and state law currently play, and what roles they ought to play, particularly among the general public interviewed.

Remote Villages

In the remote villages visited, the process of sanctioning wrongs mainly falls to the elders of the communities, a task that they willing do. Given their geographical distance, the police only visit every couple of years, which suits the local inhabitants. When I asked how the villages deal with criminal or wrong behaviour I was consistently told of the *wan bel* process. If someone has committed a wrong, the elders, including the village councillor, will gather together and approach the wrongdoer. They will talk and encourage him or her to change his or her behaviour. If the behaviour has led to a dispute between families, the elders bring the two parties together to agree on a suitable resolution, normally a compensation payment using traditional shell money. If there is animosity between the two families, the elders will first go to the two families separately to encourage them to compromise before they meet. When the two families are brought together they will agree on a settlement, shake hands, and eat together in a ceremonial feast, including chewing betel nut, and peaceful relations will be restored. This process may take anywhere from a few weeks to a number of months.

If the parties cannot reach agreement, the elders may refer the matter to the village court, which in these villages is an extension of the elders group and *wan bel* process. I was told that for a more serious wrong, such as robbery, the wrongdoer may face a beating prior to the mediation process. While beatings take place, payback killings are virtually non-existent and I was told they would not be tolerated. Compensation payments are the main sanction used. The main escalation in these villages is to refer the matter to the police. However, this is done reluctantly and is mainly used as a threat in an effort to gain agreement between the two parties. I was told that the only cases of people going to jail in these remote villages concerned: a persistent burglar who had kept on breaking into a village store; some distillers of alcohol, whose activities had led to significant social disruption; and some young men who had stolen goods from a local plantation. In the first two cases, these people had become nuisances and eventually the community simply had enough. In the latter case, the plantation owners went directly to the police to demand action. While the *wan bel* process is used for all but the most serious of wrongs, I was repeatedly told that if there were to be a killing or rape, the matter would be referred straight to the police. However, I was also told that such crimes did not happen in these communities.

The headmaster of the primary school expressed a commonly held view that customary justice exercised through the elders and the village court is more effective and less costly than using the police and formal courts. He told me it also brings peace and harmony to the village. There was also a belief that increased jail terms or a police presence would not really help these communities, as they consider it best to solve these matters at home. There was also a concern that jail will neither help the offender nor the community, with the offender learning bad practices and bringing them back the village when released. I was told that when someone goes to jail the matter still needs to be settled when the offender returns, which is hardly surprising given that the offender and victim (or at least members of their families) are likely to interact on a daily basis. Therefore, regardless of a state sanction, there still needs to be mediation and a customary settlement to ease the tension between the families.

Problems with the Current Arrangements

While the current legal arrangements coincide with relatively safe and peaceful communities, concerns were still raised. In particular, there was a deep and widespread dissatisfaction with the police, both in terms of their brutality and their inability to effectively sanction wrongdoers, and that customary sanctions can be too light.

Poor perceptions of the police and the state criminal law were widespread. In particular, the police were perceived to be corrupted by *wantokism*. There was a strong feeling that imprisonment was arbitrary and usually reserved for the unlucky ones who had a small or ineffective kinship network, although this perception varied considerably by province and community visited. The perception of the police was much worse on Buka Island, partly due to confusion over their role given the Autonomous Region of Bougainville's relatively new Constitution and that the state criminal law cannot sanction accidental deaths.[12] The public perception of the police in East New Britain was much better, as the informal arrangements for allowing customary sanctions to substitute for state sanctions seemed to be the more clearly defined.

A common complaint directed towards the police concerned their brutality, both in the towns and in the remote villages. In one of the remote villages visited, part of the reason for their preference for customary law was that when the police come, which is normally only every couple of years, they can be brutal. A teacher told me that 'if the police hear stories they come in they are cruel and punish indiscriminately'. I was told of a story by numerous sources where the police came following thefts from a plantation close by; they cut down some tree branches and used them to indiscriminately beat the young men of the village. In the remote villages there were also complaints that access to the state legal order costs money and therefore it is only accessible to the wealthy. For instance, the plantation owners paid for the fuel to get the police to the village. For the police to come out, they also charge a summons fee, and poor villagers cannot pay for this or their transport.

Taking Customary Law Seriously in the Kieta Region of Bougainville

In the Kieta region of Bougainville Island, most wrongs, grave or minor, are sanctioned using customary law and presided over by clan and village chiefs, with the police and state mostly providing a supportive role in the enforcement of customary sanctions. The 'chief' system is the most powerful institution, and evidently more powerful than the state and its agents, including the police.

These legal circumstances developed partly out of necessity, as during the Bougainville Crisis the state and its police were forced to flee. However, it also stems from a strong pre-existing customary law movement that continues to grow, aided by the Autonomous Region of Bougainville Constitution (Bougainville Constitution). The Bougainville Constitution promotes customary law even more than Papua New Guinea's Constitution. In addition, a landmark National Court ruling in late 2008, by Justice Kandakasi of Papua New Guinea's National and Supreme Courts in the *Mattau* case[13] has also had a strong impact on the treatment of grave wrongs, which is discussed in detail in Larcom (2013b).

From my interviews, a consistent account of the normal course of events in the treatment of grave wrongs in the Kieta district emerged.

In the case of a homicide, for example, the police will typically place the accused in a police cell straight after the killing, mainly for his or her own protection due to the risk of being killed for payback. In the days following, the family of the killer will provide a part payment of money to the family of the wronged. Tensions will be high, and the initial payment provides a signal that the wrongdoer's family wishes to solve the issue peacefully, and is aimed at 'cooling the hearts' of the family that has suffered a death. Issues of guilt or innocence seem to be rarely discussed, as it is normally clear in the minds of both parties who the killer is. In the following weeks, the two families, represented by the fathers and maternal uncles of those directly involved, meet to work out a mutually agreeable compensation payment with the help and guidance of their village and clan chiefs. The two clans explain their viewpoints on the matter, the root causes for the action, and the sanction. The sanction usually focuses on the magnitude of compensation and whether the perpetrator should also go to jail. When the killing is deliberate, understanding the root cause is important; one chief told me that 'there is always a reason for a killing' and this can affect the compensation payment. Compensation payments can range between K50,000 ($20,000) for an accidental killing and up to K130,000 ($52,000) for a deliberate killing. While the compensation agreed on depends on many factors, including the relative strength and wealth of the families and clans involved and the circumstances surrounding the killing, the most common sum reported to me was K100,000 ($40,000) for a murder. This is a considerable sum in a country where the average income per capita is approximately K3,250 ($1,300) and many of the wrongdoer's extended family will need to make a contribution. In addition to paper money, the payment also usually consists of shell money, pigs and other mostly ceremonial food such as taro, and may also involve the exchange of land. The 'compensation' package is seen as a tangible expression of remorse by the wrongdoer and his family, a form of punishment, and compensation to the wronged family for their loss.

Following agreement, normally within a few months, a ceremony takes place where the compensation is exchanged and peaceful relations are restored. The two families will eat betel nut from the same basket, signalling peace between the two families and clans. In addition to the customary ceremony, the two chiefs write and sign a letter, or memorandum of understanding, to the police telling them that the matter has been remedied by custom and both parties are satisfied with the outcome. The decision as to whether the wrongdoer is tried in the state court is made by the public prosecutor of the ARB. However, I was told that a state trial will not be initiated if a customary settlement has been reached. If the wrongdoer is in police custody, he or she will be released, and free to return to the community. Those who have committed a serious wrong and avoid jail through their family or clan paying compensation on their behalf know that they are indebted for some time, and that if they re-offend they face the risk of severe punishment. It is also the duty of the wrongdoer's family to keep a close eye on the offender to ensure that he or she does not reoffend, and after a period of time, to fully reintegrate him or her into the community.

Sometimes a customary settlement cannot be reached, usually because the victim's family is unwilling to accept a compensation payment or the wrongdoer's family is unwilling to pay. In these circumstances, the chiefs refer the matter to the police and the wrongdoer will face the state courts. Where the wrongdoer goes to jail, compensation is still necessary to restore peaceful relations between families and clans, and a ceremony would be performed by the two clans prior to the wrongdoer's release. The compensation would normally be a quarter to a half of what would have been paid if the wrongdoer had not gone to jail.

All the customary leaders I interviewed considered that compensation is the best remedy for the commission of serious wrongs. With the primary sanction for grave wrongs being compensation payments, albeit in the shadow of state imprisonment, the Kieta district is safer and more peaceful than many other parts of Papua New Guinea. I was also told that crime is lower and residents feel safer than in the pre-crisis days when the state was the dominant legal order.

Summary

In all these communities, with the exception of the town centres and the special case of the Kieta district, most wrongs were sanctioned through councillors, elders or individual victims who have no state authority over such matters. While village courts existed in most communities, they too seemed to play a limited role compared to councillors and elders. Overall, customary law was considered to be fairer than the state criminal law, both in terms of process and sanction, as it involves the community as well as the families of both the victim and offender, who act to counterbalance each other.

The state criminal law was seen as too removed from the community and too easily corrupted. However, very few of those interviewed considered that it did not have a legitimate role to play in the sanctioning of wrongs, particularly in town centres and as a fallback when a customary settlement cannot be reached. Others also considered that state law enforcement should be increased, as they felt customary law is generally inadequate and that jailing offenders is necessary for a range of wrongs, both to act as a deterrent and to satisfy victims. Apart from those on Bougainville Island, many of those interviewed craved a strong, impartial and effective state criminal justice system that, when called upon, could sanction wrongdoers and support local communities to control wrongs.

The finding that below the surface the state legal order plays a secondary role to customary law is hardly surprising if one considers the history of state law enforcement in the New Guinea Islands. The state has always had limited success in enforcing its criminal law, whether it be a foreign colonial administration or the independent Papua New Guinean state. The resilience of the customary legal order is remarkable, given that it has been officially suppressed, to varying degrees, for more than one hundred years.

Following this qualitative description of the sanctioning of wrongs in the New Guinea Islands is a quantitative analysis based on the results from a survey. This allows a more precise description of the extent of wrongdoing in these communities and how they are sanctioned, along with testing the prevalence of elements of substantive customary law.

Descriptive Statistics from Survey

In addition to suggesting that these communities have relatively low rates of crime, the results also demonstrate a demand for both the customary legal order and the state legal order, and their sanctions. In particular, they demonstrate that both legal orders enjoy legitimacy among the population in sanctioning wrongs, and therefore indicate a high degree of deep legal pluralism.

Crime Victimization Data

Of the two hundred respondents, forty-two reported being a victim of a crime within the last five years.[14] As can be seen in Figure 3.2, the most prevalent crime was assault, with a victimization rate of 8 per cent, followed by theft, property damage, and sorcery. The violent crime rate reported (which includes assault, threats of violence, robbery, armed robbery, and one case of rape) was 11 per cent over a five-year period.[15]

There is a general perception that the New Guinea Islands are safer than many other parts of Papua New Guinea, and the survey results support this view. While the sample size is small and comparisons should be made cautiously, the violent crime rate reported here is broadly in line with, or lower than, many Western societies.[16] In relation to the developing world, these rates are much lower than in many other societies where data are available, including in Papua New Guinea itself.[17] It is widely accepted that many of Papua New Guinea's urban centres are among the most dangerous in the world. While somewhat dated, the only cross-country victimization survey that included Papua New Guinea took place in 1992 and reported extremely high rates of crime in Port Moresby, Lae and Goroka, with the rate of assaults and threats of violence at 31.4 per cent, robbery at 26.3 per cent, and sexual incidents at 32.5 per cent over a five-year period (Egan, Zvekic and Alvazzi del Frate 1995: 200–212). These results were some of the highest crime rates recorded in any of the countries and cities surveyed.[18] More recent crime victimization surveys of Port Moresby (Guthrie, Hukula and Laki 2006a) and Lae (Guthrie, Hukula and Laki 2007) suggest that violent crime rates remain extremely high, but perhaps lower than earlier estimates for Port Moresby.[19] While the prevalence of violent crime in some parts of Papua New Guinea is a severely debilitating factor in these societies, this does not seem to be the case on the New Guinea Islands, including their urban centres. The only other known victimization survey conducted in the fieldwork area was conducted in the Autonomous Region of Bougainville in 2005 (see Guthrie, Hukula and Laki 2006b). This survey, with a

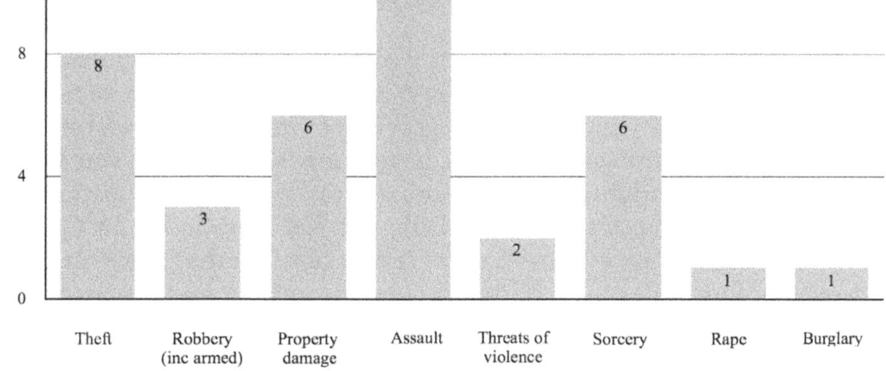

Figure 3.2. Crime by type

larger sample size, produced a similarly low violent crime rate; however the rates for less grave crimes, such as theft, were markedly higher.[20]

Further evidence that the level of wrongdoing in the areas surveyed of the New Guinea Islands is not considered overly problematic is based on the perceived prevalence of wrongdoing. In addition to actual crime victimization, respondents were asked to rate on a scale from one to five (with 1 being 'not serious' and 5 being 'extremely serious') the perceived seriousness (or prevalence) of wrongs in their communities.[21] As can be seen from Figure 3.3, few wrongs exceed an average of three, which suggests that there is a perception that while the prevalence of some wrongs is considered problematic in the communities, none approach the 'extremely serious' level of five. It is also noteworthy that the grave wrongs of homicide, rape and robbery score relatively lowly at below two. Those that score most highly are the spreading of false rumours, domestic violence, sorcery, adultery, theft and assault. This would suggest that the grave customary wrongs of sorcery and adultery are not being adequately controlled compared to other grave wrongs in the community. Domestic violence is the second most prevalent wrong (which would be included in the data under 'assault'), suggesting that women face considerable hardship in Papua New Guinea.

Response When Wronged

In relation to the choice of legal order and sanction of those who reported to be a victim of crime, 43 per cent reported that they sought redress using customary law, with 24 per cent seeking compensation payments and 19 per cent using violent payback.[22] As can be seen from Figure 3.4, only 21 per cent sought redress using the state legal order, and 26 per cent chose to do nothing.[23] In addition, 10 per cent chose to seek redress under both legal orders.

These results indicate that there is a high degree of legal pluralism in choice of redress, both in terms of legal order and sanction. In addition, this does not seem to relate to the gravity of wrong, as the victims of violent crime almost evenly sought a sanction between the two legal orders. It also highlights an important shortcoming in most victimization surveys, such as those by van Dijk, van Kesteren and Smit (2008: 110) who suggest that crimes that are not reported to the police are not adequately sanctioned. While this may be the case in some societies, it is not the case in the New Guinea Islands where customary law plays an important role in the control of wrongdoing.

Of those victims who reported their satisfaction with the end outcome, only one out of eight respondents who sought redress from the police were

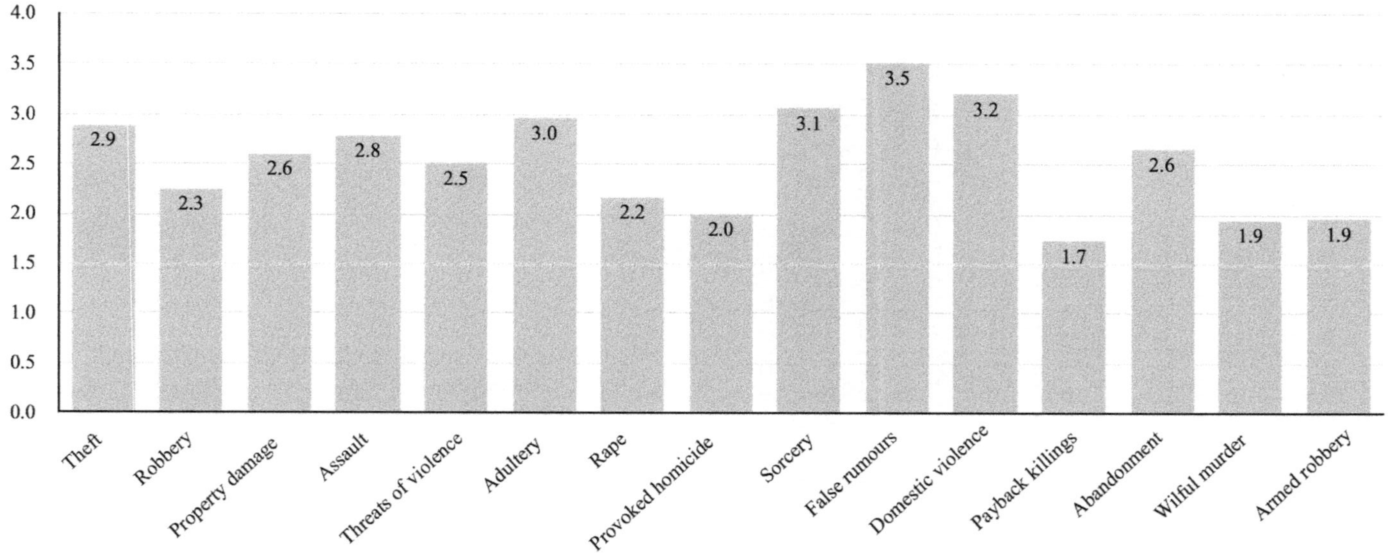

Figure 3.3. Perceived seriousness of wrongdoing

satisfied compared to four out of fourteen under customary law. While this sample is too small to make any statistical inference, it suggests that on the whole both legal orders fail to completely satisfy victims, with the state legal order faring much worse.

This high degree of pluralism is also reflected in the stated answers of the respondents when asked what their response *would* be in relation to a robbery. While the response of going to the police was the single most popular choice, the majority of respondents stated that they would seek redress from the village court or use customary sanctions. When plural responses are excluded, along with the response of 'doing nothing', approximately 45 per cent stated that they would go to the police, while 55 per cent stated that they would utilize customary law or the village courts.[24]

Similarly, when excluding plural responses, when asked what was the main deterrent against crime the respondents were again almost evenly split, with 50 per cent responding with the police and court system while 40 per cent responded with the customary legal order or village courts. Similarly, when asked how crime could be lowered, 50 per cent suggested through a greater police presence or tougher sentencing, while 20 per cent suggested greater use of customary law and 20 per cent suggested greater support and funding for village courts. Interestingly, 10 per

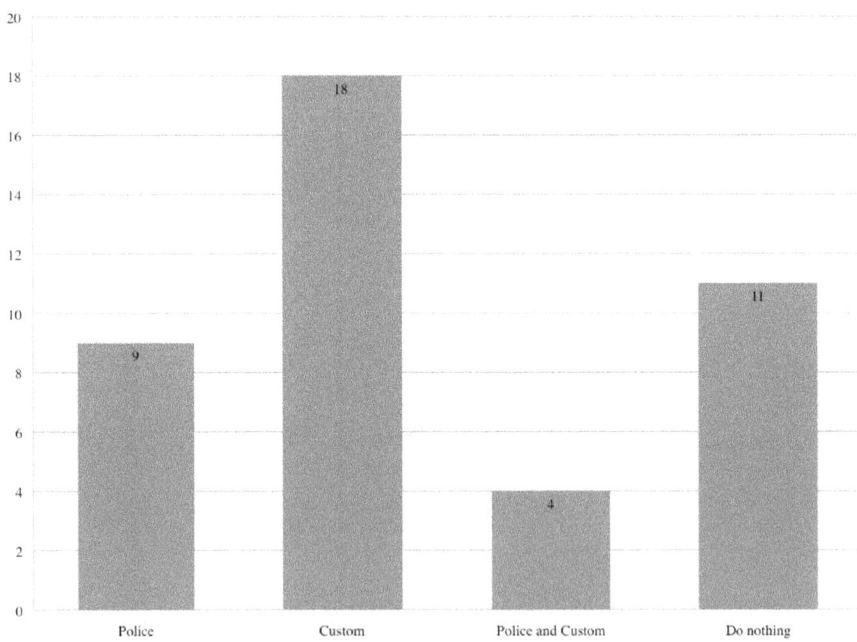

Figure 3.4. Victim response to crime

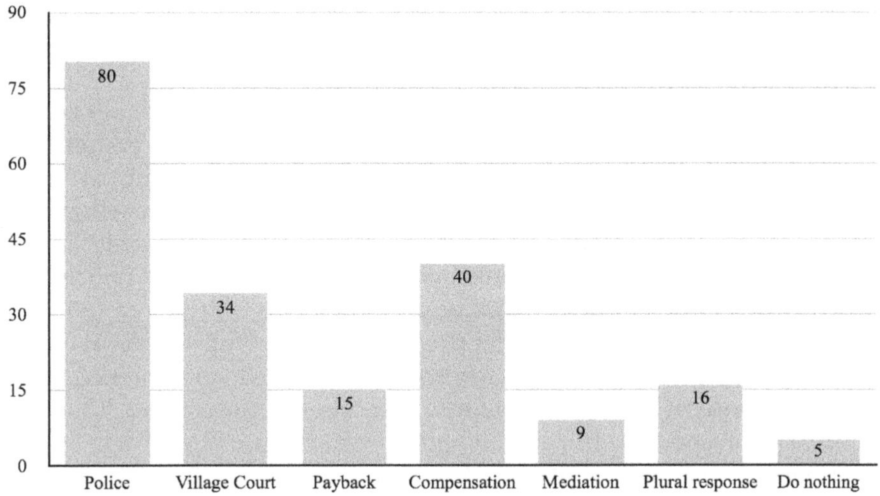

Figure 3.5. Stated response to a robbery

cent of respondents to both questions gave a different answer to either the state or customary legal orders, and most related to the internalization of behaviours, such as parents teaching their children respect for others and teaching Christian values. These results suggest that the state and customary legal orders play an almost equal role in the control of wrongdoing.

Prevalence of Customary Notions of Wrong and Sanctions

While the importance of strict liability under customary law, and the use of payback and compensation payments, have been well documented in the past, very little (if any) empirical analysis has been undertaken to ascertain to what extent these notions are currently held.

To test to what extent the notion of strict liability is internalized, a scenario was put to the respondents based on a case heard in the Kokopo District Court in 2010.[25] The scenario presented to the respondents was as follows:

> Imagine the following scenario. It is very late on a Friday night and Joseph and his friend have been drinking alcohol and are walking back to their village. Given their level of drunkenness they sit down on the side of the road and fall asleep. Not long after, a van comes past and runs over Joseph and his friend. The driver stops but both Joseph and his friend are dead. The police interview the van driver and conclude that he was driving within the speed limit and that the death of Joseph and his friend was an

unfortunate accident. Indicate how you feel about the actions taken by Joseph's family.

The respondents were then asked whether they agreed or disagreed with various potential actions taken by the family of the two young men who had died. The results indicate that the majority of respondents consider an accidental death to be a wrong, regardless of whether the driver was 'at fault' or not. As can be viewed in Figure 3.6, only 12 per cent agreed that the family should accept the decision of the police and do nothing more. The vast majority of respondents considered that the driver should be sanctioned under the customary and/or state legal order.

As respondents were asked whether they agreed or disagreed with various responses, multiple affirmative responses were possible. Allowing for multiple responses, 15 per cent agreed with the use of payback, 69 per cent agreed with the family demanding compensation from the driver, and 69 per cent agreed with the family going back to the police and demanding that the driver be charged.

While the majority of respondents agreed with the use of more than one sanction, this should not be taken that they agreed to the application of multiple sanctions on an offender; while some did, many others raised concerns over the 'double punishment' of offenders, which is discussed in the next section under the heading of substitutability of sanctions.

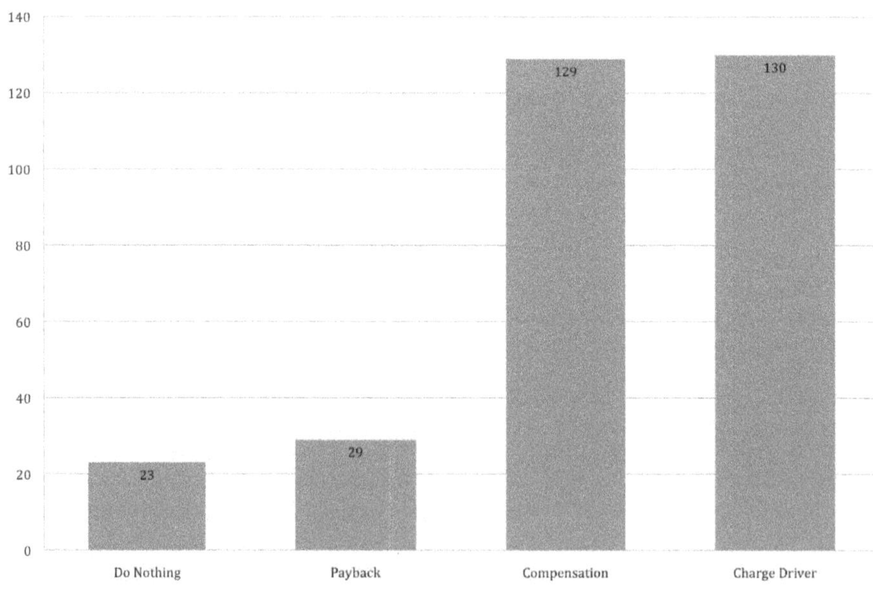

Figure 3.6. Kin's response to accidental death

To test the degree of acceptance towards the use of customary sanctions, including those that are crimes under the state criminal law, another scenario was put to the respondents that involved a deliberate killing following a heated argument. It read as follows:

> Imagine the following scenario. Two men from the same village, John and Anthony, got into a heated argument and things got out of hand. Anthony attacked John with a bush knife, chopped his arm off and killed him. Indicate how you feel about the following actions of John's brother.

Again respondents were asked whether they agreed or disagreed with various potential actions taken by the family of the murdered man. As can be seen from Figure 3.7, and allowing for multiple responses, 81 per cent agreed with going to the police and jailing the offender, 56 per cent agreed with demanding a compensation payment, and 29 per cent agreed with a payback killing.

These results indicate that most respondents agreed with the use of jail for a deliberate killing, suggesting a strong demand for the state legal order's most potent sanction. However, a significant portion of respondents also agreed with the use of compensation payments and payback

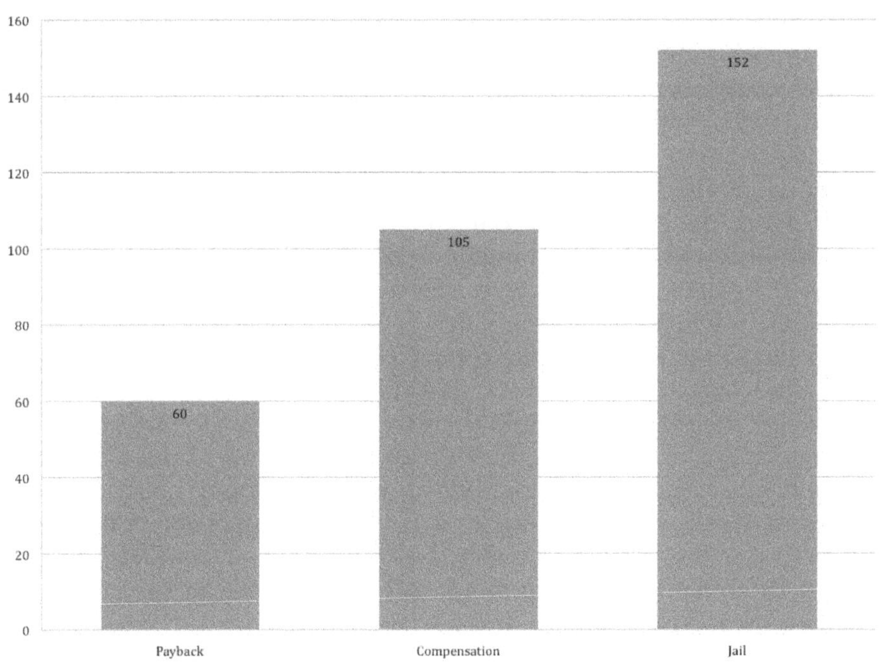

Figure 3.7. Sanction for deliberate killing

killings, indicating that these customary sanctions are also considered legitimate by a sizeable portion of the population. It also suggests the potential for legal dissonance to occur through the interaction of the two legal orders.

Comparing these results to those of the scenario of an accidental killing suggests that while an accidental killing is seen as a wrong by most respondents, a deliberate killing is seen as a graver wrong, particularly highlighted by the almost doubling of respondents who agree with payback under this scenario compared to an accidental killing.

It is worth briefly clarifying the customary concepts of payback and compensation based on interviews that were conducted in parallel to the survey questionnaire. Both concepts must be considered in line with reciprocity. In relation to a killing, 'payback' refers to a retaliatory killing of the offender or a member of his kin. For lesser wrongs, such as a robbery or assault, it normally refers to a beating. From the interviews conducted within these provinces, the view was that for a payback killing to be permissible under customary law it must occur on the same day that the initial wrong was committed. If payback cannot be enforced on the same day, it is generally accepted that compensation should be demanded instead. The only exception to this rule is when a compensation demand is not met. Under these circumstances a payback killing may again be permissible. Compensation payments are generally seen as a substitute for a payback killing and often follow the *wan bel* process which focuses on both compensation and reconciliation. The families of the wronged and wrongdoer will come together and agree on a settlement. During the compensation ceremony the two families will normally take part in a joint ceremonial feast to indicate that peaceful relations will be restored. From the interviews, compensation payments for a death vary considerably geographically, ranging from K20,000 ($8,000) to K30,000 ($12,000) in East New Britain to well over K100,000 ($40,000) in the Autonomous Region of Bougainville.

In relation to the customary concept of group liability, of those surveyed who agreed with payback, slightly more agreed with killing a member of the offender's family than the actual offender, highlighting the importance of the principle of group liability under customary law. Group liability also strongly manifests itself in relation to compensation payments. Given their magnitude, it is virtually impossible for the offender to pay the whole amount by him or herself. It is widely accepted that the offender's kinship group will pay the bulk of the payment, placing a great burden on the whole kinship group.

The respondents were also asked what state sanction should be applied to a payback killing. As can be viewed in Figure 3.8, the majority of respondents considered that the state should punish payback killings, with 42 per cent stating a preference for life imprisonment, although 38 per cent considered the sentence should be reduced in recognition of customary law. However, a sizeable minority of 20 per cent stated that there should be no state penalty attached to a payback killing.

The final customary concept tested is the importance of kinship, both in terms of a respondent's choice of legal order and its effect on the practice of state criminal law. As discussed earlier, the respondents were first asked how they would respond if they were the victim of a robbery, and 45 per cent said they would go to the police while 55 per cent stated they would seek a customary sanction. To test whether this stated choice of legal order, and therefore sanction, depended on *who* committed the wrong, the respondents were then asked if this answer would change if the perpetrator was (a) close family or kin, or (b) a member of the same or neighbouring community. As can be seen from Figure 3.9, when the perpetrator is kin only 25 per cent stated that they would go to the police, while when the perpetrator is a neighbour 36 per cent responded that they would go to the police.[26] These responses suggest that the closer the relationship the less likely it is that a victim will seek a state sanction and more likely that the wrong will be sanctioned using customary law.

In relation to testing kinship obligations and their interaction with the practice of the state criminal law the respondents were given a scenario where a police officer's cousin had committed a payback killing. The respondents were then asked if they agreed with (a) the police officer

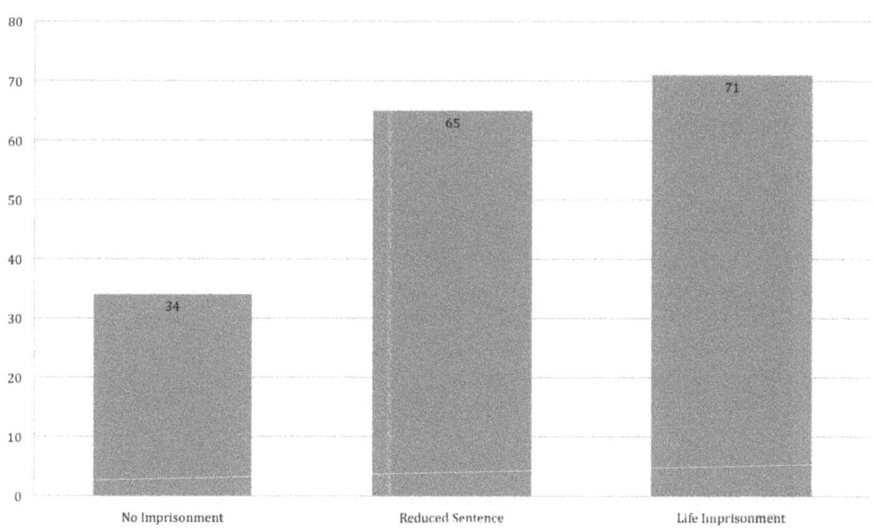

Figure 3.8. Appropriate state sanction for payback killing

arresting his cousin, (b) secretly warning him to flee, or (c) declaring a conflict of interest and asking to be taken off the case. The vast majority of respondents stated that the police officer should arrest his cousin for murder. Counting single responses, 82 per cent stated that he should arrest his cousin, 12 per cent stated that he should declare a conflict of interest, and only 6 per cent stated that the police officer should help his cousin to flee.[27]

Given the often talked about intensity of kinship ties, widespread claims that the police force was infested with *wantokism* and the fact that a sizeable minority of respondents see payback as a legitimate form of punishment, this result is surprising. At the end of the survey I asked some respondents why they agreed with the police officer arresting his cousin. I received three main responses. The first was that the state legal order was separate from customary law and that, as the police officer was being paid, he had a duty to do his job impartially. The second response was that while they agreed that the police officer should arrest his cousin, in actual fact he would help him flee. The third, and perhaps most interesting in terms of the interaction of the legal orders, was that the police officer needs to arrest his cousin and place him in custody for two related reasons: if he is not protected in police custody, he may become a victim of a payback killing; and second, if the police officer is seen to show favouritism to his cousin, it increases the chance that another family member will be the subject of a payback killing. The responses relating to kinship were particularly interesting in that they point to a general

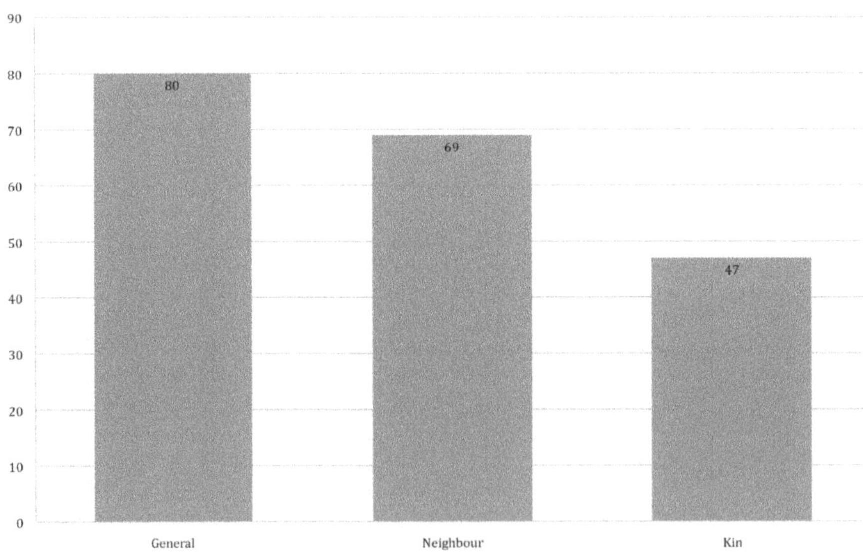

Figure 3.9. Use of police depending on relationship to perpetrator

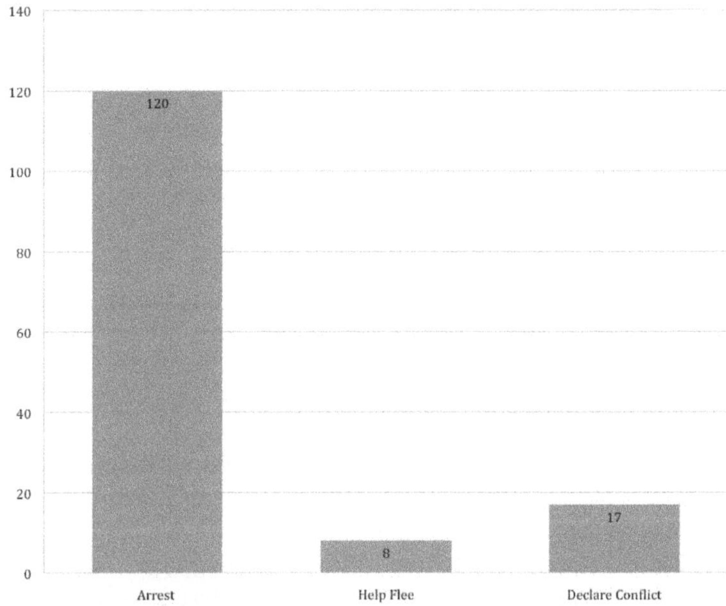

Figure 3.10. Kinship ties and police officer's response

community acceptance – or perhaps more accurately, 'demand' – that the state's agents should act in a fair and impartial manner.

Testing the Substitutability of Legal Orders

The qualitative research found that the police in the New Britain provinces show considerable discretion in prosecuting offenders, and this effectively allows customary sanctions to substitute for state sanctions.

A key rationale of the survey was to test whether state sanctions and customary sanctions are perceived as being substitutes, complements, or unrelated among the users of the law – and, in particular, whether the relatively high magnitude of customary sanctions in the New Guinea Islands made them substitutes rather than complements.

To test this perceived relationship, two related scenarios were put to respondents who agreed to take the survey. The first scenario, as explained in the previous section, concerned a van driver who accidentally killed two drunken men who fell asleep on the side of the road. Following a police investigation they conclude that the death of the two men was an unfortunate accident and therefore do not charge the driver. As explained earlier, only 12 per cent of respondents agreed that the family should accept the decision of the police and do nothing more, whereas the vast majority of respondents agreed that the van driver or his family should be sanctioned under the state criminal law (and customary law).

The next question was aimed at gleaning the degree of substitutability between state law and customary law sanctions. Respondents were asked to reconsider the actions of the family of the two young men if the driver was found guilty of reckless driving and causing death, and was jailed for ten years.

As can be seen in Figure 3.11, of the 163 respondents who answered both scenarios, 13 per cent agreed with doing nothing under the first scenario when there is no state sanction, while 44 per cent agreed with doing nothing more under the scenario when the van driver is to be jailed for ten years. This suggests that the state sanction is perceived as a complete substitute by a minority of respondents.

Allowing for multiple affirmative answers, agreement with demanding compensation from the van driver only fell from 67 per cent to 56 per cent, while the use of payback fell from 13 per cent to 7 per cent. However, it must be noted that these results are aggregate numbers. When the answers of individual respondents are analysed with the imposition of a jail term on the driver, the results are broadly compatible, with one important exception. While they are small numbers, of the

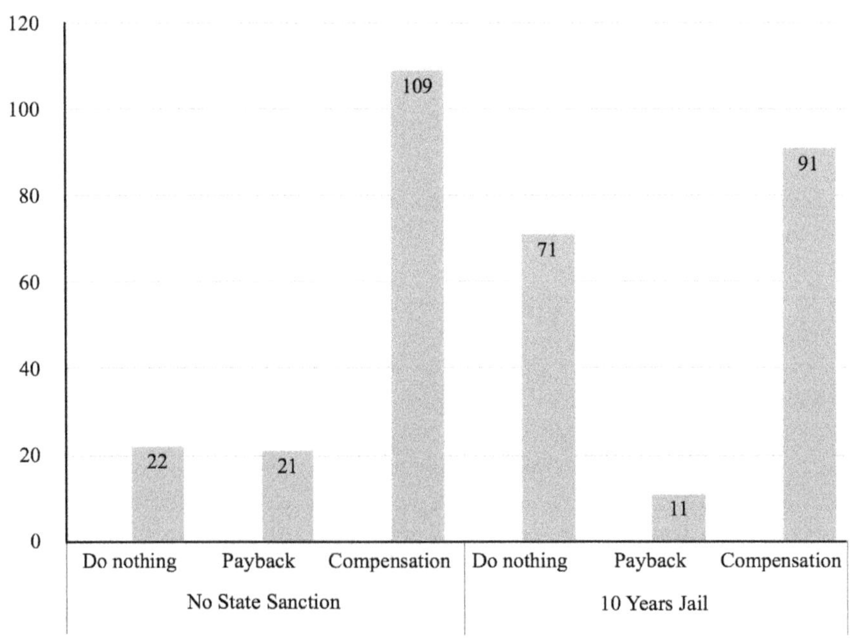

Figure 3.11. Substitutability of sanctions

twenty-one respondents who initially agreed with a payback killing only three agreed under the scenario of the van driver being jailed. This suggests an especially high degree of substitutability between jail terms and payback killings.

Taking into account individual responses, 11 per cent of respondents actually agreed with increasing the magnitude of the customary penalty in light of the driver being found guilty under the state legal order – and, in some instances, changed from agreeing to do nothing to agreeing to payback. This indicates that a significant minority see the two legal orders as something approaching complements. In this case they have adopted the state law's conception of a wrong, no fault and criminal negligence, and applied a customary sanction to it, quite often payback, in addition to the state punishment. These results indicate that there are mixed perceptions concerning the relationship between state and customary law sanctions.

From the interviews and discussions with respondents, the concern of 'double punishment' arose where it was considered unfair that an offender is both jailed and the family is required to make a large compensation payment. While the majority of respondents agreed with demanding compensation from the van driver under both scenarios, from the many discussions I had on this topic the usual response was that if someone has been jailed then the compensation payment demanded is often, but not always, lowered to around a quarter to a half of what would have been demanded if the offender had not been jailed. Unfortunately, the survey did not capture the magnitude of compensation.

However a common response, especially in the villages, was that a wrong first needs to be settled using customary law, and then if the police get involved, so be it. This suggests that a compensation payment could not be lowered due to sequencing on the sanction, unless part of the compensation payment was refunded, a possibly that was not mentioned. Another sequencing issue that affects the degree of substitutability of sanctions concerns the use of payback, which should normally be enforced immediately and thus would not allow the state time to sanction the wrongdoer. However, this sequencing issue is not as problematic as it may seem, as those involved in a serious car accident will normally flee the scene and/or, as in the case on Bougainville Island, the police will detain the perpetrator of a customary wrong for his or her own safety.

These results, while providing some evidence of perceived substitutability particularly in relation to the use of payback and jail time, highlight the complexity of the way in which the two legal orders interact and the very different perceptions of how they should interact. The data also suggests that a significant portion of respondents see the sanctions as largely unrelated, while a minority seem to perceive the sanctions of the two legal orders in a complementary manner, with the imposition of a state penalty leading to an imposition of a customary penalty.

Conclusion

This empirical analysis provides some valuable insights into the degree to which the two legal orders are practised and the sanctions they attach to wrongdoing. It also provides insight into the relationship between the two legal orders and the degree to which their sanctions both act and are perceived to act as substitutes by those subject to plural legal orders.

Those who stress Papua New Guinea's internal diversity and caution against generalizations do so for good reason; for instance, those in West New Britain were less likely to agree with payback killings, or with life sentences for payback killers. They were also more likely to agree with the greater use of customary law and less likely to see state sanctions as adequate substitutes for customary sanctions.

Perhaps the more important factor is the actual and perceived relationship between the two legal orders that also varied between provinces. From the interviews conducted in conjunction with the survey there seemed to be a much clearer understanding of the relationship between the two legal orders in East New Britain, despite the police's recognition of customary law being informal. This was in contrast to Buka Island, where there seemed to be considerable confusion between the role of each legal order. Despite the Autonomous Region of Bougainville having its own Constitution and an official prosecution policy that elevates customary law, this seems to only be practised on Bougainville Island, and not well understood on Buka Island where the bulk of the surveys for this province were collected.

Another important insight from the empirical investigation is that the practice of customary law seems to be the most problematic where state law enforcement is highest – in urban environments. Urban respondents had a significantly higher propensity to agree with the use of payback killings, which along with official corruption through kinship obligations is the most problematic interaction between the legal orders. While this higher propensity may be explained through ethnic heterogeneity, it presents a policy problem that is not easily resolved. That is, where state law is most needed, and wanted, the potential for negative interactions is highest.

Notes

1. I am extremely grateful to a number of people for their assistance with the survey and interviews, almost all having an association with the Salesian Communities of Kokopo (Vunaboso Agro-Technical Secondary College) and Boroko (Don Bosco Technical Institute). It was only with their help as guides, translators, hosts and surveyors that this ambitious empirical exercise was possible. In particular, Fr. John Cabrido SDB, Fr. John Dixon SBD, the Salesian Communities of Kokopo and Boroko, Henry Billy, Moses Banako, Christopher Torona, Peter Ikalum, Sam Raralo, Michael Rabia Dominic Lorpo, Ralph Utunga, and many others, some of whom wished to remain anonymous.
2. The sampling method was aimed at gaining a cross section of the community, given a lack of residency records and the difficulties of a unrecognised visitor entering some communities uninvited (both urban and rural). In towns and villages, the aim was to have a respondent from every third residence encountered, however in some villages and urban communities we were guided by local officials or relied on kinship networks. While the need for a random sample was stressed, and appreciated, the sampling method was not strictly randomised. In an effort to gain a more representative cross section of communities, household sampling was supplemented by sampling at marketplace and village stores due some residential 'no go' areas (for outsiders). For consistency with the market samples, there were no follow-ups with the household samples. Of the 200 responses, 23 were from the Autonomous Region of Bougainville (19 from Buka Island), 115 from East New Britain and 62 from West New Britain. The refusal rate of those asked to participate in the survey was approximately 36 per cent. The questionnaire was read out in either Pisin or English. Where respondents were asked to rank or chose responses from a list, the potential responses were presented in a random order to minimize sequencing bias.
3. All population estimates are taken from the 2000 census (Turner 2006), which for the Islands Region are only estimates.
4. Kokopo was formerly known as Herbertshöhe.
5. Of course there were exceptions, such as Bougainville Island. See May (2004) for a detailed discussion of traditional leadership in Papua New Guinea, including the differences and debates.
6. In 1929 Governor Murray, of the (at the time) administratively separate Papua, reported 'there are even two cases – sorcery and adultery – in which native custom has compelled recognition by the criminal law (Jinks, Biskup and Nelson 1973: 129). What form this recognition took and when it was granted in the Territory of New Guinea is not known. From Gore's (1965) accounts it seems to have manifested itself in extremely low sentencing (as low as the rising of the court for some homicide cases motivated by customary beliefs) from Supreme Court judges whose circuits included both Papua and New Guinea.
7. See Shaw, van Dijk and Rhomberg (2003) for a breakdown of regional policing levels, which demonstrates that Papua New Guinea has particularly low levels of policing, and lower than Africa as a continent (which approximates 800 people per officer). East Africa is the only sub-region with similarly low numbers of inhabitants per police officer. Police officers per head of population in Europe is approximately 400, and in North America 300. It should be noted that the results calculated for Papua New Guinea overstate the level of policing per head due to Papua New Guinea's fast-growing population: the policing figures used are from 2006 and population estimates are derived from the 2000 census (census figures from Turner 2006).

8. However, as Port Moresby is the administrative capital, many of these uniformed police officers would not be engaged in direct policing.
9. There were differing accounts concerning the interaction of the village court with the ('peace' or 'law') and justice committees. Some considered these institutions to be the same entity, while others talked of a three-tiered hierarchy in which the lowest level is the councillor-led committees, then the village courts, and then the district courts (through police involvement). This hierarchy was not so much in terms of the gravity of the wrong, but more in terms of a process. If agreement could not be reached using the justice committee, then the disputants would go to the village court; and if agreement could not be reached there, then the police would be informed. Others also stated that if they were wronged they would go to the village court, rather than the justice committee.
10. This sum was either K500 ($200) or K1,000 ($400), depending on whose account was correct.
11. I did not raise this matter with the police.
12. The effective jurisdiction of the police on Buka Island seemed to be restricted to the towns themselves and limited to minor crimes. I was told by a number of people that many grave wrongs go unreported to the police and that payback killings occur.
13. *The State* v. *Mattau* [PGNC 269; N3865].
14. Victimization surveys are not without their problems, including surveyor error, reluctance of victims to report crimes (due to embarrassment or some other reason), categorization issues, and issues associated with recollection and perception of past events. In addition to these, there may be political reasons for not reporting crime (see Guthrie, Hukula and Laki 2006b).
15. As the survey was based on individual crime victimization, no homicide rates were able to be attained.
16. See van Dijk, van Kesteren and Smit (2008) for comparisons of both developed and developing country crime rates. For instance, they report the annual average victimization rate for robbery at 1 per cent, and 2.4 per cent in cities, for all countries surveyed. For the United States, Truman (2011) reports the annual violent crime victimization rate in 2010 at 1.47 per cent.
17. Victimization data reported by van Dijk, van Kesteren and Smit (2008) suggests that violent crime victimization rates in the developing world are generally higher, particularly in urban environments. For instance, annual victimization rates for robbery in developing country cities surveyed (which do not include Papua New Guinea) are reported to be 6.1 per cent. The victimization rates recorded in van Dijk, van Kesteren and Smit (ibid.) suggest that violent crime in many developing cities is extremely high and individual violent crime rates can exceed 10 per cent – for example, they report Johannesburg as having a victimization rate for assault (and threats of violence) at over 10 per cent per year.
18. The other cities surveyed included Kampala, Dar es Salaam, Johannesburg, Cairo, Tunis, Buenos Aires, Rio de Janeiro, Costa Rica, Beijing, Bombay, Jakarta and Manila. However, the results should be treated with some caution as, for example, they record the theft of bicycle rate at 6.7 per cent. Having lived in Port Moresby, I saw very few bicycles and would suggest that less than this percentage of the population own a bicycle.
19. The victimization rates for these surveys are in terms of households, which does not make them easily comparable.
20. While using a measure of 'household victimization', which makes a direct comparison difficult, both the survey results suggest low rates of violence (including rape).

However, it must be noted that the authors said that respondents may have felt pressure not to report such crimes and suggested that their questionnaire technique did not encourage full reporting. While this may be the case, the same survey technique was used for the other surveys reported by Guthrie, Hukula and Laki (2006a, 2006b and 2007) in Port Moresby and Lae. The crime rate, especially for violent crime, was substantially higher in these cities, especially Lae.

21. One aim of the survey that was not fulfilled was to get a measure of the relative gravity attached to various wrongs in the communities visited. Therefore respondents were asked: 'On a scale of 1 to 5, how would you rate the seriousness of the following crimes (see list below) in your community (1 being "not serious", 5 being "extremely serious")?' However, it became apparent very early on in the survey that this question in terms of 'seriousness' was being taken to mean 'prevalence' or 'problematic', rather than 'perceived gravity'. Therefore, the data from this question is now taken as 'prevalence', with little or no relation to 'gravity'.
22. Of those who chose violent payback, all were in West New Britain in response to four cases of assault, three cases of sorcery and one case of property damage. While it was not asked what form this took, it would be likely to involve a beating rather than homicide, at least for the cases of assault and property damage.
23. These results broadly accord with Guthrie, Hukula and Laki (2006a, 2006b) who record that crimes reported to the police in other parts of Papua New Guinea are in the range of 20 to 40 per cent. It should be noted that the literature suggests that the rate of reporting a crime to the police varies both in terms of type of crime and country but rarely approaches anything near 100 per cent. The cross-country data reported by van Dijk, van Kesteren and Smit (2008: 110) suggests that the average across countries is 47 per cent for a list of non-violent crimes; however, the rate is lower in developing countries, ranging from as low as 12 per cent in Sao Paulo to 35 per cent in Johannesburg. In relation to violent crime, Truman (2011: 5) reports that approximately half were reported to the police in the United States in 2010.
24. Despite their name, village courts operate both in urban and rural communities.
25. *The State* v. *Bonot* [2010] PGNC 41; N4042. In the judgement great emphasis was placed on why the van driver could not be found guilty of reckless driving causing death.
26. Note that 184 responded to the general question whereas 191 responded to the perpetrator specific questions. Therefore, percentages are a better measure of the effect of relationship on choice of legal order. However, for consistency actual responses are presented in Figure 3.9.
27. Like for most of the questions, a sizeable portion of respondents agreed with more than one answer, in this case for example agreeing with arresting his cousin and also with declaring a conflict of interest, although for this question, at only 18 per cent, it was less than for most of the other questions in the survey – this is comforting, as in this scenario the affirmative answers are mutually inconsistent. When multiple affirmative answers are counted the results are little changed, with 83 per cent agreeing with arresting his cousin, 24 per cent with a conflict of interest, and 13 per cent with helping him to flee.

Chapter 4

Legal Dissonance in Papua New Guinea

As the legal pluralism literature tells us, legal pluralism is everywhere and most probably the natural state of any society. We also know that non-state regulation, whether it is in the form of law, norms or internalized morals, often provides a supportive and crucial role in ordering social interactions. However, legal pluralism can also be problematic. This chapter applies the formalized theoretical framework outlined in Larcom (2014) to the existing legal arrangements in Papua New Guinea.

First of all, if the two legal orders assert jurisdiction over the same people and place, but not behaviours (where 'behaviours' includes both actions and omissions), legal pluralism will not be problematic. Take a trivial example of a game of cricket in Port Moresby. Here, the Laws of Cricket made by the Marylebone Cricket Club govern how the game is played, how a team wins, how a batsman is dismissed, etcetera, across the world. However these same players come under the jurisdiction of the laws of the state, including Papua New Guinean criminal law. Under the Laws of Cricket a batsman is sanctioned (that is, lawfully penalized) for being caught on the full by being dismissed; however the state and its criminal law are not concerned with such behaviours and consequently there is no state sanction.[1] Conversely, under the laws of cricket there is no law concerning the murder of a teammate. Such an example highlights that where jurisdictions overlap in terms of place and person, but not in terms of behaviour, problematic legal pluralism should not arise. There are many such examples, including religious groups, ethnic enclaves, clubs, societies, collectives and cooperatives that co-exist with the state and are concerned with regulating behaviours outside of those over which the state asserts jurisdiction.[2] Therefore, for problematic legal pluralism to arise, the legal orders must assert jurisdiction over the same place, people and behaviours.

The first type of problematic legal pluralism relates to customary sanctions that are considered wrong by the state legal order. At its most extreme, under customary law a sorcerer may be executed or someone may be killed as payback for a homicide. However, such behaviour is considered a grave crime by the state, and the enforcer of these customary sanctions could face the death penalty or life imprisonment. Less extreme customary sanctions such as violence or a compensation demand may also attract state sanctions.

The second relates to situations of 'rivalrous compliance'. Rivalrous compliance is characterized when avoiding wrong behaviour under one legal order necessarily leads to wrong behaviour under the other. When placed in a situation of rivalrous compliance an individual must choose between committing a wrong under customary law or doing so under the state criminal law. The most common causes of rivalrous compliance in Papua New Guinea relate to opposite conceptions of wrong.[3] Opposite conceptions of wrong arise when a given act is deemed to be an imperative under state law but prohibited under customary law, or vice versa. For instance, take a police officer in the Royal Papua New Guinea Constabulary who is required to arrest his (or her) *wantok* under the dictates of the Criminal Code. If the police officer does not arrest his *wantok* it is considered a wrong under the criminal law which can be sanctioned, whereas if he does arrest his *wantok* it is considered a breach of her customary obligations where sanctions may also be attached. In situations of rivalrous compliance, problematic legal pluralism will necessarily arise. It is problematic both in terms of those subject to it, as whether they act or fail to act they will have committed a wrong under one of the legal orders, and in terms of the legal orders themselves, as whatever the decision a wrong has been committed that requires a sanction.

The third type of problematic legal pluralism arises when both legal orders deem the same behaviour to be wrong but fail to coordinate their sanctions, which can lead to excessive punishment and replicated effort. This situation can be considered unjust as both legal orders sanction the wrongdoer in isolation, and therefore the sanctions the individual faces are in excess of what each legal order alone considers just. This problematic aspect of legal pluralism was a common complaint from interviewees in Papua New Guinea and was also highlighted by Forsyth (2009) in Vanuatu. This problematic form of legal pluralism can be thought of as a situation where customary sanctions and state sanctions are substitutes (in essence) but this substitutability is not recognized by at least one of the legal orders. That is, while being substitutes in terms of their job (punishing wrong behaviour), one or both legal orders misidentify the other's sanction as a complement to their own sanction, rather than correctly identifying it as a substitute.

In order to better conceptualize problematic legal pluralism in Papua New Guinea, the analysis is divided into problems related to 'common wrongs' and 'idiosyncratic wrongs'. Common wrongs are those behaviours which both legal orders deem to be wrong, while idiosyncratic wrongs are those behaviours that only one legal order deems to be wrong.

Conceptual Overview of Common Wrongs and Problematic Pluralism

In relation to common wrongs (behaviours deemed wrong by both legal orders) legal pluralism can be problematic in two situations. The first is when those who commit a common wrong are sanctioned by both legal orders, leading to double punishment of the offender. Where both legal orders act independently and do not consider the sanction of the other as an acceptable substitute for their own, the offender could be sanctioned by both legal orders. This is clearly unjust, as those who enforce each legal order, acting in isolation, would normally consider that their own sanction is sufficient and just in itself for a given wrong. Papua New Guinea thus differs from Western societies, where non-state sanctions are much lighter and generally act as complements to the state sanction of wrongs.

It should be noted that facing the probability of heavy sanctions by two legal orders can lead to an increase in deterrence for common wrongs. Deterrence is generated by the 'expected sanction', which is equal to the probability of being sanctioned multiplied by the magnitude of the sanction. For instance, if the state attached a prison sentence of ten years to a given wrong and the probability of being sanctioned was 0.5 (that is, a 50–50 chance) then the expected sanction is five years' imprisonment. Where there is legal pluralism and common wrongs exist, the expected sanction is an *aggregate* of the expected customary sanction and the expected state sanction. However, it must be remembered that the overall effect on deterrence will depend on how the legal orders respond to the presence of the other; a legal order could adjust the magnitude of sanction or the level of enforcement effort. If both legal orders keep their sanctions for a given wrong fixed but reduce their level of enforcement, the potential for double punishment can co-exist with no increase in the overall level of deterrence against common wrongs. Furthermore, if the legal orders impose net negative costs upon one another, double punishment can even co-exist with an overall decrease in the expected sanction in relation to common wrongs. Net external costs are most evidently caused by rivalrous compliance that affects state law enforcement practitioners or agents, and when customary sanctions are deemed crimes. If this occurs, the end result of legal pluralism can be individual injustice and low levels of deterrence – something that seems to characterize the current legal arrangements in much of Papua New Guinea.

The second problem that can arise in relation to the control of common wrongs is when a sanction used by one of the legal orders is considered a wrong by the other. When this is the case, it is problematic for both legal orders. It is problematic for the legal order whose sanction is considered a wrong, as those who enforce sanctions could be sanctioned themselves by the other legal order.[4] This imposes a significant cost of enforcement on this legal order and can severely limit its ability to provide a deterrent against common wrongs. It is also problematic for the legal order that sees the other legal order's sanction as a wrong, as it now has two wrongs to sanction, the initial common wrong and the sanction of the other legal order. The extent to which this is problematic in terms of deterrence (and excluding the injustice of double punishment) will depend on: the propensity of each legal order to impose sanctions that are considered wrong by the other; the degree of perceived substitutability between the sanctions of the two legal orders; and the degree that a legal order actually sanctions the other legal order's sanction that it considers wrong.

Common Wrongs in Papua New Guinea and Problematic Legal Pluralism

The interviews and survey results suggest that most crimes are considered wrongs by the general population in the New Guinea Islands and under customary law.[5] While, I did not generate a quantitative measure of gravity attached to each wrong listed in the survey, from the interviews with community leaders and others it was apparent that the wrongs listed in the survey were common to both legal orders.[6] Of most importance was the finding that offences that directly threaten personal security, such as murder, rape and robbery, are conceived as grave wrongs under customary law and can be sanctioned in the most severe fashion.

The gravity of rape in Papua New Guinea requires some discussion in this analysis. According to Justice Gore (1965), the gravity of rape varied in parts of Papua New Guinea, and in some areas he suggests that, while it was considered a wrong, it was not considered a grave wrong. The Constitutional and Law Reform Commission of Papua New Guinea (1986: 5) also concluded that the 'rape of women from an enemy group or in a "payback" conflict between men was traditional in many areas'. From my own research I found that compensation payments in relation to rape were lower than for murder in both the Autonomous Region of Bougainville and East New Britain. On the face of it, this provides some evidence that this wrong is not considered as grave as murder in the communities surveyed. While it is true that compensation payments are considerably less than for a murder, all of the customary leaders with whom I discussed the matter considered it a grave wrong, and listed it along with murder when discussing 'serious crimes'. Similarly, in discussions with survey respondents on serious crimes, murder and rape were considered the most serious of possible wrongs. Therefore, it is concluded that, in the New Guinea Islands at least, there is not a significant divergence between state criminal law and customary law in their conception of the gravity of rape.[7] However, this is not the case for accidental killings, adultery or sorcery, which are considered much more grave under customary law than under state law, and therefore are included in the discussion of idiosyncratic wrongs.

In relation to grave common wrongs such as murder, rape and robbery, the real divergence between the two legal orders lies in relation to the sanctions each applies and the processes involved. In Papua New Guinea this difference primarily results from two factors. First, the official state policy is unwilling to recognize customary law sanctions as substitutes for their own; and, to a lesser extent, those who enforce customary sanctions are unwilling to recognize state sanctions as substitutes. Second, some customary sanctions, in particular payback killings and beatings (and compensation demands when considered to be extortion), are deemed to be grave wrongs by the state. It should be noted that in practice this is only a problem for 'grave wrongs', as the state already allows wrongs it considers less serious to be sanctioned solely by village courts.[8]

However, for grave wrongs, the official unwillingness of the state to recognize customary sanctions as valid substitutes, irrespective of whether they *are* or *are not* state wrongs, leads to some offenders (and their kinship groups) being excessively sanctioned for a common wrong. Among those interviewed, many considered the current arrangements to be unjust, particularly when a large compensation payment is paid and the offender is also given a long prison term. Given that the customary legal order often works faster in sanctioning wrongs, a customary settlement can be made but the offender is subsequently imprisoned. As stated earlier, while the courts take a compensation payment into account in sentencing, it normally sees a long sentence reduced by only two to five years. Therefore, the courts generally see a customary compensation settlement as a partial (inadequate) substitute.[9] Despite this view on the part of the courts, most of those surveyed considered a long prison sentence and a customary sanction (whether it be a compensation payment or a payback killing) to be substitutes.[10]

The most problematic interaction of the two legal orders in relation to common wrongs is the use of customary sanctions that are deemed to be crimes by the state. Customary law's most potent sanction is physical retaliation – payback; or the use of sorcery which is widely believed to be able to cause death or great misfortune. As explained earlier, the threat of payback or sorcery is a potent deterrent against wrongdoing, not only in itself, but also as a means to ensure that compensation demands are met between different groups. Even if payback is not exacted, the possibility hangs over an offender's head (and his or her clan) and provides a strong incentive for the payment of compensation. Without the use of physical force or a belief in the power of sorcery, customary law loses much of its deterrent effect in controlling serious wrongs between different kinship groups.[11] The threat of physical force, sorcery and large compensation payments also provides a powerful form of social control within groups, as each member within the group has an incentive to control and monitor the behaviour of others within that group, as under group liability they may be held liable for the wrongs committed by others. As discussed in some detail in Chapter 1, the courts now take an extremely tough stance towards payback killings with extremely long sentences, and the use of the death penalty also seems imminent. While the reasons behind the stance of parliament and the judiciary are understandable, nonetheless it greatly decreases the deterrent effect of customary law. However, as outlined in Chapter 2, this stance is relatively new. The colonial regime used to impose relatively light sentences for customary sanctions it considered wrong, including payback killings. More importantly, prior to the Derham reforms the state was geographically confined, and practised a non-intervention policy that meant most offenders of the criminal law did not face court. The growth of the state in geographical terms, a willingness to penalize the use of customary sanctions, and the extremely tough stance now being taken by the higher courts has significantly reduced the potency of customary law, while also imposing significant additional costs on state law enforcement, leading to the dilution of finite crime-fighting resources.[12] The overall effect on the deterrence of common wrongs from the state penalizing customary sanctions will depend on the response of those who enforce customary sanctions. However, it is a real possibility that severe state sanctions imposed

Table 4.1. Sources of problematic legal pluralism in Papua New Guinea – common wrongs

Description of problem	Types of wrong	Effect	Reaction by state	Reaction by customary law – community	Remaining problems
Double Punishment – when both legal orders act independently and impose a sanction that either would consider sufficient and just if imposed in isolation.	Potential to arise in relation to most grave wrongs such as murder, rape, robbery, and most crimes under the Criminal Code.	Should increase deterrence against common wrongs, although it can undermine the legitimacy of both legal orders in sanctioning wrongs. Injustice for those who incur high magnitude punishments from each legal order.	State does not consider violent customary sanctions as substitutes for imprisonment. Compensation payments effectively treated as a minor mitigating factor in sentencing.	Imprisonment generally seen as a substitute for violent customary sanctions. Differing perceptions of imprisonment as substitute for compensation payments – ranging from no recognition to complete recognition. Majority of respondents consider some significantly smaller payment still required if offender is imprisoned.	Continued failure by state to recognize customary sanctions as substitute for state sanctions. Differing views within society on applicability of customary sanctions and their degree of substitutability with state sanctions.

Customary sanctions considered wrong by the state.	Customary sanctions that involve violence, including payback killings. Demands for compensation can also be considered extortion, or when combined with an agreement not to involve the state as perverting the course of justice.	Significantly reduces the deterrent effect of customary law in relation to common wrongs. Places greater burden on state law enforcement. Some consider that those who enforce customary law and are sanctioned are treated unjustly.	The state has grown increasingly intolerant of violent customary sanctions. They are seen by the courts as a cause of disorder. In particular, payback killings attract the highest possible prison sentences. The killing of sorcerers and adulterers now carries high prison sentences. The state can and does punish compensation payments when they are perceived as extortion or perverting the course of state justice.	Violent customary sanctions are still used throughout Papua New Guinea, despite the high state sanctions attached. However, compensation demands are more common. Given the weakness of the state in sanctioning wrongs this is not surprising. Customary law derives much of its deterrent effect from violence and the threat of violence. Despite its use, many of those interviewed, including customary leaders, consider the use of violence to sanction wrongs as undesirable or no longer acceptable.	The state has aimed to eliminate violent customary sanctions but has only been moderately successful. While severely reducing the ability of customary law to deter common wrongs it has been unable to provide a sufficient deterrent itself. This is partly due to the intensity of kinship ties that severely weaken the ability of the state to enforce its sanctions. If the state were able to eliminate violent customary sanctions it would make customary law effectively impotent. For compensation payments to be an effective deterrent they require some threat of harm to ensure they are paid.

on those who impose customary sanctions could lead to an overall fall in the level of deterrence against common wrongs. This result is most likely if both legal orders continue to enforce their sanctions but at a lower level of enforcement than if they were operating in isolation. This result is more likely when someone who breaches the Criminal Code motivated by customary law faces a higher probability of being sanctioned by the state than a wrongdoer motivated by other factors. This seems plausible in the case of customary killings, as under customary law payback is normally instantaneous, an alleged sorcerer's 'executor' is often well known, and a killing over the non-payment of compensation could be easily traced by police.[13]

The current situation seems to be one where both customary law and the state criminal law enforce sanctions against common wrongs, but both with low probabilities of enforcement. Those who enforce customary law will continue to enforce sanctions considered wrong by the state, albeit at a reduced level, when state law enforcement is weak or when such sanctions are considered more effective deterrents than those not considered wrong by the state. A summary of problematic legal pluralism in relation to common wrongs is presented in Table 4.1.

Conceptual Overview of Idiosyncratic Wrongs and Problematic Pluralism

Legal pluralism has the potential to be problematic not only in the case of common wrongs, but also in the case of idiosyncratic wrongs. Idiosyncratic wrongs are those unique to one legal order. However, the mere existence of idiosyncratic wrongs does not necessarily lead to problematic pluralism. Rather, where idiosyncratic wrongs exist, problematic legal pluralism can arise in two situations.

The first situation is when the sanctions used to 'correct' or punish an idiosyncratic wrong by one legal order are considered a wrong by the other. As in the case of common wrongs, this scenario leads to those aiming to sanction idiosyncratic wrongs under the customary legal order facing a probability of being sanctioned themselves under the state legal order. At the same time, in aiming to penalize the use of customary sanctions, the state legal order faces increased levels of wrongdoing and increased costs. Clearly, more idiosyncratic wrongs, and a higher propensity for a legal order to use sanctions that the other legal order considers wrong, will amplify these problems. Where this occurs, the legal order aiming to sanction idiosyncratic wrongs will be restricted in its ability to control these wrongs, while the legal order attempting 'to sanction the sanctions' will face an increase in wrongs and costs of enforcement.

The second problematic case occurs when there is rivalrous compliance between the legal orders. This occurs when, given a certain set of circumstances, a wrong will be committed under either customary law or state law. Conceptually, this is the most troublesome type of problematic legal pluralism, as when these situations arise it is inevitable that a wrong will be committed – unless the situation itself can be avoided.

Idiosyncratic Wrongs in Papua New Guinea and Problematic Legal Pluralism

It has been well documented that certain acts or omissions in Papua New Guinea are considered as wrongs by one legal order and not by the other, however this is not necessarily problematic in itself. For example, under customary law there are various rules relating to customary authority, personal relations and family relations (including inheritance). Failure to follow these rules would attract sanctions under customary law; however such wrongs are not necessarily considered wrongs under the state law. Similarly, the state law has many rules relating to the operation of government, such as taxation, elections, and external relations. Failure to observe these rules is not considered a wrong under customary law. These sorts of idiosyncratic wrongs are not necessarily problematic so long as the sanctions used to control them are not considered wrong by the other, or the conceptions of a wrong held by each legal order are not in direct opposition. In relation to customary law, these wrongs are normally sanctioned using non-violent, or at least non-fatal, means. While the state may use imprisonment or fines to sanction its idiosyncratic wrongs, this is not problematic if the state enjoys a degree of legitimacy in enforcing its laws; that is, society accepts the state's behaviour in such cases. The findings from the fieldwork show that there is general acceptance of the state's legitimacy in enforcing its own laws, albeit probably not to the same extent as in some Western societies.

Material problematic legal pluralism arises in Papua New Guinea in relation to the idiosyncratic customary wrongs of adultery, sorcery and accidental death. While the state has made efforts at accommodating each of these wrongs, the end effect is that in regard to all three wrongs the state's response is often seen (or was seen in the case of sorcery) as an inadequate substitute for customary sanctions. This underscores the difficulties with any state, particularly a weak one, in adopting another legal order's wrongs as their own. While the act of 'forbidden sorcery' under the now repealed Sorcery Act 1971 could see a sanction of up to five years' imprisonment, very few sorcery cases went through the higher courts, and when they did it was difficult to secure a conviction due to the evidence required by the courts.[14] Indeed, from my own fieldwork, I was told that most alleged sorcerers were sanctioned through customary tribunals, village courts or direct action (by those who perceived they have been harmed). Given that sorcery remains under the jurisdiction of the village courts, these arrangements can continue – and in this sense the repeal could be seen as an act of practical wisdom. Although, unless customary settlements can be made in the shadow of sufficiently large state penalties (which *is* still possible through the village courts system) it is suggested these reforms will fail. In relation to adultery, while the state treats it as a civil wrong under the Adultery and Enticement Act 1998 with damages awarded up to K1,000 ($400), this amount is often far below the customary sanction. Again, most of these cases seem to be dealt with through customary means or through the village court system (which often shows considerable discretion in relation to its state powers). In relation to accidental deaths, the Motor Vehicles (Third Party Insurance) (Basic Protection Compensation) Act 1974 and the Compulsory Third Party Motor Vehicles Insurance Industry Act 2002 allows those injured or the families of those killed to claim compensation, regardless of fault, from an insurance pool funded by the owners of registered vehicles. In the case of death, courts can award up to K5,000 ($2,000). While such a scheme has attempted to obviate the need for a customary settlement, the sum is much lower than that normally expected for a death under customary law. It should also be noted that of all the people surveyed (the survey included a set of questions relating to a death caused by a car accident) only one person referred to this scheme. This may reflect either its lack of functionality or a low level of awareness among the general population, or both. Although the state has made efforts to accommodate the three most important idiosyncratic wrongs, under customary law, given their gravity, they will generate a high-magnitude customary sanction if the state is unable (or unwilling) to sanction them.

In Papua New Guinea the other class of problematic idiosyncratic wrongs are those which lead to rivalrous compliance between customary law and the state law. Customary law relies on strong kinship ties, whether it is for the control of wrongs or any other aspect of life. Intense kinship ties, or *wantokism*, mean that when a kin member asks for or needs help it is provided, even if it comes at considerable personal cost, on the understanding that help will be forthcoming in each member's time of need. Strong kinship ties are necessary for customary law to function and sanction both idiosyncratic and common wrongs. Conversely, the state criminal order relies on its agents acting in an impartial manner in order to function effectively and provide a credible deterrent against wrongs. These conflicting conceptions mean that state officials often face a stark choice in relation to their customary and official duties.[15] When kin are involved, officials presiding in the state sanctioning process (police or prison officials) must choose whether to abide by their customary obligations and commit a wrong under state law or abide by their state obligations and commit a customary wrong. In such cases an act is considered a wrong by one legal order while the corresponding omission is considered a wrong by the other. When these officials put their customary obligations first it is referred to as corruption or *wantokism* and it severely limits the state's ability to sanction wrongdoing, including serious wrongs against the person.[16] In the age of Wikileaks, Dorling (2011) reports that United States officials based in Port Moresby consider that Papua New Guinea's most urgent problem is the near-collapse of its police force. This collapse has taken place despite decades of external funding, equipment, training, and capacity-building exercises. Opposite conceptions of wrongdoing, and the tendency of many law enforcement officials to choose to abide by their customary obligations rather than their state obligations is the most serious problematic aspect of legal pluralism for the state legal order, as it severely reduces its productivity and therefore its ability to enforce sanctions for wrongs under the Criminal Code.[17] A summary of problematic legal pluralism in relation to idiosyncratic wrongs is presented in Table 4.2.

The importance of enforcement in relation to problematic legal pluralism cannot be overstated. While the legal orders may have differing conceptions of wrong and different sanctions, the problematic instances of legal pluralism only manifest themselves when one or both legal orders (depending on the circumstances) insist on enforcing their sanctions. Importantly for the state, enforcement is not merely related to police presence and numbers. From discussions with survey respondents and interviews with customary leaders it seems that the state, primarily through the discretion shown by the police in the prosecution of offenders, is sometimes willing to accept customary sanctions as a valid substitute. In the villages surrounding the towns a consistent account emerged of the police sending victims back to the customary leadership to sanction and remedy wrongs for all but the most serious of crimes. If this is indeed the case, it demonstrates a practical solution to the complex problems associated with legal dissonance. Similarly, in the remote rural areas the state law is only called upon to ensure wrongdoers are sanctioned when customary law is unable to, or when those who enforce customary law are unwilling to enforce violent sanctions. In the Kieta region of

Table 4.2. Sources of problematic legal pluralism in Papua New Guinea – idiosyncratic wrongs

Description of problem	Types of wrong	Effect	Response by state	Response by customary law – community	Remaining problems
Customary sanctions considered wrong by the state	(i) Payback for accidental deaths (ii) Violence towards (including killing) sorcerers (iii)Violence towards (including killing) adulterers.	Significantly reduces the deterrent effect of customary law in relation to the idiosyncratic grave customary wrongs of accidental death, sorcery and adultery. This can have the effect of destabilizing communities when such wrongs are not sanctioned. (i.e. lawfully punished)	State has made accommodations to customary law in all three idiosyncratic wrongs (although the Sorcery Act 1971 was repealed in 2013). All may be sanctioned using the village court system. In addition, the state runs a motor accident insurance scheme that sees kin compensated up to K5,000 ($2,000) for a death (regardless of fault); up until 2013 'forbidden' sorcery was considered a crime with imprisonment of up to 5 years; and adultery a civil wrong with damages awarded up to K1,000 ($400).	Continued use of customary sanctions that are considered wrong by the state. Also widespread use of the village court system and compensation payments. Few cases taken to the higher state courts for application of state sanctions.	State court evidence requirements make it difficult for sorcerers to be convicted of a crime. State sanctions generally seen as too light, given the gravity of the offences under customary law. Highlights the difficulty of the state attempting to incorporate wrongs from another legal order and sanction them.

Rivalrous Compliance	Failure of a state official to show impartiality is an offence under the Criminal Code and is commonly referred to as official corruption. Conversely, failure by state officials to perform kinship obligations under customary law can be sanctioned. State officials, particularly police and prison officials, face situations where an action, such as the arrest or prosecution of kin, or someone from their *wantok* group, is considered wrong under customary law while the omission to arrest or prosecute is considered a wrong under state law.	In such situations one legal order's ability to sanction wrongdoers will be diminished. If state officials choose to abide by customary law, which they often do, this sees a severe reduction in the ability of the state to sanction wrongs under the criminal code. If they choose to commit a wrong under customary law it can lead to a loss of customary law's ability to sanction wrongs and a breakdown of kinship ties and potential social disintegration.	A seemingly endless string of capacity-building and governance programmes aimed at reducing official corruption, as well as various investigations, and the practice, at least in some parts of Papua New Guinea, of stationing of police and other state law enforcement officials to regions other than their own. However as the police force is mainly contained within cities and towns, which are multi-ethnic, this has a limited effect.	The vast majority of those interviewed expressed a strong desire for an impartial state criminal justice system. Despite this, many Papua New Guineans would expect kin and *wantoks* obligations under customary law to override state obligations if they committed a wrong under the state legal order. There is evidence from the survey results that if a state official fails to perform his or her duties by not arresting or prosecuting an offender, customary law sanctions will be enforced.	A severe weakening of the state legal order's abilities to enforce sanctions on wrongdoers in relation to both common and idiosyncratic wrongs. This weakening is due to a loss of productivity, and therefore increases in policing numbers, or better equipment or training, will only have a limited effect. This failure leads to the imposition of customary sanctions that are often considered wrong by the state. However, the customary law's ability to sanction wrongs is also limited due to opposite conceptions of wrong.

Bougainville Island, while the Criminal Code is in force, the prosecution policy sees wrongdoers only prosecuted when a customary settlement cannot be reached. The widely held belief of those interviewed is that the rate of wrongdoing has significantly decreased. Here the state legal order provides a credible default if a customary settlement cannot be reached (see Larcom 2013a, 2013b). In both instances, one informally and the other formally, the state considers customary sanctions as viable substitutes for their own.

The above analysis informs the discussion for the next two chapters on possible legal reforms to address Papua New Guinea's problematic legal pluralism. In evaluating these potential legal reforms the most weighting is given to how likely they are to achieve personal security. This criterion is used because of its fundamental importance for any society to function. Unfortunately, ranking legal reforms in Papua New Guinea primarily on their practical consequences seems to be a novel approach, as the writings of the legal reformers of the past, such as Derham (1960) and even Narokobi (1996), showed little interest in such matters. However, using personal security as the sole criterion to evaluate potential legal reforms would be too narrow, and therefore human rights considerations and conceptions of justice are also discussed where relevant.

Conclusion

In this chapter it has been shown how problematic legal pluralism may arise (conceptually) and the likely consequences for Papua New Guinea. It has shown that a necessary condition of problematic legal pluralism in relation to the control of wrongs is that both legal orders must assert jurisdiction in terms of the same place, people and behaviours. However, when this is the case, it does not necessarily result in problematic legal pluralism. In relation to idiosyncratic wrongs, it arises when there is rivalrous compliance or if one legal order's sanction is considered a wrong by the other. In relation to common wrongs it arises when both legal orders sanction an offender, which can lead to excessive sanctions being imposed on the offender and, depending on the type of sanction used, increasing the enforcement costs for one or both legal orders. The analysis above demonstrates that problems in legal pluralism are not so much related to legal orders differing in their conceptions of wrong, but more to the decisions over whether or not to sanction (that is, legally penalize) a wrong, and to the choice of sanction.

In Papua New Guinea many behaviours are deemed wrong by both legal orders, particularly those that threaten personal security such as murder, rape and robbery. However, both legal orders have idiosyncratic wrongs. As stated earlier, adultery, sorcery and accidental death are considered grave wrongs under customary law in most parts of Papua New Guinea. While adultery and sorcery are wrongs under the state (even with the repeal of the Sorcery Act 1971 due to sorcery remaining an offence under the jurisdiction of the village courts) they are considered far less grave than under customary law. The state legal order also has many idiosyncratic wrongs about which the customary law has little to say one way or the other, such as treason, the non-payment of taxes and duties, disclosure of official secrets, forgery, and various breaches of official rules and procedures. In relation to these idiosyncratic wrongs, there is nothing necessarily problematic except, as highlighted earlier, in the special case where it leads to rivalrous compliance. This is problematic, especially in relation to government agents who often face considerable pressure to act or not to act from their *wantok* group, and this is commonly labelled corruption. In such an example, a police officer's kin may ask: what is the point of providing assistance to him (or her) in the future as would be expected under customary law if he cannot help in a time of need? Furthermore, the police officer knows that he will eventually retire. While the example used is a police officer, similar situations can arise in relation to other public offices, and indeed in other societies. To some extent they are unavoidable, but it is suggested that in Papua New Guinea they are both amplified and extensive.

However, what is avoidable (at least conceptually) is conflict between the legal orders relating to the sanctioning of common wrongs. In Papua New Guinea most wrongs against the person are common to both legal orders, however what *is* different are the sanctions. The state legal order relies mostly on imprisonment and fines, while the customary legal order relies mostly on retributive violence and compensation payments. Furthermore, most customary sanctions are wrongs under the state legal order, especially anything involving violence, and even compensation when the state considers it extortion. This has the potential to put the two legal orders in direct conflict and may lessen the ability of both legal orders to deter common wrongs.

Notes

1. Sanctions, for the purpose of this analysis, are defined as 'harms permitted by the legal order as punishment for a wrong' (see Larcom 2015: 199).
2. This book is concerned with the regulation of wrongs; however it is acknowledged that law (including customary law) has many other jobs, including the recognition of agreements made between private parties. Even in this area the consequences

of jurisdictional overlap in terms of place, person and action raise the prospect of problematic pluralism. However, the consequences are likely to be less 'problematic' and more 'inconvenient'. As in the case of wrongs, the potential for a difficulty arises where this overlap of jurisdiction is not acknowledged by one or more of the legal orders present. For instance Turkey's state Civil Code only recognizes the legitimacy of a secular wedding rite while most religious authorities only recognize the legitimacy of a religious wedding rite. Therefore if a couple in Turkey wish to have recognition under both their religion and the state they are required to marry twice, and many do (Yilmaz 2004). In other societies, such as the United Kingdom, while the state may recognize a religious wedding rite if it fulfils certain requirements under the Marriage Act 1994, the religious authorities may not. For example, under the Code of Cannon Law 1983, the Catholic Church will not normally recognize a civil wedding in which one of the parties is Catholic. In this case, religious law does not recognize a state marriage.

3. The other cause of rivalrous compliance is the closely related concept of 'rivalrous imperatives'; this arises when both the customary legal order and state legal order require the commission of an imperative act but they are mutually exclusive. This is most likely to arise when there are finite resources, usually time.
4. Presumably, from the point of view of the person who enforces such a sanction, it may also be considered unjust.
5. The analysis in this chapter is based on the description of customary law as an 'ideal type' in Chapter 1 and is informed by the empirical results outlined in the previous chapter.
6. Unless they were themselves used as a customary sanction, such as demands for compensation, assault or a payback killing. The wrongs listed in the survey were: theft, robbery, property damage, assault, threatening violence, adultery, rape, provoked homicide, sorcery, spreading of false rumours, domestic violence, payback killing, abandonment, murder, and armed robbery. As explained elsewhere, technically adultery is treated as a civil wrong under state law.
7. Under the Criminal Code (1974) the crime of wilful murder can be penalized by death (Section 299). The maximum sentence for the crime of rape is fifteen years' imprisonment. However, when committed in the circumstances of aggravation, it is life imprisonment (Section 347).
8. It should be noted that this is a generalization, as the Government of Papua New Guinea: Law and Justice Sector (2010) states that in 2003, of the country's 3,682 prison inmates (including those on remand), most were imprisoned for '[m]inor offences such as assault, break and enter, stealing, and white collar crimes'. For a country that has extremely high rates of violent crime this may seem surprising. However, it highlights the inability of the state legal order to offer an effective deterrent against serious wrongs such as murder, rape and robbery.
9. To the best of my knowledge, and as would be expected, the courts give no weight to a payback killing of a member of a wrongdoer's family as a substitute for state punishment.
10. It must be noted, however, that a sizeable minority did not see these two sanctions as substitutes. Still others considered that if a wrongdoer is imprisoned it would eliminate the need for a payback killing, but still require a part compensation payment of around a third to a half of what would normally be required.
11. As discussed in Chapter 1, while self-control and non-violent sanctions are used to control wrongs within a kin or *wantok* group, payback and large compensation payments are the primary deterrent against wrongs committed between members of

different groups. This would suggest that violent sanctions are more likely in ethnically diverse areas, such as Papua New Guinea's cities and towns, and the settlements that surround them.

12. Police numbers have been static in Papua New Guinea since independence despite an almost doubling in population (see Levantis 2000).
13. This result would also hold when a person motivated by customary considerations is more risk averse (in terms of being sanctioned by the state) than other wrongdoers. This will effectively see low levels of customary law enforcement, even under relatively low levels of state law enforcement activity.
14. Indeed this was one of the conclusions reached by the Constitutional and Law Reform Commission (2012) and one of the reasons for its repeal. In an interview, the commission's secretary, Dr Eric Kwa, said that sorcery is a 'spiritual matter' and that 'Law cannot deal with "spiritual" matters. It's very difficult to prove it as evidence' (ABC Radio 2012). This is also alluded to in the Second Reading Speech and Explanatory Memorandum of the Sorcery (Repeal) Act 2013. Also see *State* v. *Miritok* [2007] PGNC 164; N3466 (4 October 2007), where Justice Kandakasi acquitted a man accused of homicide through sorcery due to the lack of evidence provided by the prosecutor (highlighting the problem of evidence in order to secure a conviction in sorcery cases).
15. This reality was long recognized by both the German and Australian administrations. For instance, Gore (1965: 177) describes a payback raid where those who initially objected were told by their kinship group: 'If you don't like payback go and stay with the government official'.
16. The relationship between state officials and customary obligations is complicated. For instance from the fieldwork some respondents suggested that customary obligations required a police officer to arrest his kin if he or she committed a serious crime to protect him or her from payback and the kinship as a whole from payback. In this sense, arresting a *wantok* is not so much abiding by his or her official duties but actually protecting the kinship group.
17. Given the reciprocal nature of customary law, state officials who refuse to break the laws of the state face the risk of being effectively expelled from their kinship group. Once expelled, the individual must rely solely on his or her own resources and on the protective capacity of the state for security. We can expect the individual to weigh up the expected costs and benefits. If the protective power of the state is weak and the probability of being punished for breaking the laws of the state are low, then the net benefits of defection are likely to be negative, even if the penalties for breaching the state law are high. If the protective power of the state is strong and the probability of being punished high, the net benefits are likely to be positive. This suggests that the power of the dominant legal order is self-reinforcing.

Chapter 5

Past Reforms that Failed

The survey data in the New Guinea Islands suggests that 'traditional' customary notions of kinship, group liability, strict liability, belief in sorcery, and the use of compensation and payback as legitimate sanctions remain among a significant portion of respondents. The results also demonstrated that there is strong demand for both legal orders and that there is a high degree of perceived substitutability between their sanctions and sanctioning processes. While the survey results cannot be extrapolated across the whole of Papua New Guinea, it is noteworthy that the people of the Islands Region have had a relatively high level of exposure to the transplanted state law and Western norms, so if these traditional customary notions remain there they are likely to remain elsewhere. However, the overview of legislation and sentencing trends showed that both parliament and the courts have become increasingly intolerant of crimes motivated by customary beliefs, despite the passing of the Underlying Law Act 2000.

This book analyses how customary law and state law in Papua New Guinea interact with one another and sanction wrongs, to shed some light on the country's law and order problem with the hope of offering some constructive policy advice to improve the personal security of its citizens. The key finding is that the both legal orders have similar aims, but that each often undermines the other, leading to legal dissonance. The dissonance effects arise from the fact that the legal orders have very different processes and use very different sanctions to control wrongdoing – and these negative interaction effects are exacerbated by the existence of idiosyncratic customary wrongs.

Some may suggest that time is the answer to legal dissonance in Papua New Guinea. Perhaps these effects will dissipate over time as the two legal orders converge, or at least evolve, so as to avoid the more problematic interactions that have been identified. Indeed Aldashev et al. (2012) argue that customary law will converge towards the state law with greater exposure and access to it. In this sense they see the state law (and state courts) acting as magnets that will draw customary law closer to it. This argument suggests that the costly and traumatic disorder generated by the transplant process may only be temporary. Given that it was not until the late 1960s that there was any serious attempt by the colonial government to impose the transplanted law on the whole of the indigenous population of Papua New Guinea, perhaps the current problematic interactions are simply teething problems.[1] However, there are reasons to be sceptical of this view. It is shown in Larcom (2015) that, once controlling other factors, those who have greater access and exposure to the state legal order (measured in geographic terms) are more likely to condone the use of payback killings.[2] This suggests that if the state law is acting as a magnet, there are more powerful forces countering its magnetic effect. Furthermore, as explained below, there are numerous examples across the globe of non-state rules persisting (seemingly indefinitely) despite being in opposition to the state law.

Whether or not problematic legal pluralism in the post-colony of Papua New Guinea is merely a phase on the path to self-correcting unification and harmony cannot easily be answered, however it seems likely that both legal orders will continue to sanction wrongs and hold onto their idiosyncratic elements for the foreseeable future. Given that the state is growing no stronger over time (and perhaps weaker), and given the adverse and debilitating consequences the current interactions seem to be having, it would be cavalier to wait the necessary decades or centuries to find out. For those who are reluctant to consider the legal circumstances in Papua New Guinea as problematic (or exaggerated) they should consider that in addition to having some of the highest victimization rates in the world (see Egan, Zvekic and Alvazzi del Frate 1995: 200–12; Guthrie, Hukula and Laki 2006a, 2006b, 2007), the state is largely unable to sanction grave crimes. The state legal order aims to suppress large parts of customary law but it is largely dysfunctional. While official data are rare the Papua New Guinea Law and Justice Sector Secretariat (2007: 11–39) reported data on victimization, reported crimes, arrests, and prison escapes. Remembering that most crimes go unreported, for those that are, the data suggests that the national arrest rate for murder is 27 per cent, rape 22 per cent and robbery 16 per cent.[3] Of those who were arrested, found guilty and imprisoned, many escaped. With an estimated total prison population of 4,169 inmates (of which 1,421 were on remand) over the four-year period to 2006 a total of 1,116 inmates escaped, which is an average escape rate of 7 per cent per year.

Legal Monism

A State Surge

Perhaps the most obvious legal reform for Papua New Guinea would be for it to become legally monistic. If there are large net external costs generated through legal pluralism, the existence or enforcement of only one legal order could result in an improvement in the legal arrangements of Papua New Guinea. Legal monism could be achieved by either one legal order withdrawing or by one legal order aiming to eradicate the other. Hirshleifer (1982) likens this struggle for existence at the expense of the eventual elimination of the other, to Rome and Carthage's duel for survival.

The aim of the Derham reforms, which continues to be state policy, was to effectively eliminate the need for customary law by replacing it with state law enforcement. It was anticipated that this would lead to a legally monistic society. Many of Papua New Guinea's elite continue to favour efforts towards legal monism as they may see it as a necessary step towards development. For instance, an editorial of the *Post Courier* (2011) called for all serious crimes to be solely sanctioned by the higher state courts and for an end to the use of customary compensation payments.[4] If the state were able to sufficiently sanction common wrongdoers then enforcement of customary sanctions should fall, especially those sanctions that are grave wrongs under the state law (e.g. payback killings) as there is a high degree of perceived substitutability between imprisonment and payback among those surveyed. In addition, if the state was able to adequately sanction idiosyncratic wrongs, it would also greatly reduce the need for customary sanctions in relation to these most prominent idiosyncratic wrongs. Alternatively the state could aim to eliminate the use of all idiosyncratic customary wrongs and sanctions through the use of brute force.

While the Derham reforms have failed to date, one possible solution would be for them to be properly implemented. Levantis (2000) and Dinnen (2006) rightly point out that Papua New Guinea has a relatively small police force for its population, and advocate an increase in enforcement effort. The Papua New Guinea Law and Justice Sector Secretariat (2007: 6) records 4,789 uniformed police officers in 2006 which, using 2000 census data, equates to one police officer for every 1,084 people. This compares to the global average of one police officer for every 400 people as reported by Shaw, van Dijk and Rhomberg (2003). More, better trained, and better resourced police and criminal law enforcement officers would enable the Derham reforms (and recent extensions) to be more forcefully implemented.

However, any increase in enforcement activity would have a diluted effect in the sanctioning of wrongdoers due to the negative productivity effects generated by *wantokism* and the other dissonance effects that have been identified. Presumably, a significant portion of the increased enforcement effort would be directed against those customary sanctions that are crimes. As such, it would face higher costs than if it were only sanctioning common wrongs, and would also be further eliminating the deterrent effect that customary law currently provides in relation to common wrongs. Also, if the state law is too out of step with the internalized beliefs or prevailing morality of the citizenry (or is considered too draconian in terms of magnitude of sanction), those tasked with enforcing it may simply refuse to do so, either explicitly or tacitly.[5]

These factors suggest that, for the Derham reforms to be implemented given the current productivity levels of state law enforcement, substantial increases in numbers would be needed – most likely multiples of current levels. To give some indication of the increase that may be required, the Papua New Guinea Law and Justice Sector Secretariat (2007: 6) records that approximately one-third of the uniformed police force (1,632 officers) are stationed in Port Moresby. However, as mentioned earlier, many of these will have management or administration roles at the headquarters in Port Moresby and so will not be involved in direct policing. Notwithstanding, this number approximates to one police officer for every 156 residents, which is higher than in many highly urbanized Western societies (Shaw, van Dijk and Rhomberg 2003). Despite this, Port Moresby still suffers from high rates of violent crime (Guthrie, Hukula and Laki 2006). Therefore, while 'properly' implementing the Derham reforms may be technically feasible, it is unclear whether the state of Papua New Guinea, or any other state for that matter, could afford the required increase in enforcement. It should also be noted that if the productivity of criminal enforcement is so low, as it seems to be in Papua New Guinea, it may actually be rational for the state to have low per capita police numbers, as scarce government resources could be spent more productively elsewhere. Indeed, this is the essence of legal dissonance – a 'high crime–low state enforcement' trap that is generated by negative interaction effects between the two legal orders.

Given the low levels of state law productivity in sanctioning wrongdoers, which has not been overcome despite decades of capacity-building exercises supplied by foreign aid donors, one option would be to have the transplanted criminal law enforced by 'transplanted officials'. Seeing foreign officials assume the general policing duties in Papua New Guinea may be what is necessary for the state criminal law, as it currently stands, to have a chance of being enforced. Such a reform would probably lead to higher productivity levels of enforcement as these officials would not be conflicted by kinship obligations, and would be less likely to have sympathy for other customary notions that may inhibit policing of the transplanted criminal law.[6] After decades of talk of an escalating law and order problem, the Australian and Papua New Guinea governments entered into an agreement in 2003 which resulted in hundreds of Australian Federal Police being stationed in Port Moresby and other urban centres to engage in direct policing. However, in 2005 the Supreme Court ruled that the Enhanced Co-operation between Papua New Guinea and Australia Act 2004 was inconsistent with the Constitution on several grounds, including that the indemnity against prosecution granted to the Australian police was inconsistent with the guaranteed rights and freedoms of persons contained in the Constitution, and that the prosecution powers granted to the foreign police under the Act interfered with the discretionary powers of the public prosecutor as outlined in the Constitution.[7] After this judgement the Australian police returned home, although there are still occasional reports that they will return – in a direct policing role.[8] The Supreme Court's ruling was in response to a challenge brought forward by the then Governor of Morobe Province, as a large contingent of armed foreign police was seen by some as an unwelcome encroachment on Papua New Guinea's sovereignty and an attempt at re-colonization.[9] While such a move was undoubtedly a challenge to Papua New Guinea's sovereignty, so is its inability to provide basic security for many of its citizens. However, given the gulf of difference between the two legal orders and their ability to undermine each other as they are currently configured, it is unclear whether this approach, which would come at great cost to self determination, would work in any case.

Woodman (2012: 138) suggests that a unification of laws, whereby the state attempts to eliminate legal pluralism, would most likely be impossible, but if it were to have any chance it 'would require a totalitarian policy'. On this, it is noteworthy that Massell (1968) has documented the failure of a well-resourced and highly motivated totalitarian state to suppress another very different legal order. His account relates to Soviet attempts (led by the Troika which included none other than Josef Stalin) to introduce 'revolutionary' state laws and ideals to Soviet Central Asia in the late 1920s. Massell (ibid.: 226) concluded that despite almost 'ideal' conditions, which included the Soviet state's 'undisputed and centralized political power, overwhelming superiority of force, and authoritarian dispositions coupled with the absence of democratic constraints', the state failed in its efforts to use 'law as an autonomous strategic instrument of rapid, administered social change'. In short, it is suggested that the elimination of conflicting legal orders (or deeply held internalized beliefs) through criminal sanctions, is not as easy as some legal reformers may think. Numerous authors have provided accounts of the persistence of non-state rules, beliefs and organizations that can be at odds or in competition with the state.[10] In addition, even where the state is strong, problematic legal pluralism can persist in pockets for long periods of time.[11] This is partly a result of the fact that groups often place great value in maintaining and adhering to their own legal order, and will fight encroachment. The work of Iannaccone (1992), while focused on religious groups, suggests that laws and norms that are in direct opposition to state laws can persist for indefinite periods, and even be deliberately maintained in an effort to encourage commitment among tightly knit groups, and to reduce defection.

While the eventual domination of state law over customary law was an unquestioned assumption of colonizers and remains so among many policymakers today, the state legal order seems to have diminished in both geographical terms and actual ability to sanction wrongs in Papua New Guinea since independence. While many of Papua New Guinea's elite continue to favour legal monism, the empirical works suggests that the general population see an important role for customary law, especially in relation to the payment of compensation, the restoration of peaceful relations, and the sanctioning of customary wrongs. Therefore, in addition to the practical difficulties associated with renewed efforts to eliminate the practice of customary law, which have been continually underestimated by past legal reformers and current advocates for change, if one is to take the preferences of Papua New Guineans seriously, any legal reforms should allow customary law to play an important role in the sanctioning and remedying of wrongs.

The State Withdraw?

Of course, another obvious solution to problematic legal pluralism is for the state to completely withdraw, or at least to withdraw from sanctioning wrong behaviour. Indeed, some such as Woodman (2012: 130) have questioned the presumption that 'the rule of law must mean the rule of state law', and Tamanaha (2012: 36) states that 'If a state legal system is stuck in a dysfunctional state, viewed negatively by the populace, with reform efforts persistently failing, it is sensible to explore alternatives that might satisfy legal functions'.

These alternatives could presumably see a partial withdrawal of the state and a greater role for customary law in sanctioning wrongdoing. However, Tamanaha acknowledges that such an approach is not without its practical problems.[12] More fundamentally, however, many would argue that providing security and sanctioning wrongdoing is the state's reason for being; if it cannot do this there seems very little reason for its existence.[13] Therefore the withdrawal of the state seems as unlikely as the complete eradication of customary law. Evidence of this can be found from the recent history of Bougainville Island. Despite having been pushed out during the crisis, the state and its legal order is re-establishing itself, albeit in a modified form (see Larcom 2013a, 2013b). Finally, the results from the survey and interviewees made it clear that the state does enjoy legitimacy in sanctioning wrongs. Indeed many craved an effective state criminal system. So it would seem that both legal orders will have to learn to live with each other.

Perhaps the most binding constraint to greater recognition of customary law by the state is human rights concerns, including concerns over customary law's treatment of women and children. Customary law in most parts of the world contains many elements that are 'repugnant' to Western values and sensibilities. It is often male-dominated, hierarchical and undemocratic. It often uses sanctions that consist of violent retribution, can determine guilt or innocence using divination, and readily relies on group and strict liability. While many laud its focus on restorative justice and encourage its practice, as Pimental (2010: 5) diplomatically tells us, 'there are limits to the principle of respect for indigenous rights'. While the term 'repugnancy' is now out of favour, seemingly due to its association with the excesses of European colonialism, the term has simply been replaced, quite literally in Papua New Guinea's case, with 'human rights' provisions, which have the same intention and effect.

Customary law's perceived treatment of women makes some feminists particularly wary of encouraging its practice.[14] At the more extreme end of resistance, and written in relation to those who live in enclave communities in the West, is Okin (1999: 22–23), who considers that such groups might be much better off if their cultures were to 'become extinct' so that women would be subject to a less sexist culture, although her preference is for these cultures to be 'encouraged to alter' themselves. Taking a less combative stance is Nussbaum (1999: 108–9) who only demands the 'political equality of women'. Acknowledging that good things can come from traditional cultures, she considers a key determinant in whether or not governments should suppress them is whether women are able to have a real choice to exit them, or their rules, should they wish.

The role and status of women in Papua New Guinea is complicated, as many women hold positions of authority in both state and non-state organizations.[15] Evans, Goddard and Paterson (2011: 20) recently concluded in relation to the village courts, which much more closely resemble the practice of customary law, 'that *overall*, women disputants fare as well as, and frequently better than, male disputants'. However, this should be contrasted with Jessup (2010) who provides evidence of sex discrimination and harsh treatment of women by some village courts in relation to family law matters, and the recent findings of Forsyth (2009) who found that in Vanuatu, another Melanesian country that is culturally similar to Papua New Guinea, customary law discriminates against women and youth. In addition, the results of the survey suggest that domestic violence is one of the most prevalent wrongs in the communities surveyed. Therefore, perhaps the greatest impediment to greater recognition of customary law by the state is fear over its treatment of women. Indeed, this seemed to be a major factor in the repeal of the Sorcery Act 1971.[16]

Legislative Reform (State Legal Pluralism)

Given the constraints that the post-colonial state of Papua New Guinea faces, both in terms of the workings of its transplanted criminal law and pressures from external sources, it could be argued that it has already made significant efforts at recognizing and incorporating elements of customary law into its own legal order. Many of the Law Reform Commission recommendations under the leadership of Bernard Narokobi were actually made state law: customary law is now explicitly recognized by the Constitution and is part of the nation's Underlying Law; village courts are the most used state courts; amendments were made to the Customs Recognition Act 1963 that among other things removed the repugnancy clause; the grave customary wrongs of sorcery and adultery were made wrongs under state law;[17] and the families of those involved in fatal car accidents can receive compensation regardless of fault. Notably, however, the Law Reform Commission's (1977a) recommendations for the role of customary law in relation to criminal law were never passed by parliament. If enacted this would have seen assaults motivated by customary law attract no state penalty while killings (except paybacks) or very serious injuries would have attracted a maximum prison sentence of three years. While these reforms would have seen very different treatment of state crimes motivated by customary law than current treatment, they would really only have been a return to colonial times, except in relation to payback killings which were also, for the most part, treated leniently by the colonial courts. Some even hold up Papua New Guinea as a model for state recognition of customary law. However, it is suggested that *state* legal pluralism, where the state aims to appropriate another legal order's wrongs and prosecute them itself or tries to incorporate the other legal order into its own, is severely limited in meaningfully ameliorating the severity of the problematic legal pluralism found in Papua New Guinea.

Perhaps the greatest fault of the Law Reform Commission under Narokobi was placing too much trust in legislative reforms. Narokobi (1996), Corrin-Care and Zorn (2001) and many others have been frustrated by the higher courts' interpretations of legislation aimed at elevating customary law and allowing for it as a motivating factor when it clashed with the criminal law. With some notable exceptions outlined in earlier chapters, the judiciary has been reluctant to embrace customary law within the criminal law. There should be considerable sympathy for the judiciary's stance because, in addition to the practical considerations concerning rules of evidence and standards of proof, if they did give much greater weight to customary law it would, in many cases, turn the practice of criminal law on its head. With the recent repeal of the Sorcery Act 1971 it seems that both the Constitutional and Law Reform Commission (2012) and parliament are finally acknowledging this fact.

Like the Derham reforms, getting the legislative change advocated by the Law Reform Commission under Narokobi is one thing, but actual implementation is another. After decades of urging and prompting, which culminated in the Underlying Law Act 2000, the judiciary of the higher courts, who are now overwhelmingly indigenous Papua New Guineans, have made it clear that customary law should only play a minor role in the practice of state criminal law. While some, such as Corrin (2014: 2, 14), continue to urge for a state 'legal system based firmly on Melanesian values, beliefs and customs', and as she renews her call for 'judicial activism', it is suggested that this is a vain hope as the transplanted state law and customary law are just too different. Indeed, how could the state courts meaningfully incorporate the widely held customary principles of primacy of kinship over all other relations, group liability, strict liability, belief in sorcery, and the use of compensation and payback as legitimate sanctions in its substantive rules?

While state legal pluralism has much intuitive appeal, it has been a spectacular failure in relation to criminal law in Papua New Guinea, with substantial human costs. The state cannot, through legislative fiat, simply pick and choose which elements of customary law are to be retained and which elements are to disappear. Such an approach fails to fully account for customary law's force and legitimacy beyond that which is granted to it by the state; that is, deep legal pluralism. This was an analytical error made by Derham (1960), who sought to incorporate as much customary law as he considered tolerable and eradicate the rest. This mistake was also made by Narokobi (1996), and it is suggested that this is why his reforms (and proposed reforms) also failed. While Narokobi was much more sympathetic towards 'custom' than Derham (1960), his analysis also suffered from the state-centric conception of legal pluralism as it sought to incorporate substantive customary laws into state criminal law. Joining the long list before me, I too could argue for greater recognition of substantive customary law or better implementation of existing legislation. However, it seems that at some point defeat must be acknowledged and a new approach considered.

Conclusion

The state-centric Melanesian Jurisprudence Movement led by Bernard Narokobi failed primarily due to the inability (not necessarily unwillingness) of the state legal order to substitute for the enforcement of customary law sanctions and to acknowledge that some crimes are in fact customary sanctions. In relation to common wrongs, low levels of enforcement are primarily driven by extremely low productivity levels brought about by administering a foreign legal order, including the effects of *wantokism*; in relation to idiosyncratic wrongs, it is due to the inability of the state legal order to adequately sanction grave customary wrongs and recognize customary motivations for state crimes.

If the most problematic elements of legal pluralism are to be ameliorated, one or both legal orders will have to make greater efforts at coordination than they currently do. Forsyth (2009: 204) rightly suggests that the state's structural characteristics give it a practical advantage in implementing reforms in contrast to the dispersed nature of customary law which makes it 'difficult to obtain leverage for substantial changes'.[18] Therefore, in the short term, perhaps only the state has the ability to ameliorate problematic aspects of legal pluralism.

Both Forsyth (2009) and Dinnen and Braithwaite (2009) provide an important insight into the historical interactions between state and customary law in Melanesia in terms of the importance of a gatekeeper between the two legal orders that helped to ameliorate problematic legal pluralism in the past. In colonial Vanuatu, court assessors acted as flexible gatekeepers between customary and state law, and Forsyth advocates their reinstatement in relation to minor wrongs. Similarly, in colonial Papua New Guinea, this gatekeeper role was performed by the colonial *kiap*, and Dinnen and Braithwaite also call for their return, albeit in a modified form. Both the assessor and the *kiap* effectively, and often outside of their state mandate, decided which cases would and would not be sent to the higher state courts. It is suggested here that a broader way of conceptualizing the role of a gatekeeper is the importance of the ordering of legal orders when considering legal pluralism.

By acknowledging the reality of deep legal pluralism, the analysis of the interaction of customary and state criminal law in Papua New Guinea is enriched. This allows the legal orders to be analysed from a horizontal rather than a vertical perspective, and acknowledges that both legal orders have their own largely independent sources of legitimacy – however, they can still adversely affect one another to a significant and potentially debilitating degree. By going below the surface and acknowledging legal pluralism, it is the enforcement undertaken by the two legal orders which is highlighted. Therefore, rather than attempting to incorporate customary law into state criminal law, or attempting to make special sentencing provisions for those who have committed a crime motivated by customary law, a legal re-ordering is proposed so that customary law has the first opportunity to sanction a wrong. It is proposed that the state would only attempt to enforce its criminal sanctions if customary law is unable to sufficiently sanction a wrong. Under the arrangements formalized in the Autonomous Region of Bougainville, the state accepts a customary sanction as a valid substitute for its own sanctions, even for the most serious wrongs, and its own sanctions support, rather than undermine, the practice of customary law. The merits and impediments to extending this legal re-ordering across Papua New Guinea are discussed in the Conclusion.

Notes

1. Rouland (1994) suggests that in many post-colonial African states as well, attempts to enforce a transplanted law on a whole population only began after the start of self government.
2. Both in absolute terms, and when other variables were controlled for, such as personal characteristics and province, urban respondents were more likely to agree with the use of payback. It is also noteworthy that non-legal channels (i.e. the ability to speak English) had a strong negative relationship with agreeing with payback, suggesting that it may be a more powerful tool for changing internalized beliefs than the criminal law. See Larcom (2015) for a complete discussion, outline of a theoretical framework, and econometric analysis.
3. The actual crime data for the period from January to June 2006 was: 278 murders reported to the police, 75 arrests made; 417 rapes reported, 90 arrests made; and 737 robberies reported, 115 arrests made. Over this period, 82 people escaped police custody and 28 were re-arrested.
4. Editorial 4 October 2011.
5. The lack of cooperation by witnesses and the failure of police to adequately address victims' concerns (presumably due to widespread internalized beliefs concerning sorcery) is a very real issue in relation to violence against alleged sorcerers. See Constitutional and Law Reform Commission of Papua New Guinea (2012).

6. On this, Berkowitz, Pistor and Richard (2003b: 171) suggest: 'They may be unfamiliar with dispute settlement through adversarial litigation rather than mediation and negotiation or with the rigidity of legal rights independent of kinship relations or norms of social obligations. Moreover, the social, economic and institutional context often differs remarkably between origin and transplant country, creating fundamentally different conditions for effectuating the imported legal order in the latter.'
7. Special Reference Pursuant to Constitution Section 19; Special Reference by the Morobe Provincial Executive [2005] PGSC 32; SC785 (13 May 2005).
8. There are currently approximately fifty Australian Federal Police Officers deployed in Papua New Guinea. While they have a uniformed presence, they will not be 'arresting or charging any person for an offence against PNG domestic law' (Australian High Commission, Papua New Guinea, 2013).
9. It is another question whether the average Papua New Guinean, who yearns for an impartial police force and a heightened level of personal security, would mind such a trade-off if it could be delivered. While it is no justification for further challenges to Papua New Guinea's sovereignty, the Australian Government donates approximately AU$ 500 million per year which equates to around 17 per cent of total Papua New Guinea government expenditure (AusAID 2009). This funding, which consists of direct budgetary support and support for various law and order, health, education and infrastructure programmes, also buys considerable 'leverage'.
10. See, for example, Basu (2000); Aoki (2001); Bicchieri (2006); and Greif (2006).
11. See Wilkinson-Ryan and Baron (2008) for a case concerning attitudes to divorce laws in the United States. In Europe, non-state legal orders with different and opposite conceptions of wrong can also persist and even flourish, albeit at the margins of society. Examples include Ruffini's (1978) Sardinian shepherds, vendettas in parts of the Mediterranean, drug cartels, football hooligans, and biker gangs. It is also noteworthy that the Republic of Turkey, founded in 1923, has had, and continues to have, limited success in implementing its secular constitution.
12. As Tamanaha (2012: 40) points out, customary courts might not be 'adequate substitutes for state law on all horizontal matters', such as when a dispute involves members of different communities or one person who is 'attached to traditional ways' and another person who rejects them, which results in an outcome 'contrary to the prior expectations of at least one of the parties'. He also highlights the fact that customary law sanctions cannot deal with 'erecting legal restraints on government officials'; that is, the state would at least need to sanction wrong behaviour by its own officials.
13. Ellickson (1994: 124) notes the risk that non-state control could lead to feuds and even civil war – a concern which has led prominent libertarians to endorse the prevailing view that only the state should have a monopoly on forceful sanctions.
14. Okin (1999: 10) defines feminism as 'the belief that women should not be disadvantaged by their sex, that they should be recognized as having human dignity equal to that of men, and that they should have the opportunity to live as fulfilling and as freely chosen lives as men can'.
15. In regard to Bougainville, see Braithwaite et al. (2010). Women's groups took the lead role in establishing peace in Bougainville drawing on their customary law. They continue to play an important role and have considerable status in Bougainville.
16. See Constitutional and Law Reform Commission of Papua New Guinea (2012); 'PNG Law Reform Commission Urges Sorcery Act Repeal', ABC Radio Australia (2012); Amnesty International (2013); Second Reading Speech of the Sorcery (Repeal) Act 2013; and 'PNG Repeals Sorcery Law and Expands Death Penalty', BBC (2013).

17. Note that sorcery remains an offence under the jurisdiction of the village courts.
18. Such a view is consistent with Roland's (2004) conception of fast-moving and slow-moving institutions in understanding institutional change, where the state law is more able to change than dispersed institutions such as norm and customary law.

Conclusion

Reforming the Prosecution Process

It has been shown that customary law and criminal law undermine each other. It has also been argued that state legal pluralism in relation to criminal law, where the state appropriates another legal order's wrongs and aims to prosecute them itself or tries to incorporate the other legal order into its own, has severe limitations and has largely failed in Papua New Guinea. Therefore, it is suggested that further attempts should be avoided. In any case, the repeal of the Sorcery Act 1971 in 2013 suggests that the current Papua New Guinean government has no interest in such an approach. However, given Papua New Guinea's seemingly ever-escalating law and order problem, something needs to be done, and it is suggested that this should be a change in the state's prosecution policy. In Woodman's (2012) language this would be a case of 'passive institutional recognition' of customary law by the state. By conceptualizing the problematic relationship between customary and criminal law (in Chapter 4) it is suggested that this reform should move the relationship from the current situation, where they undermine each other, to one where they provide mutual support for each other. In short, the reform proposed is for the state to recognize high-magnitude customary compensation payments as valid substitutes for its own high-magnitude sanctions (imprisonment and the death penalty). This practice was once common place in England and other European countries (Friedman 1979, 1984; and Garoupa and Klerman 2010) and is currently practised in a number of post-colonial states (Badar 2011).

Whether or not the Papua New Guinean state can bring itself to accept customary sanctions as valid substitutes for their own across the entire country will depend on how it sees itself and the job of criminal law. Here it is useful to draw on Damaska's (1986) theory of criminal procedure, which places great weight on the perceived role of the state in society. Specifically, Damaska (ibid.: 11) contrasts the ends of a *policy implementing* state, that aims to 'manage the lives of people and steer society', with those of a *conflict solving* state, that aims to 'maintain the social equilibrium and merely provide a framework for social self-management'. He goes on to suggest that when the state is seen primarily as 'policy implementing', a *hierarchical* structure of procedural authority is more likely, whereas when it is seen as 'conflict solving' a *coordinator* model is more likely.[1]

A Change in the Prosecution Process

One notable procedural difference between customary law and criminal law relates to who initiates the prosecution process. Under state criminal law the public prosecutor (or police with delegated authority) makes the decision whether to prosecute, while under customary law it is the responsibility of the wronged or his or her kin. Following the landmark *Mattau* judgement, in the Kieta region of Bougainville Island a situation has developed where the state only prosecutes offenders under the Criminal Code when a customary sanction is deemed unenforceable; that is, when one or both of the parties cannot reach agreement on the payment of a suitable compensation settlement. In negotiating a settlement both parties know that if an agreement cannot be reached the offender will face a state criminal court and a potentially long period of imprisonment. Such a change in process has the ability to address the key causes of problematic legal pluralism, particularly in relation to grave common wrongs which have the sharpest effect on personal security.

This change in the prosecution process deals directly with the two most prominent causes of problematic legal pluralism in relation to common wrongs. The state, through prosecutorial discretion, only prosecutes an offender when a customary settlement cannot be agreed. This sees the state recognize the customary sanction as a substitute that significantly reduces the chance of double punishment. In addition, negotiating compensation settlements in the shadow of imprisonment also lessens, but does not eliminate, the probability of payback. It must also be remembered that the more effective the state is at sanctioning those common wrongdoers it is asked to sanction, the less likely that payback killings will occur. If the state is able to sufficiently sanction those wrongdoers who refuse to pay adequate compensation, it should eventually eliminate its use. The threat of lengthy imprisonment should replace the need for payback and provide a strong incentive for the wrongdoer and his or her kin to pay an adequate level of compensation, show remorse, and ensure that relations between the two parties are restored. It must be stressed that such a change in process would not see the state condoning payback killings or executions, but rather would allow these to be solely sanctioned using customary law.[2]

The key element of this reform is a change in legal ordering. The practice of customary law would become the default legal order for sanctioning all wrongs, and the decision to involve the state criminal justice system (through the prosecution process) would depend on whether both parties are satisfied that the customary sanction is both appropriate and adequate. Its effectiveness, both in deterring common wrongs and eliminating the practice of payback killings, would rely on the state's ability to sanction those wrongdoers brought before it. This should be more likely because the police and courts would have fewer wrongs to investigate and sanction.

Such arrangements would also help to reduce, but not eliminate, problematic legal pluralism in relation to idiosyncratic wrongs, as customary sanctions could be imposed with less state interference. When a customary sanction is imposed that is a wrong under the state criminal law it would only be prosecuted if it was deemed inappropriate and could not be adequately sanctioned itself under customary law. In relation to rivalrous compliance these arrangements should also help, as the offences prosecuted would only be those that had failed to be settled under customary law. This should increase the legitimacy of the state criminal law as it would now work to support customary law. However, it would not eliminate the incentives for public officials to give more weight to kinship ties over their state duties. A policy of posting police to other parts should however reduce the extent of *wantokism*.

In Bougainville the actual mechanism used to decide whether to prosecute or not was a jointly signed letter by customary leaders from the two sides providing evidence that the wrong had been adequately sanctioned and resolved under customary law. For other parts of Papua New Guinea, where customary leadership is not as strong or has broken down, such a mechanism would not be possible.

One possibility would be for the police or the Office of the Public Prosecutor to only prosecute crimes that were not sufficiently sanctioned under customary law or shown to be customary sanctions themselves. Such an approach would allow customary law to operate with minimal state interference where it is strong, and the state legal order to operate where customary law is unable to sanction wrongs. However, if such an approach were to be formalized it would require the state legal order to collect and document evidence that the victim has been satisfied by the customary legal order. One theoretical benefit of such an approach, assuming the state had the capacity, is that it would allow the state to investigate the type of sanction used and to reject those that are deemed to contravene human rights. While this approach could be pursued, it would seem to be beyond the current administrative capacity of the state legal order.[3] Another variant of this reform could be to allow village court magistrates to decide which matters are prosecuted and which are not. For instance, to avoid prosecution a letter could be required stating that the matter has been resolved without the need for state prosecution, and signed by a village court magistrate and the two parties. However, not all communities have functioning village courts, and village court magistrates do not always have legitimacy under customary law. Alternatively, Papua New Guinea could even borrow and adapt the procedures that a number of post-colonial Muslim-majority states have adopted in relation to the recognition of a *diyya* (a specified or mutually agreed compensation payment under Islamic law) wholly substituting for a death sentence or imprisonment (Badar 2011).

However, it is suggested that perhaps the simplest and most feasible legal reform that could allow this re-ordering of legal orders to be implemented across Papua New Guinea would be for the public prosecutor to delegate the decision of whether to prosecute to the *victim*, or to kin in the case of a killing. While the victim (or the kin in the case of a killing) would be free to initiate a prosecution at any time (subject to any normal statutes of limitation) they would waive the right of prosecution if a compensation payment was paid and accepted for this purpose. What constitutes acceptance (and by whom) could be outlined by the Public Prosecutor (or even by legislation if deemed necessary). This change in prosecution policy would make the victim the 'gatekeeper' of the state legal order and could be made under the state's existing legal framework; Section 176 of the Constitution grants 'absolute discretion' to the public prosecutor in deciding whether to refuse or consent to any prosecution, and Section 525 of the Criminal Code provides for the public prosecutor to decide whether to indict the offender or decline to lay a charge. If the prosecutor deemed that such a change in prosecution policy was in the national interest, and there are strong grounds, such a change in legal ordering could proceed. If the public prosecutor were to make such a change in policy, it would have to be applied consistently across crimes and persons to provide certainty of outcome. The only exception would be in the case of crimes against children and other vulnerable people, where the public prosecutor would automatically initiate a prosecution.

Such a change in prosecution policy would allow both the customary law and state criminal law to be better coordinated in the sanctioning of wrongs, which should lead to a reduction in problematic legal pluralism and therefore increase the deterrent against common wrongs. Rather than the state attempting to incorporate substantive customary rules into its own legal order, this change would allow customary law to be practised more freely. This should result in state sanctions mainly acting to support rather than undermine the practice of customary law. It would also allow customary law to take a considerable burden off the state legal order, which it cannot currently handle, and therefore allow it to more ably prosecute and sanction those wrongs that would be directed towards it. The success of such a change would very much depend on the ability of the state to sufficiently sanction those wrongs that are referred to it.

While this change would address the two main problems associated with the sanctioning of common wrongs, it would see a significant change in the way criminal law is enforced, which is likely to raise two broad concerns. The first relates to whether the state should allow victim discretion in the prosecution of crimes – indeed some may argue that this is one of the defining characteristics of criminal law.[4] Second, such a move may raise some important human rights concerns, particularly as the Constitution obliges the state to protect fundamental human rights. It will be argued that both of these concerns are surmountable although, as stated earlier, much depends on what the Papua New Guinean state considers to be the purpose of criminal law; in particular whether it sees itself as a 'conflict solving' coordinator rather than a 'hierarchical policy' implementer.

Finally, for such a change in process to work for all wrongdoing, all idiosyncratic customary wrongs would have to be state wrongs and ideally have sanctions attached that are broadly commensurate to their gravity as customary wrongs. This is necessary so that a compensation payment could be negotiated in the shadow of a state sanction, rather than in the shadow of retributive violence. This is already broadly the case in Papua New Guinea, as even with the repeal of the Sorcery Act 1971, sorcery still remains an offence under the Village Court Regulations and there is no upper limit on the amount of compensation for cases involving death. Furthermore, while village courts do not generally have the power to impose prison sentences, they can if a person disobeys a court's ruling when also approved by a District Court magistrate. Nonetheless, if violence is to be avoided, the threat of imprisonment, for whatever the customary wrong, must be sufficient to negotiate a mutually agreeable compensation payment.

The Prosecution Process in Criminal Law

It is argued here that the state would do better to see itself as a conflict solver and coordinator. While the post-colonial state of Papua New

Guinea inherited essentially English law, which is meant to be of a conflict solving and coordination type, the act of transplantation paradoxically seems to have resulted in it being explicitly used as a tool for steering society. The current conception of the state legal order seeing itself as a hierarchical manager is one that it has inherited from its colonial masters; Derham (1963) consciously aimed to use the Criminal Code as a tool for social engineering, while earlier colonial administrations, being gentler in their implementation, also saw the criminal law as primarily playing an educative role. This view seems to accord with the Supreme Court of Papua New Guinea, which stated in *Kumbamong* v. *State* [2008] (para. 19) that the 'Criminal Code prescribes the kinds of conduct that are unacceptable in our society'.

The legitimacy for this expressive element of criminal law in a Western democracy is expressed by Lacey (2008: 281) as 'a collective judgement about what is not acceptable, and enunciate a general standard of social behaviour which is assumed at some level to be shared and which constitutes a significant expression of the identity of the social order'.

In relation to the prosecution process, this expressive role can manifest itself in the view that there are certain behaviours that require the state to regulate and prosecute directly.[5] In the West, legitimacy for state criminal law to take such a role is often derived from the concept of a social contract combined with democratic and liberal underpinnings.[6] While such a rationale may apply to a Western liberal democracy, it would be foolhardy to attempt to apply it to a post-colonial state such as Papua New Guinea, which was saddled with a foreign Criminal Code in every sense. Indeed, in relation to the legitimacy of customary law, Corrin-Care and Zorn (2001: 84) point out that in the parliamentary debates leading up to the passing of the Underlying Law Act 2000, '[e]very member who spoke – both those in favour of the Bill's passage and those against – presumed that they were voting for an Act that would require the courts to apply customary law generally and in regard to most matters that would come before the courts'.

Allowing victim discretion in relation to prosecutions under the Criminal Code would allow the state to move from being a hierarchical manager to a conflict solver and coordinator, while avoiding the perils of state legal pluralism. While there are no doubt strong political or jurisprudential grounds for any state conceiving itself as either a manager or coordinator, the reality of the current legal circumstances in Papua New Guinea would seem to give it little choice. It would be difficult to imagine how efforts at using the criminal law as a tool for social transformation could have failed more spectacularly. In this respect, Damaska (1986: 13) considers that '[a] state with many independent power centres and a powerful desire to transform society can be likened to a man with ardent appetites and a poor instrument for their satisfaction'.

While it is true that if such a reform was implemented it would see many individuals who have breached the Criminal Code not face a state sanction, this outcome must be compared with the current circumstances. In addition to an unacceptable lack of personal security for many citizens and countless individual injustices for those who come into contact with the state legal order, most individuals who currently breach the Criminal Code do not face a state sanction anyway, and many who do end up as prison escapees.

When such a reform is considered historically and comparatively, it is not as radical as it first appears. The common law tradition has a long history of prosecutorial discretion and victim participation. When the state in England was much weaker than it currently is, few wrongs were considered public wrongs (including homicide), there was considerable discretion shown in the prosecution process, and grave crimes were often sanctioned solely by compensation payments.

Musson (2008: 256) suggests that the notion that a grave wrong was an infringement of the king's peace in English law developed during the tenth and eleventh centuries and that 'the idea that it was in the public interest to punish offences committed by individuals' did not emerge until the Anglo-Norman period (1100–1500). Before this, those found guilty of homicide or robbery could be punished by death, but primarily as a measure for compensating a victim (or their kin) and re-establishing their honour and respect. Up until the mid-sixteenth century, homicide was still often regarded as a private wrong remedied with a settlement and compensation. The seventeenth and eighteenth centuries continued to see discretionary and mainly private approaches to sanctioning wrong behaviour. Handler (2008: 257) concludes that during this period '[c]rime was perceived in local, rather than national terms, and the law was enforced selectively' and mainly 'determined at the point of application'. Before the establishment of police forces in the mid-nineteenth century, almost all crimes were privately prosecuted. Sanders (2008: 949) suggests that '[o]nly serious public order and political matters were prosecuted by government'. Victims who wished to prosecute a wrongdoer initiated the action, did their own detective work, located witnesses, arranged for them to appear in court and undertook most of the functions that are now associated with the public prosecutor. Many formal prosecutions did not proceed beyond the preliminary hearing as the Justice of the Peace hearing the case often brokered a compensation settlement between the victim and the wrongdoer (Handler 2008: 258). Friedman (1996: 103) also claims that the aim of private prosecutions was often not to have the wrongdoer punished by the state per se but 'in the hope of being paid to drop them'. However, with the growth of the state in England, gradually the police took over the prosecutions, albeit with no more formal powers than private citizens. It was only towards the end of the nineteenth century that the Office of the Director of Public Prosecutions was established and later the Crown Prosecution Service – in part, according to Sanders (2008: 949), to 'curtail police dominance' of the prosecution process.

In terms of cross-country comparisons, it is noteworthy that a number of post-colonial Muslim-majority states (for example Pakistan, Saudi Arabia, Iran and parts of Nigeria) recognize compensation payments (*diyya*) as complete substitutes for the highest magnitude state sanctions available, including the death penalty. Even in contemporary civil law states, which could be considered to be the most hierarchical and managerial in type, allow for significant prosecutorial discretion and victim participation in the prosecution process (although granted not to the extent proposed here).[7]

If the state were to adopt the stance of a conflict solver and coordinator by only prosecuting offences under the Criminal Code when initiated by the victim or his or her kin (or alternatively allowing the victim or kin to halt the prosecution process on the grounds of a mutually agreed compensation payment) we would expect greater use of customary law sanctions and potentially a fall in the use of state sanctions. We can expect this outcome given the high degree of perceived substitutability between the two legal orders and their sanctions amongst those surveyed and interviewed.[8] While this would not concern a conflict solver and coordinator, as long as it provided an acceptable level of personal safety and both parties were satisfied with the customary outcome, it may raise other concerns particularly by those who may consider the practice of customary law as being contrary to human rights or unable to act as a substitute both in the type of sanction and in serving as a deterrent against wrongdoing, as discussed below.

The Constitution and Human Rights

In relation to human rights, Papua New Guinea's Constitution (1975: 5) provides its citizens with 'Basic Rights': 'all persons in our country are entitled to the fundamental rights and freedoms of the individual, that is to say, the right, whatever their race, tribe, places of origin, political opinion, colour, creed or sex … [to] life, liberty, security of the person and the protection of the law'.

Unfortunately the state is currently unable to secure many of these rights for its citizens, particularly in relation to security of the person and protection of the law. The proposed reform would allow individuals to secure these rights using customary law *or* the state criminal law. While a greater role for customary law is often lauded, it is also treated with suspicion, particularly in the human rights discourse (Pimental 2010). In addition to concerns over the process of customary law, its sanctions are often opposed from two sides. Violent customary sanctions are considered inhumane and therefore in breach of human rights, while the use of compensation payments to sanction wrongs is considered inadequate in terms of justice for the victim, and is therefore also seen as a breach of human rights. Sadly, within this discourse there seems to be a belief that any sanction other than long-term imprisonment is either brutality or impunity.

It is undeniable that many aspects of the customary law sanctioning process such as its rules of evidence, liability rules, conceptions of wrong, sanctions and male domination are concerning and some have been ruled to contravene the Constitution.[9] However one chooses to characterize customary practices and sanctions, it must be remembered that the proposed reform would not see the state condoning any human rights breaches or encouraging impunity, it would simply be allowing the victim of a crime to choose whether to have the offender prosecuted under the state criminal law. It would not stop a victim from seeking to prosecute a wrongdoer under the criminal law or enforcing their Constitutional rights, unless they themselves chose not to. The substantive elements of criminal law would remain as they are, and customary sanctions that are crimes would remain crimes. Similarly those who are subject to customary practices that contravene the Constitution's human rights provisions would also still be able to have their rights vindicated under the state legal order. However, rather than the state automatically initiating prosecution (in theory at least), the victim of a crime or human rights violation would be empowered with this decision. If implemented and then challenged, a ruling as to whether such a reform in the prosecution process is inconsistent with the Constitution would be a matter for Papua New Guinea's Supreme Court. However, it seems unlikely that it would be inconsistent. Supreme Court Justice Kandakasi in the *Mattau* case[10] allowed a customary sanction to wholly substitute for a custodial sentence for wilful homicide based on the grounds that the victim's family were satisfied with the customary settlement and that it would lead to greater community harmony in the Autonomous Region of Bougainville. While the Autonomous Region of Bougainville has its own Constitution and special provisions within the Constitution of Papua New Guinea, there is no apparent reason to suggest that the basic rights of the Papua New Guinea Constitution do not apply.

On this, the Constitution is most concerned with the 'principles of natural justice' in terms of legal procedure as evidenced by Section 37 of the Constitution, which explicitly exempts the village courts from providing various procedural protections granted to an offender under the 'right of protection under the law'. Their only requirement is to act 'in accordance with the principles of natural justice', defined under Section 59(2) of Constitution as 'the duty to act fairly and, in principle, to be seen to act fairly'.

In relation to general human rights provisions in international law, Article 5 of the United Nations-sponsored Vienna Declaration and Program of Action as adopted by the World Conference on Human Rights in 1993 decrees that it is the 'duty of States, regardless of their political, economic and cultural systems, to promote and protect all human rights and fundamental freedoms'. Interpreting this declaration in its strictest sense would seem to severely limit a greater role for customary law, and no doubt this is a view that many hold. However, it is the opinion of some such as Kinley (2012) that international human rights law does allow individual rights to sometimes be legitimately limited in order to protect other individual or group rights, especially in the provision of public order, health and security. The whole purpose of this proposed reform would be to improve public order and provide some more personal security for Papua New Guinea's citizens.

Practical Human Rights Concerns

It is argued that the proposed reform of the prosecution process would enhance freedom of choice when seeking redress and vindicating breached rights, by allowing the victim to choose from which legal order to seek redress. If the reform was to have its intended effects it should also increase personal security among the population. However, given the importance of kinship in Papua New Guinea, it is unlikely that the decision to prosecute would be made solely by the victim but rather collectively depending on whether a customary settlement can be reached. The decision to prosecute would also depend on the preferences of the victim and his or her kin; given that the kinship group is likely to benefit directly from a customary settlement compared with the offender being imprisoned under a state sanction, the individual victim may face pressure not to prosecute the offender under the state criminal law but to accept a customary settlement. This raises a practical concern that an individual victim may become marginalized in the decision to prosecute, in contrast to the current approach where the state attempts – in theory – to prosecute all offenders. This practical concern is particularly worrying for those who are subjugated by traditional social structures or whose voice is less well heard. One group of particular concern is women, as domestic violence is prevalent in the parts of Papua New Guinea surveyed.

Violations of women's rights are unacceptable and they are inconsistent with the rights granted to every Papua New Guinean under the Constitution. It is a sad fact that human rights abuses towards women, children, prisoners and many others are common in Papua New Guinea. It must be remembered that currently, due to the suppression of customary law and the inability of the state to enforce the criminal law, few women have the ability to vindicate their rights and see wrongdoers sanctioned under either legal order. Rates of violence and sexual crimes against women in parts of Papua New Guinea are intolerably high. After fifty years of no progress, and most likely regression, in building the rule of state law across Papua New Guinea, including countless capacity-building exercises aimed at 'strengthening the justice sector', there must be recognition that the current approach has failed. Efforts at using criminal law to bludgeon the 'repugnant' elements of customary law, whatever they may be, have failed, with the consequence being an unacceptable lack of personal security, especially for women. However, the cooperative relationship between the legal orders in the New Guinea Islands may be a way forward. In the Kieta region of Bougainville, I was told that women's freedom of movement and personal security has increased markedly. It is unclear what cost, if any, was incurred in terms of the exercise of women's rights.[11] If it has come at a cost, Papua New Guinean women should decide whether it is worth this cost, and the proposed reform will allow for this more than the current arrangements. Okin (1999: 23) suggests that 'it would take significant factors weighing in the other direction to counterbalance evidence that a culture severely constrains women's choices or otherwise undermines their well-being'. While it is unclear whether there would be any such trade-off with such a reform, it does seem there are significant factors in terms of personal security weighing in the other direction. The basic rights granted in Papua New Guinea's Constitution, especially 'life, liberty and security of the person', have striking similarities to Bentham's (1843a) subordinate ends of government of 'subsistence, equality and security'. He concluded that without security, equality would not last a single day. Some basic level of personal security is necessary for a society to function and allow the enforcement of all basic rights, including women's rights.

While it is argued here that the Papua New Guinean state should adopt the stance of a conflict solver and coordinator in administering the Criminal Code, based upon the consequences of its current stance, there is no suggestion that the state should not try to effect social transformation and the promotion of human rights. On the contrary, it is suggested that the state should take concrete and effective measures to promote human rights as outlined in the Constitution. Prioritizing non-legislative measures, such as education programmes, over legislative measures (including imposing extremely high magnitude sanctions on wrongdoers) may well be more effective and certainly less traumatic and destructive. The importance of internalization of norms in promoting human rights should not be understated, however it will likely require much time.[12]

Given that school enrolment rates in Papua New Guinea remain low, one concrete measure to promote human rights would be take actual steps to reverse this and to ensure that the teaching is of high quality. Therefore, specific measures that could be taken in relation to the promotion of women's rights should include special efforts to encourage girls' education and schooling, promoting gender equality, and to encourage the training of female village court magistrates and higher court judges.

The alternative to a customary sanction for grave crimes, whether they be motivated by customary law or not, is for the state to seek to imprison the offender. While few criminals face imprisonment due to the state's inability to sanction wrongdoers, because of poor policing and mass prison escapes, those who are imprisoned have their Constitutional rights violated by the state.[13] While the Office of the High Commissioner for Human Rights (2011) reported 'poor prison conditions and lengthy pre-trial detention' in Papua New Guinea, this can be taken as an understatement. Abuses, inhuman treatment and unsanitary conditions are rife within Papua New Guinea's prisons (Reed 2004). For example, in November 2010 prison officials shot dead five prisoners who were part of mass breakout to avoid a cholera outbreak inside Baisu jail (AAP 2010). It should also be noted that many who suffer these violations have not been convicted of a crime, as anywhere from a third to a half of Papua New Guinea's prison population are pre-trial detainees.[14] While Papua New Guinea's prison inmates face extreme human rights abuses, inmates in the richest and most liberal societies also suffer inhumane treatment and abject abuses. Since it became the primary form of state punishment for grave crimes, reformers such as Bentham (1843b) and many others have called for humane treatment of prisoners, but with little effect. Long-term imprisonment cannot be described as one of the West's finest exports. Acknowledging the reality of imprisonment, Justice Kandakasi ruled in the *Mattau* case[15] that 'imprisonment is undoubtedly a form of violence'.

Substitutability of Sanctions in Terms of Deterrence

In relation to the degree of substitutability between the sanctions of the two legal orders it must be noted that the current circumstances can see excessive punishments for common wrongs. As noted earlier, in Western societies non-state sanctions are generally minor and act as complements to criminal sanctions, whereas in Papua New Guinea they are often of extremely high magnitude. While existing legal defences or doctrines may not provide literal support for the recognition of customary law sanctions as adequate substitutes, the reasons behind them should – particularly if customary law is recognized as *law*, as is the case in the Underlying Law Act 2000. The defence of double jeopardy is based on the ideal that a defendant should not be placed in jeopardy or punished twice for the same conduct, based on the notion of fairness.[16] In relation to the sole use of customary compensation payments to sanction a wrong, while they often contain a strong ceremonial element and the mending of broken relationships, some may still consider that they should only be a complement to a criminal sanction and not a substitute, analogous to seeking civil damages in addition to a criminal prosecution. While being a technical possibility under English law, in most cases it is rare to see an individual face both criminal and civil sanctions – and sometimes it is explicitly ruled out.[17] However, this must be contrasted with many civil law systems, where the victim of a crime can attach a civil tort claim or request the court to issue an order for reparations as a collateral criminal sanction.[18] It should be noted that the Criminal Law (Compensation) Act 1991 allows a judge to award up to K5,000 ($2,000) compensation to victims. However, the magnitude in terms of average income is many times greater under customary law in Papua New Guinea than damages awarded under tort or civil claims. All that is suggested here is that the decision on whether customary law sanctions can substitute or complement criminal sanctions should be made by the victim of the crime, not the state.

While allowing the victim to choose whether a customary sanction is a complement or a substitute to a criminal sanction, there may be a concern that this will not provide a sufficient deterrent against wrongdoing. The field of law and economics suggests that the use of criminal sanctions should be made on empirical grounds. As noted in the introduction, deterrence theory suggests that a potential wrongdoer will commit a wrong if the expected punishment/sanction is less than the expected benefit, where the expected punishment/sanction is calculated by multiplying the magnitude of the punishment/sanction by the probability of it being enforced. Posner (1985: 1195) argues that civil law sanctions in contemporary Western societies are unable to provide a sufficient deterrent as the optimal damages that would be required for deterrence would frequently exceed the offender's ability to pay, and that therefore public enforcement and non-monetary sanctions such as imprisonment are required. That is, the offender is 'judgement proof'. Similarly, Polinsky and Shavell (1984) suggest that due to issues of insolvency, imprisonment is necessary when fines are unable to achieve sufficient deterrence effect. Bowles, Faure and Garoupa (2008: 401) suggest that under the principles of civil law where sanctions are normally based on compensation, rather than punitive sanctions, there will be 'significant under-deterrence' *unless* the probability of enforcement approaches unity.[19] For Papua New Guinea these assumptions are unlikely to hold in relation to the practice of customary law, as: kinship ties mostly solve collective action problems; most people live in communal societies in close proximity to one another, which makes detection of wrongdoing (and wrongdoers) much easier; and most offenders are *not* judgement proof as compensation payments are borne by the wrongdoer's extended kinship group. An offender would spend many years, perhaps a lifetime, paying back the group and often forfeits property.

The sole use of a customary sanction should not be seen as impunity for wrongdoers, but rather as recognizing the legitimacy of customary law. The Papua New Guinean state should allow the greater use of customary sanctions because: a customary settlement can substitute for a criminal sanction in the eyes of the victim; it can provide a sufficient deterrent against wrongdoing; and there is no inherent benefit of imprisonment in terms of deterrence, or in vindicating the rights of the wronged.[20] While the practice of customary law should not be overly romanticized, if a system were to develop where compensation payments combined with the restoration of peaceful relations were primarily used to sanction even grave wrongs, it may not be an adverse outcome. Given Papua New Guinea's strong kinship networks that guard against the problem of offenders being judgement proof, compensation payments in the shadow of state sanctions may provide a sufficient deterrent against crime, but without the need for mass imprisonment. Perhaps such an outcome would be an advance on current Western practices.

Conclusion

The experiment of using criminal law for social change has failed in Papua New Guinea. The state has taken on customary law and lost, with serious negative consequences for its citizens in terms of personal security. It is time for the state to adopt the stance of a conflict solver and coordinator in the administration of its criminal law across the country. Perhaps this result and prescription is not surprising, as it seems that whenever the state aims to suppress widely held and embedded beliefs through the criminal law it will face trouble – if not immediately, then eventually. While gentle nudges may be possible, hard shoves are much more problematic, and this seems to be the case even for the most able of states. Papua New Guinea's experience suggests that merely punishing behaviour, no matter how severely, is insufficient to stop it, particularly when there is a low probability of punishment due to the weakness of the state. Where there is a desire to change customary practices, then prioritizing indirect legislation, such as education programmes, over direct legislative measures and sanctions may prove to be more effective and less destructive. However, such an approach would require patience on behalf of reformers, something they rarely seem to have.

The damage done by the Derham reforms and the continued attempt to implement them cannot be overstated. It has resulted in the reduced capacity of customary law to sanction common wrongs, while the state criminal law has been unable to take on this role. The end result has been an overall decline in deterrence against the common wrongs such as murder, rape and robbery, with devastating effects on personal security in parts of the country. However, there is a potential way forward: a change in prosecution policy that would allow customary law to be the default in sanctioning wrongdoers, regardless of the gravity of the wrong, and in the shadow of the threat of state sanction. This should ameliorate the problematic interactions of the two legal orders in Papua New Guinea. Where the state has sued for peace in its battle with customary law, both officially and unofficially, the empirical work suggests that the sky has not fallen in. On the contrary, the communities of the New Guinea Islands enjoy relatively high levels of personal security. However, for such a legal reform to have its intended effects, the state must be able to adequately sanction those wrongdoers that come before its courts, and this would require a more functional state criminal justice system. The incentive structure generated from this legal re-ordering should encourage this. By sanctioning only those wrongs that are referred to it, the state legal order should grow in legitimacy and this would make it easier for its agents to sanction these wrongdoers. In addition, as the number of wrongs it is required to sanction would fall, it would have more resources to devote to each referral. Furthermore, if the state is able to sanction those wrongs which are referred to it, it would greatly reduce the need for payback, as the empirical research provides evidence that long prison terms and payback are seen as close substitutes.

Notes

1. Specifically, Damaska (1986) suggests that when these types are combined, civil law systems combine 'hierarchical' and 'policy implementing', whereas common law systems combine 'coordinate' and 'conflict solving'. In doing so he acknowledges that such conceptions and structures are ideal types and that in reality they are a blend.
2. As outlined in Chapter 3, all the customary leaders interviewed in this area were vehemently opposed to the use of payback, and told me they would not tolerate such behaviour. If a payback killing did occur, the customary leadership and the families of those concerned would decide whether it was to be prosecuted under the Criminal Code. If the payback killing was itself adequately sanctioned using a customary settlement, and if agreed by both kinship groups (families) and their customary leaders, presumably the killing would not be prosecuted under the criminal law. Similarly, if the killing was seen as a legitimate sanction by both kinship groups involved, it also might not be prosecuted; however, it is likely that some compensation would be necessary given that many customary leaders now see payback as an unacceptable form of sanction. Furthermore, as a payback killing is a wrong under the state criminal law and will be prosecuted unless agreement can be reached between the two sides, it is likely that compensation will be paid as otherwise the payback killer faces a lengthy prison term.
3. For instance, at the very least, some type of registration of customary leadership would be required. If such evidence could not be collected and documented it could lead to further arbitrariness in prosecution of offenders and encourage official corruption, problems which are already recognized as significant shortcomings of the state legal order.
4. Simester and Sullivan (2007: 4) suggest this can 'be seen in the rule that a victim who forgives his attacker may discontinue his civil suit for damages, but cannot stop the prosecution of that attacker'.
5. Damaska (1986: 200) considers that a 'pure hierarchical activist system of justice does not permit the victim to control such important matters as the initiation and termination of prosecutions'.
6. See, for example, Braithwaite and Pettit (1990) who use republican theory to legitimize the state's role. Bowles, Faure and Garoupa (2008: 393) like many others rely on the concept of a social contract to legitimize criminal law, suggesting '[t]he right of the state to punish derives from the idea that the citizen has given up some rights of self-defence in exchange for protection by the state'.
7. Mack (2008: 229) suggests that there are two basic prosecutorial principles: 'the legality principle', where officials must bring charges when there is sufficient evidence of a suspect's guilt; and 'the opportunity principle', where officials have wide discretion in bringing charges taking into account the public interest. France follows the opportunity principle: in criminal proceedings, before deciding whether or not

to prosecute, public prosecutors often seek to apply intermediary solutions including mediation. As discussed by Elliot (2001), following legislative change in 1993 the prosecutor can bring the victim and offender together under mediation where compensation, the return of goods and other sanctions can be negotiated. If successful the public prosecutor can decide not to pursue the prosecution, however if it is unsuccessful the prosecution will be commenced. While Germany, Italy and Spain follow the legality principle, there is still room for some discretion: Mack (2008: 253) highlights a special section of the German Penal Code that allows for the 'option of abstention of punishment where the offender has made or honestly attempted to make amends, in both financial and non-financial ways' for less serious cases; and Nelken (2002) notes that even while mandatory prosecution is entrenched in the Italian Constitution, prosecutors do show discretion in deciding what cases make it to court. In addition, Germany, Spain and France also permit private prosecutions.

8. It should be noted that there was a much higher degree of substitutability between payback and imprisonment than between compensation payments and imprisonment. However, the arrangements in the Kieta region of Bougainville indicate that hefty compensation payments and prison terms are highly substitutable.
9. The courts rejected payback killings on the grounds of repugnancy to the general principle of humanity in *Public Prosecutor* v. *Apava Keru* [1985], PNGLR 85; the handing over a child for a death in *The State* v. *Joseph Kure* [1991] PNGLR 404; and giving away single girls as part of a compensation package between two clans in *In Re Miriam Willingal* [1997] NI506 and *The State* v. *Paulus Non Pable* [1999] NI873 (see Chalmers et al. 2009: XIII).
10. PGNC 269; N3865, 19 November 2008 (para. 54).
11. The practice of marrying women off to another clan was sometimes part of the customary settlement process itself, and most likely continues today in the more remote parts of Papua New Guinea. In Bougainville it was suggested by one person that this could be used as part of a customary settlement to avoid the use of violence or imprisonment.
12. How norms are internalized is a complex process, as discussed earlier. Bisin and Verdier (2008) suggest that internalized norms are transmitted by interactions from one generation to another and within generations. Transmission from one generation to another (i.e. children learning norms and values from their family) is known as 'vertical' transmission, and transmission across generations (i.e. learning from peers) is known as 'horizontal' (or oblique) transmission. Such models presume that children are born without a defined preference, but that they are first exposed to their parent's norm trait, which they adopt with a certain probability. While parents and family are the most likely source, the state can also attempt to internalize norms. Most states have considerable control over the education provided to children, along with owning or controlling various forms of media, and conducting various 'public education' campaigns. States also use honours, awards and praise, as well as dishonour and blame, to shape civic virtue and discourage anti-social behaviour. An extreme example of a state attempting to internalize their norms on a customary group in society are the 'Stolen Generations' of Australia and Canada, where Aboriginal children were forcibly removed from their parents and educated in state institutions, or were fostered or adopted out to non-indigenous parents. This practice is now widely considered to have been cultural genocide.
13. Section 36 of the Constitution provides freedom from inhuman treatment. Sections 36(1), 37(17) and 41(1) of the Constitution requires that treatment in prison shall not be harsh, oppressive, cruel or inhuman.

14. The United States Department of State (2010) reports that half of the then 4,901 prison population were pre-trial detainees, whereas the Papua New Guinea Law and Justice Sector Secretariat (2007) reports that the prison population in 2006 was 4,169, of whom 1,421 were on remand (34 per cent).
15. PGNC 269; N3865, 19 November 2008 (para. 54).
16. The right to the defence of double jeopardy is granted under Section 37(8) of the Constitution. Friedland (1969: 358) also suggests that throughout the history of English criminal law, where multiple legal orders have had competing jurisdictional claims to try an accused, the issue has normally been resolved by agreement so that he or she has only had to face one trial. While it would be a courageous leap to suggest that the defence of double jeopardy applies a customary law sanction, the principle that underlies it is important for a legally pluralistic society such as Papua New Guinea.
17. Sections 44 and 45 of the Offence Against the Person Act 1861 provide that summary criminal proceedings, whether they result in conviction or acquittal, create a hurdle to subsequent civil proceedings. In addition there is also the technical doctrine of Res Judicata, which is based partly on the principle that a defendant should not be 'oppressed by successive actions where one would do' (Clerk and Lindsell 2010: 2051). It is also noteworthy that the Law Commission (England and Wales) (1997: 122) recommended that, due to concerns over excessive punishment, the courts should be required to 'refuse to award punitive damages where the defendant has been convicted of a criminal offence involving the conduct for which punitive damages are claimed, unless there are exceptional reasons why an additional award of punitive damages is still necessary and appropriate'.
18. For instance, in Germany, France, Italy and Spain a victim of crime can bring civil proceedings, or make a financial claim against the wrongdoer, joined to a criminal prosecution. In France there is no upper limit on the amount of damages claimed. In addition, victims of crime can seek considerable compensation payments (for instance, in Italy up to 200,000 euros) from the state in relation to violent crime. However, in Germany, where the victim receives compensation from the state, any proceeds from the wrongdoer pass to the state. A European Union Council directive was adopted on 29 April 2004 that required each member state to have a national scheme in place which guaranteed fair and appropriate compensation for victims of crime. In England a criminal court conviction is required to order the offender to pay compensation to his or her victim, or to state the reasons for no order during court, although the amount is capped at £5,000. However, if the offender is imprisoned an order can only be issued if he or she has the means to pay immediately.
19. More generally Bowles, Faure and Garoupa (2008: 415) concluded that criminal law is 'likely to be particularly effective' when 'harm is diffuse, the probability of detection low, or defendants are likely to be judgement-proof'. The conclusions of Bowles, Faure and Garoupa (ibid.: 397–400) are based on the assumptions that: private enforcement is likely to suffer from collective action problems and be restricted in its ability to detect wrongdoers due to poor information and technology; many offenders are indeed judgement proof; those who are wronged are unable to able to intervene before an offence; and many will not have the incentive to prosecute due to the fear of retaliation.
20. There may also be concern that wrongs would not necessarily be sanctioned in the same way, in that some would have to pay compensation, while others would be imprisoned. However, as Strauss (2002: 1) notes, treating like cases alike as a general requirement can 'perpetuate injustice: it will require that an unjust result, reached

in one case, be replicated rather than corrected in future similar cases'. In addition, Forsyth (2009: 263) notes the main rationale for the 'rule of law' is to safeguard 'against arbitrary governance'; however, in many societies in the Pacific the state law is 'considered by many to be foreign and arbitrary', and treating everyone the same 'in reality results in substantial inequality and injustice'.

References

AAP. 2010. 'Five Escaping Prisoners Shot Dead in PNG', *Sydney Morning Herald*, 8 November. Retrieved November 2010 from http://news.smh.com.au/breaking-news-world/five-escaping-prisoners-shot-dead-in-png-20101108-17kc2.html

Abrams, D.S. 2011. 'Estimating the Deterrent Effect of Incarceration Using Sentencing Enhancements', Working Paper No. 11–13. Philadelphia, PA: University of Pennsylvania Institute for Law and Economic Research.

'AG Defends Charges against Alleged PNG Sorcerer – Sorcery Act's Repeal, Amendments not yet Certified'. 2013. *Post Courier*, 5 September. Retrieved March 2014 from http://pidp.eastwestcenter.org/pireport/2013/September/09-06-15.htm

Aldashev, G., I. Chaara, J.-P. Platteau and Z. Wahhaj. 2012. 'Using the Law to Change the Custom', *Journal of Development Economics* 97(2): 182–200.

Aleck, J., and J. Rannells (eds). 1995. *Custom at the Crossroads*. Port Moresby: Faculty of Law, University of Papua New Guinea.

Amet, A. 1995. 'Severing the Umbilical Cord from Common Law', in J. Aleck and J. Rannells (eds), *Custom at the Crossroads*. Port Moresby: Faculty of Law, University of Papua New Guinea, pp. 62–67.

Amnesty International. 2009. 'Increasing Sorcery-Related Killings in Papua New Guinea', *Amnesty News and Updates*, 11 February. Retrieved July 2011 from http://www.amnesty.org/en/news-and-updates/news/increasing-sorcery-related-killings-papua-new-guinea-20090211

———. 2013. 'Papua New Guinea: Police Must Act Urgently to Save Captured Women Accused of "Sorcery"', 10 April. Retrieved April 2013 from http://www.amnesty.org/en/news/papua-new-guinea-police-must-act-urgently-save-captured-women-accused-sorcery-2013-04-10

Aoki, M. 2001. *Toward a Comparative Institutional Analysis*. Cambridge: The MIT Press.

AusAID. 2009. 'AusAID Annual Report'. Canberra. Accessed April 2014 from http://aid.dfat.gov.au/anrep/rep10/index.html

———. 2011. 'Papua New Guinea Country Report'. Canberra. Accessed July 2011 from http://www.ausaid.gov.au/country/papua.cfm

Australian High Commission (Papua New Guinea). 2013. 'Information Sheet: Australian Federal Police Deployment to Papua New Guinea', 13 December. Retrieved April 2014 from http://www.png.highcommission.gov.au/pmsb/185.html

Axelrod, R. 1984. *The Evolution of Cooperation*. New York: Basic Books.

Badar, M. 2011. 'Islamic Law (Shari'a) and the Jurisdiction of the International Criminal Court', *Leiden Journal of International Law* 24: 411–33.

Banks, C. 1998. 'Custom in the Courts: Criminal Law (Compensation) Act of Papua New Guinea', *British Journal of Criminology* 38(2): 299–316.

———. 2001. 'Women, Justice, and Custom: The Discourse of "Good Custom" and "Bad Custom" in Papua New Guinea and Canada', *International Journal of Comparative Sociology* 42: 101–22.

Barron, P., C.Q. Smith and M. Woolcock. 2004. 'Understanding Local-Level Conflict in Developing Countries: Theory, Evidence and Implication from Indonesia', in *Social Development Papers, Conflict Prevention and Reconstruction Paper 19*, Washington, D.C.: World Bank.

Basu, K. 2000. *Prelude to Political Economy: A Study of the Social and Political Foundations of Economics*. Oxford: Oxford University Press.

Becker, Gary S. 1968. 'Crime and Punishment: An Economic Approach', *Journal of Political Economy* 76, 169–217.

———. 1976. *The Economic Approach to Human Behavior*. London: The University of Chicago Press.

Benda-Beckmann, F. von, and K. von Benda-Beckmann. 2006. 'The Dynamics of Change and Continuity in Plural Legal Orders', *Journal of Legal Pluralism and Unofficial Law* 38(53–54): 1–44.

Bentham, J. 1789. *An Introduction to the Principles of Morals and Legislation*. Oxford: Clarendon Press.

———. 1843a. 'Principles of Morals and Legislation, Fragment on Government, Civil Code, Penal Law', in *The Works of Jeremy Bentham*, Volume 1, published under the Superintendence of his Executor, John Bowring. Edinburgh: William Tait.

———. 1843b. 'Proposal for a New and Less Expensive mode of Employing and Reforming Convicts', in *The Works of Jeremy Bentham*, Volume 11, published under the Superintendence of his Executor, John Bowring. Edinburgh: William Tait.

———. 1843c. 'Rationale of Judicial Evidence', Part 2, in *The Works of Jeremy Bentham*, Volume 7, published under the Superintendence of his Executor, John Bowring. Edinburgh: William Tait.

———. (1802) 2011. 'Place and Time', P. Schofield and S.G. Engelmann (eds), in S.G. Engelmann (ed.), *Selected Writings: Jeremy Bentham*. New Haven, CT: Yale University Press.

Benton, L. 2012. 'Historical Perspectives on Legal Pluralism', in B. Tamanaha, C. Sage and M. Woolcock (eds), *Legal Pluralism and Development: Scholars and Practitioners in Dialogue*. Cambridge: Cambridge University Press, pp. 21–33.

Berkowitz, D., K. Pistor and J. Richard. 2003a. 'Economic Development, Legality, and the Transplant Effect', *European Economic Review* 47(1): 165–95.

———. 2003b. 'The Transplant Effect', *American Journal of Comparative Law* 25(3): 457–91.

Berman, H. 1983. *Law and Revolution: The Formation of the Western Legal Tradition*. Cambridge, MA: Harvard University Press.

Bicchieri, C. 2006. *The Grammar of Society: The Nature and Dynamics of Social Norms*. New York: Cambridge University Press.

Bisin, A., and T. Verdier. 2008. 'Cultural Transmission', in S.N. Durlauf and L.E. Blume (eds), *The New Palgrave Dictionary of Economics*, 2nd Edition. New York: Palgrave Macmillan. Retrieved 1 May 2014 from http://www.dictionaryofeconomics.com/article?id=pde2008_C000549&q=culture&topicid=&result_number=2

Bowles, R., M. Faure and N. Garoupa. 2008. 'The Scope of Criminal Law and Criminal Sanctions: An Economic View and Policy Implications', *Journal of Law and Society* 35(3): 389–416.

Braithwaite, J., H. Charlesworth, P. Reddy and L. Dunn. 2010. *Reconciliation and Architectures of Commitment: Sequencing Peace in Bougainville*. Canberra: The Australian National University E Press.

Braithwaite, J., and P. Pettit. 1990. *Not Just Deserts: A Republican Theory of Criminal Justice*. Oxford: Oxford University Press.

Brown, B.J. (ed.). 1969. *The Fashion of Law in New Guinea*. Sydney: Butterworths.

Chalmers, D.R., and A.H. Paliwala. 1984. *An Introduction to the Law in Papua New Guinea*, 2nd Edition. Sydney: The Law Book Company.

Chalmers, D.R., D. Weisbrot, S. Injia, A.J. Warwick and D. Nicol. 2001. *The Criminal Law and Practice of Papua New Guinea*, 3rd Edition. Sydney: The Law Book Company.

———. 2009. *Criminal Law and Practice of Papua New Guinea: With a Forward by the Honorable Sir Arnold Amet*. Reprint of Third Edition first published in 2001 with no updates. Port Moresby: University of Papua New Guinea Press and Bookshop.

Chanock, M. 1998. *Law, Custom and Social Order*. Cambridge: Cambridge University Press.

Clifford, W. 1976. 'Urban Crime in Papua New Guinea', in D. Biles (ed.), *Crime in Papua New Guinea*. Phillip, ACT: Australian Institute of Criminology, pp. 1–37.

Comaroff, J., and J. Comaroff. 2006. *Law and Disorder in the Postcolony*. Chicago: Chicago University Press.

Conrad, J. 1902. *Heart of Darkness*. London: Blackwood.

Constitution and Law Reform Commission of Papua New Guinea. 1975. 'Report on Abolition of Native Regulations', Report No. 2. Port Moresby.

———. 1977. 'Sorcery', Occasional Paper No. 4, October. Port Moresby.

———. 1986. 'Domestic Violence in Urban Papua New Guinea', Occasional Paper No. 19 (S. Toft ed.). Port Moresby.

———. 2012. 'Review of the Law on Sorcery and Sorcery-Related Killings', Report No. 7, August. Port Moresby.

Cooter, R. 1998. 'Expressive Law and Economics', *The Journal of Legal Studies* 27(2): 585–608.

———. 2000. 'Do Good Laws Make Good Citizens? An Economic Analysis of Internalized Norms', *Virginia Law Review* 86(8): 1577–1601.

Corrin, J. 2014. 'Getting Down to Business: Developing the Underlying Law in Papua New Guinea', *Journal of Legal Pluralism and Unofficial Law* (ahead-of-print), 1–17. Retrieved April 2014 from http://www.tandfonline.com/doi/abs/10.1080/07329113.2014.893126#.UzqiSFd7R-w

Corrin-Care, J., and J.G. Zorn. 2001. 'Legislating Pluralism: Statutory "Developments" in Melanesian Customary Law', *Journal of Legal Pluralism and Unofficial Law* 33: 49–101.

Damaska, M.R. 1986. *The Faces of Justice and State Authority: A Comparative Approach to Legal Process*. New Haven, CT: Yale University Press.

Demian, M. 2003. 'Custom in the Courtroom, Law in the Village: Legal Transformations in Papua New Guinea', *Journal of the Royal Anthropological Institute* 9: 97–115.

Department of Justice and Attorney General. 2003. 'Village Courts Manual', 2nd Edition. Port Moresby.

———. 2009. 'Papua New Guinea Country Report 2009', Pacific Islands Law Officers' Network (PILON). Port Moresby.

Derham, D.P. 1960. 'Report on the System for the Administration of Justice in the Territory of Papua and New Guinea', 21 December. University of Melbourne.

———. 1963. 'Law and Custom in the Australian Territory of Papua New Guinea', *University of Chicago Law Review* 30: 495–505.
Desailly, N., and F. Iramu. 1972. 'Report of Inquiry into the Need for Village Courts and Village Constables'. Port Moresby: Government of Papua New Guinea.
Dharmapala, D., and R.H. McAdams. 2003. 'The Condorcet Jury Theorem and the Expressive Function of Law: A Theory of Informative Law', *American Law and Economics Review* 5(1): 1–31.
Diamond, A.S. 1971. *Primitive Law, Past and Present*. London: Methuen & Co.
Dijk, J. van, J. van Kesteren and P. Smit. 2008. *Criminal Victimisation in International Perspective: Key findings from the 2004–2005 ICVS and EU ICS*. The Hague: Boom Legal Publishers.
Dinnen, S. 2002. 'Building Bridges: Law and Justice Reform in Papua New Guinea', *State, Society and Governance in Melanesia Project Working Paper 01/3*. Australian National University.
———. 2006. 'Restorative Justice and Governance of Security in the Southwest Pacific', in D. Sullivan and L.Tifft (eds), *Handbook of Restorative Justice: A Global Perspective*. London: Routledge, pp. 401–21.
———. 2010. 'Building Bridges – Law and Justice Reform in Papua New Guinea', in A. Jowit and T. Newton Cain (eds), *Passage of Change: Law, Society and Governance in the Pacific*, 2nd Edition. Canberra: ANU E Press, pp. 277–304.
Dinnen, S., and J. Braithwaite. 2009. 'Reinventing Policing through the Prism of the Colonial Kiap', *Policing and Society* 19(2): 161–73.
'Do Away with Compensation'. 2011. *Post Courier* (editorial) 4 October. Retrieved October 2011 from http://www.postcourier.com.pg/20111004/yutok.htm
Dorling, P. 2011. 'Australia, US Damn PNG's Rotten Political Practices', *The Age*, 3 September. Retrieved September 2011 from http://www.theage.com.au/world/australia-us-damn-pngs-rotten-political-practices-20110902-1jq9a.html
Egan, K., U. Zvekic and A. Alvazzi del Frate. 1995. 'The International Crime (Victim) Survey in Port Moresby, Goroka, Lae (Papua New Guinea)', in U. Zvekic and A. Alvazzi del Frate (eds), *Criminal Victimisation in the Developing World*. United Nations Publication No. 55. Rome: UNICRI. Retrieved September 2011 from http://www.unicri.it/services/library_documentation/publications/unicri_series/n55.html
Ellickson, R.C. 1994. *Order without Law: How Neighbors Settle Disputes*. Cambridge, MA: Harvard University Press.
Elliot, C. 2001. *French Criminal Law*. Cullompton, Devon: Willan Publishing.
Evans, D., M. Goddard and D. Paterson. 2011. 'The Hybrid Courts of Melanesia: A Comparative Analysis of Village Courts of Papua New Guinea, Island Courts of Vanuatu, and Local Courts of Solomon Islands', *World Bank Justice and Development Working Paper Series* 13/2011.
Fitzpatrick, P. 1980. *Law and State in Papua New Guinea*. London: Academic Press.
Forster, Christine. 2008. 'Criminal Injuries Compensation Schemes', in P. Cane and J. Conaghan (eds), *The New Oxford Companion to Law*. Oxford: Oxford University Press.
Forsyth, M. 2009. *A Bird that Flies with Two Wings: Kastom and State Justice Systems in Vanuatu*. Canberra: ANU E Press.
Friedland, M.L. 1969. *Double Jeopardy*. Oxford: Clarendon Press.
Friedman, D. 1979. 'Private Creation and Enforcement of Law: A Historical Case', *The Journal of Legal Studies* 8(2): 399–415.
———. 1984. 'Efficient Institutions for the Private Enforcement of Law', *The Journal of Legal Studies* 13: 379–97.

———. 1996. 'Beyond the Tort/Crime Distinction', *Boston University Law Review* 76: 103–12.

Garoupa, N., and D.M. Klerman. 2010. 'Corruption and Private Law Enforcement Theory', *Review of Law and Economics* 6(1): 75–96.

Geisinger, A. 2002. 'A Belief Change Theory of Expressive Law', *Iowa Law Review* 88(1): 35–73.

Ghai, Y. 1997. 'Establishing a Liberal Political Order through a Constitution: The Papua New Guinea Experience', *Development and Change* 28: 303–30.

Goddard, M. 2009. *Substantial Justice: An Anthropology of Village Courts in Papua New Guinea*. Oxford: Berghahn Books.

Gordon, R.J. and M.J. Meggitt. 1985. *Law and Order in the New Guinea Highlands: Encounters with the Enga*. Hanover and London: University Press of New England.

Gore, R.T. 1965. *Justice versus Sorcery*. Brisbane: The Jacaranda Press.

Government of Papua New Guinea. 2012. 'Judges of the National and Supreme Courts of Papua New Guinea'. Port Moresby. Accessed January 2012 from http://www.pngjudiciary.gov.pg/www/html/56-judges.asp

Greif, A. 2006. *Institutions and the Path to Modern Economy: Lessons from Medieval Trade*. Cambridge: Cambridge University Press.

Griffith, S.W. 1897. 'Letter from the Honourable Sir Samuel Walker Griffith, Chief Justice of Queensland to the Honourable the Attorney General: Forwarding Draft of a Bill to Establish a Code of Criminal Law: Presented to both Houses of Parliament by Command'. Brisbane: Edmund Gregory, Government Printer.

Griffiths, J. 1986. 'What is Legal Pluralism?', *Journal of Legal Pluralism and Unofficial Law* 24: 1–55.

———. 1995. 'Legal Pluralism and the Theory of Legislation: With Special Reference to the Regulation of Euthanasia', in H. Petersen and H. Zahle (eds), *Legal Polycentricity: Consequences of Pluralism in Law*, Aldershot: Dartmouth Publishing Company.

Guiso, L., P. Sapienza and L. Zingales. 2006. 'Does Culture Affect Economic Outcomes?', *Journal of Economic Perspectives* 20(2): 23–48.

Guthrie, G., F. Hukula and J. Laki. 2006a. 'Port Moresby Community Crime Trends 2005: Special Publication 40'. Boroko: National Research Institute.

———. 2006b. 'Bougainville Community Crime Trends 2005: Special Publication 41'. Boroko: National Research Institute.

———. 2007. 'Lae Community Crime Survey 2005: Special Publication 43'. Boroko: National Research Institute.

Halsbury, H.S.G. 2002. 'Halsbury's Laws of England'. London: Butterworths.

Handler, P. 2008. 'Crime and Punishment, 1600–1900', in P. Cane and J. Conaghan (eds), *The New Oxford Companion to Law*. Oxford: Oxford University Press. Retrieved 1 May 2014 from http://www.oxfordreference.com/view/10.1093/acref/9780199290543.001.0001/acref-9780199290543-e-521?rskey=Je4czv&result=1

Hart, H.L.A. 1997. *The Concept of Law*, 2nd Edition. Oxford: Oxford University Press.

Hirshleifer, J. 1982. 'Evolutionary Models in Economics and Law: Cooperation versus Conflict Strategies', *Research in Law and Economics* 4: 1–60.

Iannaccone, L.R. 1992. 'Sacrifice and Stigma: Reducing Free-Riding in Cults, Communes, and Other Religious Collectives', *Journal of Political Economy* 100(2): 271–91.

Independent State of Papua New Guinea. 1974. Explanatory Booklet of the Village Courts Act 1973, Village Court Secretariat, R.W. Cruickshank and I.A. Holmes, 18 January, Port Moresby.

Jessup, O. 1998. 'The Elusive Role of Custom in the Underlying Law of Papua New Guinea', *Melanesian Law Journal* 26(1): 1–24.

———. 2010. 'Customary Family Law and Gender Discrimination', in A. Jowit and T. Newton Cain (eds), *Papua New Guinea, in Passage of Change: Law, Society and Governance in the Pacific*, 2nd Edition. Canberra: ANU E Press.

Jessup, O., and A.J. Regan. 1996. 'Developing a Coherent Underlying Law: Integrating Custom and Common Law', in A.J. Regan, O. Jessup and E. Kwa (eds), *Papua New Guinea, in Twenty Years of the Constitution of Papua New Guinea*. Sydney: The Law Book Company, pp. 134–58.

Jinks, B., P. Biskup and H. Nelson (eds). 1973. *Readings in New Guinea History*. Sydney: Angus & Robertson.

Jones, M.A., and A.M. Dugdale (eds). 2010. *Clerk and Lindsell on Torts*, 20th Edition. London: Sweet & Maxwell.

Kahan, D.M. 2000. 'Gentle Nudges vs. Hard Shoves: Solving the Sticky Norms Problem', *University of Chicago Law Review* 67: 607–45.

Kaputin, John. 1973. Press Release, in A. Amet, *Severing the Umbilical Cord from Common Law*, in J. Aleck and J. Rannels (eds), *Custom at the Crossroads*, 1995. Port Moresby: Faculty of Law, University of Papua New Guinea.

Kelola, T. 2010. 'Killer Escapes Death Penalty', *Post Courier*, 14 October. Retrieved September 2011 from http://www.postcourier.com.pg/20101014/news01.htm

Kepore, K. 1975. 'Crime, Compensation and Kin', in J. Zorn and P. Bayne (eds), *Lo Bilong ol Manmeri: Crime, Compensation and Village Courts*. Port Moresby: The University of Papua New Guinea, pp. 176–80.

Kim, S.-H. 2008. 'Max Weber', in E.N. Zalta (ed.), *Stanford Encyclopedia of Philosophy*. Retrieved January 2012 http://plato.stanford.edu/entries/weber/#IdeTyp

Kinley, D. 2012. 'Bendable Rules: The Development Implications of Human Rights Pluralism', in B. Tamanaha, C. Sage and M. Woolcock (eds), *Historical Perspectives on Legal Pluralism, in Legal Pluralism and Development: Scholars and Practitioners in Dialogue*. Cambridge: Cambridge University Press, pp. 50–65.

Knight, J. 1992. *Institutions and Social Conflict*. Cambridge: Cambridge University Press.

Koczberski, G., G.N. Curry and J. Connell. 2001. 'Full Circle or Spiralling Out of Control? State Violence and the Control of Urbanisation in Papua New Guinea', *Urban Studies* 38(11): 2017–36.

Lacey, N. 2008. 'Rationale of Criminalization', in P. Cane and J. Conaghan (eds), *The New Oxford Companion to Law*. Oxford: Oxford University Press.

Larcom, S. 2013a. 'Accounting for Legal Pluralism: The Impact of Pre-colonial Institutions on Crime', *Law and Development Review* 6(1): 25–59.

———. 2013b. 'Taking Customary Law Seriously: A Case of Legal Re-Ordering in Kieta', *Journal of Legal Pluralism and Unofficial Law* 45(2): 190–208.

———. 2014. 'Problematic Legal Pluralism: Causes and some Potential "Cures"', *The Journal of Legal Pluralism and Unofficial Law* 46(2): 193–217.

———. 2015. 'Internalising Legal Norms: An Investigation into the Legitimacy of Payback Killings in the New Guinea Islands', *Law and Society Review* 49(1): 179–208.

Larcom, S., and T. Swanson. 2015. Documenting Legal Dissonance: Legal Pluralism in Papua New Guinea, *Review of Law and Economics* 11(1): 25–50.

Law and Justice Sector. 2010. 'Frequently Asked Questions Relating to the Papua New Guinea Correctional Services'. Port Moresby: Government of Papua New Guinea. Retrieved September 2011 from http://www.lawandjustice.gov.pg/www/html/191-correctional-services.asp

Law Commission (England and Wales). 1997. 'Aggravated, Exemplary, and Restitutionary Damages', 16 December. London. Retrieved September 2011 from http://www.justice.gov.uk/lawcommission/publications/aggravated-exemplary-restitionary-damages.htm

———. 1999. 'Claims for Wrongful Death', November. London. Retrieved September 2011 from http://www.open.gov.uk/lawcomm/
Law Reform Commission of Papua New Guinea. 1975. 'Report on Abolition of Native Regulations', Report No. 2, October. Port Moresby.
———. 1976. 'The Punishment of Wilful Murder: A Study by the Law Reform Commission', Occasional Paper No. 1, July. Port Moresby.
———. 1977a. 'The Role of Customary Law in the Legal System', Report No. 7, November, Port Moresby.
———. 1977b. 'Criminal Responsibility: Taking Customs Perceptions and Beliefs into Account', Working Paper No. 6., February, Port Moresby.
———. 1978. 'Sorcery Among the Tolai People' (by William Kaputin, Commissioner), Occasional Paper No. 8, April, Port Moresby.
Lawrence, P. 1969. 'The State versus Stateless Societies in Papua and New Guinea', in P.J. Brown (ed.), *The Fashion of Law in New Guinea*. Sydney: Butterworths, pp. 15–37.
Lett, L. 1949. *Sir Hubert Murray of Papua*. Sydney: Collins.
Levantis, T. 2000. 'Crime Catastrophe: Reviewing Papua New Guinea's Most Serious Social and Economic Problem', *Pacific Economic Bulletin* 15(2): 130–43.
Levine, S. 1997. 'Culture and Conflict in Fiji, Papua New Guinea, Vanuatu, and the Federated States of Micronesia', in M.E. Brown and S. Ganguly (eds), *Government Policies and Ethnic Relations in the Asia Pacific*, Cambridge: MIT Press, pp. 457–508.
Levitt, S., and T. Miles. 2007. 'Empirical Study of Criminal Punishment', in A.M. Polinsky and S. Shavell (eds), *Handbook of Law and Economics*, Volume 1, Amsterdam: Elsevier, pp. 455–95.
Licht, A.N., C. Goldschmidt and S.H. Schwartz. 2005. 'Culture, Law and Corporate Governance', *International Review of Law and Economics* 25: 229–55.
———. 2007. 'Culture Rules: The Foundations of the Rule of Law and Other Norms of Governance', *Journal of Comparative Economics* 35: 659–88.
Lipset, D. 2004. '"The Trial": A Parody of the Law amid the Mockery of Men in Post-Colonial Papua New Guinea', *Journal of the Royal Anthropological Institute* 10(1): 63–89.
Llewellyn, K.N. 1962. *Jurisprudence: Realism in Theory and Practice*. Chicago: The University of Chicago Press.
Mack, R.L. 2008. *Comparative Criminal Procedure: History, Process and Case Studies*. Buffalo, NY: William S. Hein & Co., Inc.
Mackenzie, G. 2002. 'An Enduring Influence: Sir Samuel Griffith and His Contribution to Criminal Justice in Queensland', *Queensland University of Technology Law and Justice Journal* 2(1): 53–63.
Mair, L. 1970. *Australia in New Guinea*, 2nd Edition. Melbourne: Melbourne University Press.
Massell, G.J. 1968. 'Law as an Instrument of Revolutionary Change in a Traditional Milieu: The Case of Soviet Central Asia', *Law and Society Review* 2(2): 179–228.
May, R. J. 2004. *State and Society in Papua New Guinea: The First Twenty-Five Years*. Canberra: ANU E Press.
McAdams, R.H., and E.B. Rasmusen. 2007. 'Norms and the Law', in A.M. Polinsky and S. Shavell (eds), *Handbook of Law and Economics*, Volume 2: 1573–1618. Amsterdam: Elsevier.
Merry, S.E. 2012. 'Legal Pluralism and Legal Culture: Mapping the Terrain', in B. Tamanaha, C. Sage and M. Woolcock (eds), *Legal Pluralism and Development: Scholars and Practitioners in Dialogue*. Cambridge: Cambridge University Press, pp. 66–82.
Michaels, R. 2007. 'Two Paradigms of Jurisdiction', *Michigan Journal of International Law* 27: 1003–69.

Mihalic, F. 1989. *The Jacaranda Dictionary and Grammar of Melanesian Pidgin*, Milton, Qld: The Jacaranda Press.

Miller, S., and L. Armytage. 2008. 'Legal and Judicial Reform Performance Monitoring: The PNG Approach', *The European Journal of Development Research* 20(1): 141–57.

Montesquieu, C. (1748) 1914. *The Spirit of Laws*, T. Nugent (trans). London: G. Bell & Sons Ltd.

Moore, S.F. 2005. 'Enforceable Rules Inside and Outside the Formal Law', in A. Reader and S.F. Moore (eds), *Law and Anthropology*. Malden: Blackwell.

Morse, B., and G. Woodman (eds). 1988. *Indigenous Law and the State*. Dordrecht: Foris.

Müller, H., C. Marti, E. Schiedt and B. Arpagaus. 2000. *Atlas Vorkolonialer Gesellschaften: Kulturelles Erbe Und Sozialstrukturen Der Staaten Afrikas, Asiens Und Melanesiens*. Berlin: Reimer. Retrieved March 2014 from http://www.ethnomaps.ch/hpm-e/atlas-e.html

Musson, A.J. 2008. 'Crime and Punishment: 900–1600', in P. Cane and J. Conaghan (eds), *The New Oxford Companion to Law*. Oxford: Oxford University Press. Retrieved 1 May 2014 from http://www.oxfordreference.com/view/10.1093/acref/9780199290543.001.0001/acref-9780199290543-e-520?rskey=vffecW&result=2

Narokobi, B. 1996. 'Law and Custom in Melanesia', *Point Series* No. 12. Goroka: Institute of Pacific Studies of the University of the South Pacific and Melanesian Institute for Pastoral and Socio-Economic Service.

Nelken, D. 2002. 'Comparing Criminal Justice Policy', in M. Maguire, R. Morgan and R. Reiner (eds), *The Oxford Handbook of Criminology*, 3rd Edition. Oxford: Oxford University Press. Retrieved 1 May 2014 from http://www.oxfordreference.com/view/10.1093/acref/9780199290543.001.0001/acref-9780199290543-e-375?rskey=C5yPUC&result=1

Nonggorr, J. 1993. 'Papua New Guinea', in M.A. Ntumy (ed.), *South Pacific Islands Legal Systems*. Honolulu: University of Hawaii Press, pp. 202–50.

North, D.C. 1990. *Institutions, Institutional Change, and Economic Performance*, Cambridge: Cambridge University Press.

Ntumy, M.A. 1995. 'The Dream of a Melanesian Jurisprudence: The Purpose and Limits of Law Reform', in J. Aleck and J. Rannells (eds), *Custom at the Crossroads*. Port Moresby: Faculty of Law, University of Papua New Guinea, pp. 7–19.

Nussbaum, M.C. 1999. 'A Plea for Difficulty', in J. Cohen, M. Howard and M.C. Nussbaum (eds), *Is Multiculturalism Bad for Women?* Princeton, NJ: Princeton University Press, pp. 105–14.

Office of the High Commissioner for Human Rights. 2011. 'Papua New Guinea'. Retrieved January 2012 from http://www.ohchr.org/EN/countries/AsiaRegion/Pages/PGIndex.aspx

Office of Public Prosecutor. 2008a. 'Going to Court: A Guide to Understanding the Criminal Court Process in Papua New Guinea', J. Pambel, Acting Public Prosecutor, April 2008. Port Moresby: Attorney General's Department.

———. 2008b. 'Prosecution Policy, Port Moresby: Attorney General's Department'. First published 2006. Accessed September 2011 from http://www.paclii.org/pg/opp/PPPolicy.html

Okin, S.M. 1999. 'Is Multiculturalism Bad for Women?', in J. Cohen, M. Howard and M.C. Nussbaum (eds), *Is Multiculturalism Bad for Women?* Princeton, NJ: Princeton University Press, pp. 7–26.

Oliver, D.L. 1991. *Black Islanders: A Personal Perspective of Bougainville*. Honolulu: University Press of Hawaii.

O'Regan, R.S. 1970. 'The Reception of Common Law and the Authority of Common Law Precedents in the Territory of Papua and New Guinea', *The International and Comparative Law Quarterly* 19(2): 217–28.

Otterly, B.L., and J.G. Zorn. 1983. 'Criminal Law in Papua New Guinea: Code, Custom and the Courts in Conflict', *The American Journal of Comparative Law* 31(2): 251–300.

Ottley, B. 1992. 'Custom and Introduced Criminal Law', in R.W. James and I. Fraser (eds), *Legal Issues in a Developing Society*. Port Moresby: Faculty of Law, University of Papua New Guinea, pp. 128–45.

Oxford Dictionary Online. 2011. Oxford: Oxford University Press. Accessed July 2011 from http://oxforddictionaries.com/page/about_world/about-;jsessionid=C02BC836ECD2FD8ABBF80431D4012B80

Paney, P., T. Barnett, W. Tiden, W. Bai and J. Nombri. 1973. 'Report of the Committee Investigating Fighting in the Highlands', May 1973. Port Moresby.

Papua New Guinea Justice Advisory Group. 2004. 'Law and Justice Sector: Village Court System of Papua New Guinea', 21 March. Retrieved June 2011 from http://www.justice.gov.pg/vc/images/Docs/Village%20Courts%20Appraisal%20-%20JAG%20220304.pdf

Papua New Guinea Law and Justice Sector Secretariat. 2007. 'Papua New Guinea Law and Justice Sector Annual Performance Report 2006'. Port Moresby. Retrieved January 2012 from http://www.lawandjustice.gov.pg/www/html/560-sector-performance-reporting.asp

'Papua New Guinea PM Plans to Implement Death Penalty'. 2013. *BBC*, 1 May. Retrieved May 2013 from http://www.bbc.co.uk/news/world-asia-22366075.

Parisi, F., and G. Dari-Mattiacci. 2004. 'The Rise and Fall of Community Liability in Ancient Law', *International Review of Law and Economics* 24(4): 489–505.

Pimentel, D. 2010. 'Legal Pluralism and the Rule of Law: Can Indigenous Justice Survive?', *Selected Works of David Pimentel*, July. Jacksonville, FL: Florida Coastal School of Law.

Pitts, M. 2001. 'Crime and Corruption: Does Papua New Guinea Have the Capacity to Control It?', *Pacific Economic Bulletin* 16(2): 127–34.

———. 2002. *Crime, Corruption and Capacity in Papua New Guinea*. Canberra: Asia Pacific Press at The Australian National University.

'PNG Law Reform Commission Urges Sorcery Act Repeal'. 2012. ABC Radio Australia, 6 March. Retrieved April 2014 from http://www.radioaustralia.net.au/international/2012-03-06/420954

'PNG Repeals Sorcery Law and Expands Death Penalty'. 2013. BBC, 29 May. Retrieved March 2014 from http://www.bbc.co.uk/news/world-asia-22698668

Polinsky, A.M., and S. Shavell. 1984. 'The Optimal Use of Fines and Imprisonment', *Journal of Public Economics* 24: 89–99.

———. 2001. 'Law: Economics of its Public Enforcement', in N.J. Smelser and P.B. Baltes (eds), *International Encyclopedia of the Social and Behavioral Sciences*, Volume 12. Amsterdam: Elsevier, pp. 8510–17.

———. 2007. 'The Theory of Public Enforcement of Law', in A.M. Polinsky and S. Shavell (eds), *Handbook of Law and Economics*, Volume 1. Amsterdam: North-Holland, Elsevier, pp.1573–1618.

Posner, R.A. 1983. 'The Economic Theory of Primitive Law', in *The Economics of Justice*. Cambridge: Harvard University Press.

———. 1985. 'An Economic Theory of Criminal Law', *Columbia Law Review* 85: 1193–1231.

Posner, R.A., and E. Rasmusen. 1999. 'Creating and Enforcing Norms, with Special Reference to Sanctions', *International Review of Law and Economics* 19(3): 369–82.

Prime Minister's Department (Australia). 1937. 'Official Handbook of the Territory of New Guinea: Administered by the Commonwealth of Australia'. Canberra.

Reed, A. 2004. Papua New Guinea's last place: experiences of constraint in a postcolonial prison, Oxford and New York: Berghahn Books.
Reilly, B. 2008. 'Ethnic Conflict in Papua New Guinea', *Asia Pacific Viewpoint* 49(1): 12–22.
Roberts, S. 2005. 'After Government? Representing Law without a State', *The Modern Law Review* 68(1): 1–24.
Roland, G. 2004. 'Understanding Institutional Change: Fast Moving and Slow Moving Institutions', *Studies in Comparative International Development* 38(4): 109–31.
Rouland, N. 1994. *Legal Anthropology*, P. Planel (trans). London: The Athlone Press.
Rowley, C.D. 1958. *The Australians in German New Guinea, 1914–1921*. Melbourne: Melbourne University Press.
Ruffini, J.L. 1978. 'Disputing over Livestock in Sardinia', in L. Nader and H.F. Todd (eds), *The Disputing Process: Law in Ten Societies*. New York: Columbia University Press, pp. 209–47.
Sack, P., and D. Clark (eds). 1979. *German New Guinea: The Annual Reports*. Canberra: Australian National University Press.
Sanders, A. 2008. 'Prosecution', in P. Cane and J. Conaghan (eds), *The New Oxford Companion to Law*. Oxford: Oxford University Press. Retrieved 1 May 2014 from http://www.oxfordreference.com/view/10.1093/acref/9780199290543.001.0001/acref-9780199290543-e-1764?rskey=AzXj5L&result=1
Scaglion, R. 1981. 'Homicide Compensation in Papua New Guinea: Problems and Prospects', *Law Reform Commission of Papua New Guinea*, Monograph No. 1. Port Moresby: Office of Information.
———. 1990. 'Legal Adaption in a Papua New Guinea Village Court', *Ethnology* 29(1): 17–33.
Settle, R. 1998. *'Tasol': Individual Responsibility Under Criminal Law*. Belmont, Vic: Patsey Pacific Publications.
Sezgin, Y. 2004. 'Theorising Formal Pluralism', *Journal of Legal Pluralism and Unofficial Law* 50: 101–17.
Shaw, M., J. van Dijk and W. Rhomberg. 2003. 'Determining Trends in Global Crime and Justice: An Overview of Results from the United Nations Surveys of Crime Trends and Operations of Criminal Justice Systems', *Forum on Crime and Society* (3)1/2: 35–63.
Simester, A.M., and G.R. Sullivan. 2007. *Criminal Law: Theory and Doctrine*. Oxford: Hart Publishing.
Smith, A. 1759. *The Theory of Moral Sentiments*. London: A. Millar.
Smith, M. 1982. *Evolution and the Theory of Games*. Cambridge: Cambridge University Press.
Soares, R. 2004. 'Development, Crime and Punishment: Accounting for the International Differences in Crime Rates', *Journal of Development Economics* 73: 155–84.
Standish, B. 2001. 'Papua New Guinea in 1999–2000', *The Journal of Pacific History* 36(3): 285–98.
Strathern, A. 1975. 'Compensation in the Highlands', in J. Zorn and P. Bayne (eds), *Lo Bilong ol Manmeri: Crime, Compensation and Village Courts*. Port Moresby: The University of Papua New Guinea, pp. 184–92.
———. 1993. 'Violence and Political Change in Papua New Guinea', *Bijdragen tot de Taal, Land en Volkenkunde*, Politics, Tradition and Change in the Pacific 149(4): 718–36. Leiden: KITLV.
Strauss, D.A. 2002. 'Must Like Cases be Treated Alike?', *University of Chicago Public Law Research Paper* No. 24, May 2002.

Takaku, M. 2007. 'Statement by Ms. Mathilda Takaku Minister Counsellor Papua New Guinea to the United Nations, on the Occasion of the 51st Session of the Commission for the Status of Women', 1 March. New York.

Tamanaha, B.Z. 2008. 'Understanding Legal Pluralism: Past to Present, Local to Global', *Sydney Law Review* 30: 375–411.

———. 2012. 'The Rule of Law and Legal Pluralism', in B. Tamanaha, C. Sage and M. Woolcock (eds), *Legal Pluralism and Development: Scholars and Practitioners in Dialogue*. Cambridge: Cambridge University Press, pp. 34–49.

'The List: Murder Capitals of the World'. 2009. *Foreign Policy*, 29 September. Retrieved June 2011 from http://www.foreignpolicy.com/articles/2008/09/28/the_list_murder_capitals_of_the_world

Truman, J.I. 2011. 'Criminal Victimization 2010: National Crime Victimization Survey'. Washington DC: United States Department of Justice, Office of Justice Programs – Bureau of Justice Statistics. Retrieved January 2012 from http://bjs.ojp.usdoj.gov/content/pub/pdf/cv10.pdf

Turner, B. (ed.). 2006. *The Statesman's Yearbook 2006*. Basingstoke: Palgrave Macmillan.

Twining, W. 2004. 'Diffusion of Law: A Global Perspective', *Journal of Legal Pluralism and Unofficial Law* 49: 1–45.

———. 2009. *General Jurisprudence: Understanding Law from a Global Perspective*, Cambridge: Cambridge University Press.

———. 2010. 'Normative and Legal Pluralism: A Global Perspective', The Seventh Annual Herbert L. Bernstein Memorial Lecture in International and Comparative Law. Held at Duke University School of Law, 6 April 2009.

United Nations Development Program (UNDP). 2013. 'World Development Indicators Database'. New York. Retrieved November 2014 from http://hdr.undp.org/en/statistics/

United States Department of State. 2010. 'Human Rights Report: Papua New Guinea 2009', 11 March. Retrieved September 2011 from http://www.state.gov/g/drl/rls/hrrpt/2009/eap/136005.htm

Vienna Convention on Diplomatic Relations. 1961. *United Nations Treaty Series* 500: 95. Retrieved April 2014 from https://treaties.un.org/pages/ViewDetails.aspx?src=TREATY&mtdsg_no=III-3&chapter=3&lang=en

Vienna Declaration and Program of Action. 1993. Adopted by the World Conference on Human Rights in Vienna on 25 June 1993. Retrieved April 2014 from http://www.ohchr.org/en/professionalinterest/pages/vienna.aspx

Ward, D. 2013. 'Legislating against Spirits & Amending the PNG Criminal Code', *Lexology*. Retrieved June 2013 from http://www.lexology.com/library/detail.aspx?g=9b07b46d-5b36-48d2-b498-9db86d2ca553

Watson, A. 1998. *Comparative Law*, 6th Edition, R.B. Schlesinger, H.W. Baade, P.E. Herzog and E.M. Wise (eds). New York: Foundation Press.

Weisbrot, D. 1982. 'Integration of Laws in Papua New Guinea: Custom and the Criminal Law in Conflict', in D. Weisbrot, A. Paliwala and A. Swayer (eds), *Law and Social Change in Papua New Guinea*. Sydney: Butterworths, pp. 59–103.

West, F. 1968. *Hubert Murray: The Australian Pro-Consul*. Melbourne: Oxford University Press.

Westermark, G.D. 1986. 'Court is an Arrow: Legal Pluralism in Papua New Guinea', *Ethnology* 25(2): 131–49.

Wiessner, P. 2010. 'Youths, Elders, and the Wages of War in Enga Province, Papua New-Guinea', *State, Society and Governance in Melanesia Discussion Paper* 2010/3. Canberra: School of Pacific and Asian Studies, Australian National University.

Wilkes, J. 1958. *New Guinea and Australia*. Sydney: Angus and Robertson.
Wilkinson-Ryan, T., and J. Baron. 2008. 'The Effect of Conflicting Moral and Legal Rules on Bargaining Behaviour: The Case of No-Fault Divorce', *The Journal of Legal Studies* 37: 315–38.
Williams, G. 2006. *Learning the Law*, edited by A.T.H. Smith. London: Sweet & Maxwell.
Woodman, G. 1986. 'The State and Customary Laws: The Case of Papua New Guinea', *Holdsworth Law Review* 11: 132–40.
———. 2001. 'Customary Law in Common Law Systems', *IDS Bulletin* 32(1): 28–40.
———. 2002. '"Why There Can Be No Map of Law": Legal Pluralism and Unofficial Law in Social, Economic and Political Development'. Papers of the XIIIth International Congress of the Commission on Folk Law and Pluralism, 7–10 April 2002. Chiangmai, Thailand.
———. 2012. 'The Development "Problem" of Legal Pluralism: An Analysis and Steps Toward Solutions', in B. Tamanaha, C. Sage and M. Woolcock (eds), *Legal Pluralism and Development: Scholars and Practitioners in Dialogue*, Cambridge: Cambridge University Press, pp. 129–44.
World Bank. 2014. 'World Development Indicators Database'. Washington D.C. Retrieved March 2014 from http://data.worldbank.org/indicator
World Health Organization. 2010. 'Cholera Country Profile: Papua New Guinea', WHO Global Task Force on Cholera Control, last update 14 July 2010. Retrieved April 2014 from http://www.who.int/cholera/countries/PapuaNewGuineaCountryProfile2010.pdf
Wuillenmin, D., B. Richardson and D. Moore. 1986. 'Ranking of Crime Seriousness in Papua New Guinea', *Journal of Cross-Cultural Psychology* 17(1): 29–44.
Yilmaz, I. 2004. 'Marriage Solemnization among Turks in Britain: The Emergence of a Hybrid Anglo-Muslim Turkish Law', *Journal of Muslim Affairs* 24(1): 57–66.
Zasu, Y. 2007. 'Sanctions by Social Norms and the Law: Substitutes or Complements?', *Journal of Legal Studies* 36(2): 379–96.
Zorn J., and P. Bayne (eds). 1975. *Lo Bilong ol Manmeri: Crime, Compensation and Village Courts*. Port Moresby: The University of Papua New Guinea.

INDEX